Man and Environment Ltd.

A publication of the
Institute of Social Studies,
The Hague

PROCUL CERNENS
CLARIUS OBSERVAT

Internationaal Instituut
voor Sociale Studiën - 's-Gravenhage

Man and Environment Ltd.

Natural imbalances and social justice

Edited by

Hans G. T. van Raay
Senior Lecturer in Geography and Regional Planning,
Institute of Social Studies,
The Hague

Ariel E. Lugo
Assistant Secretary of Natural Resources,
Department of Natural Resources
Puerto Rico

Rotterdam University Press / 1974

Printed in the Netherlands

Library of Congress Catalog Card Number: 74-84042

ISBN 90 237 6243 6 (Cloth)

ISBN 90 237 6296 7 (Paperbound)

Acknowledgements

First, we must record our deepest thanks to the Universities of Leiden and of Florida and to the Institute of Social Studies for the organisation of the courses that have provided the basis of this Reader. Particular thanks are due to Messrs. F. Mulder, H. Popenoe, and J. Glastra van Loon, for their personal role in facilitating the two courses so far held. We wish also to acknowledge our appreciation of faculty and participants of the courses and of colleagues at the Institute of Social Studies whose direct and indirect contributions constitute the core of this Reader. It is a measure of the enthusiasm of the contributors that in spite of the shortage of time and the pressure of other work, only one of the chapters originally planned did not materialise. For this enthusiasm their fortunate editors cannot but express their gratitude and admiration. Finally, the people who have helped to make the production of this volume possible should be noted. In particular, grateful acknowledgement is due to Mrs. J. Sanders for technical advice and for her considerable assistance in preparing the manuscript for publication and, last but not least, to Mrs. D. van Arkel for her continuous support in the editorial work.

Hans G. T. van Raay
Ariel E. Lugo

List of authors

Dik van Arkel, Professor of Social History, University of Leiden

Dieke van Arkel-Merens, Sociologist and Workshop Administrator, Institute of Social Studies

Avrom Bendavid, Visiting Lecturer in Regional Economics, Institute of Social Studies

Godfried van Benthem van den Bergh, Senior Lecturer in International Relations, Institute of Social Studies

Willem Burger, Senior Lecturer in Sociology, Institute of Social Studies

Richard B. Du Boff, Visiting Reader in Economics, Institute of Social Studies

Robert G. Gaither, Professor and Chairman, Mechanical Engineering Department, University of Florida, Gainesville

John F. Gerber, Assistant Dean for Environmental Programs and Natural Resources, University of Florida, Gainesville

Jos G. M. Hilhorst, Professor of Economics and Regional Planning for Developing Countries, Institute of Social Studies

Anton C. Kuijsten, Lecturer in Demography and Family Sociology, University of Amsterdam

Jan G. Lambooy, Professor of Economic Geography and Regional Economy, University of Amsterdam

Ariel E. Lugo, Assistant Professor of Botany, University of Florida, Gainesville

James F. Morrison, Associate Professor in Political Science, University of Florida, Gainesville

Hans G. T. van Raay, Senior Lecturer in Geography and Regional Planning, Institute of Social Studies

Ernest T. Smerdon, Professor and Chairman, Agricultural Engineering Department, University of Florida, Gainesville

Joop J. G. Syatauw, Reader in International Relations, Institute of Social Studies

Egbert Tellegen, Reader in Sociology, University of Amsterdam

Ernest Weissmann, Visiting Professor in Regional Planning, Institute of Social Studies

Contents

Introduction

In 1971, at a European airport, academics and administrators of the Universities of Florida and Leiden met and discussed the need and desirability to create opportunities for people of diverse cultural and disciplinary backgrounds to exchange ideas and information about the pressing problem of man in relation to his environment. Bold and exciting views were expressed and it was decided that further exploration was necessary. In the Fall of that same year a Workshop was held at Leiden University at which scholars from Sweden, the Netherlands and the USA discussed the problem and made arrangements for an international and interdisciplinary course on man and his environment to be organised the following year.

The first Man and Environment Course was accordingly held at Leiden in the summer of 1972, with faculty from the Universities of Florida and Leiden and from the Institute of Social Studies at The Hague. A year later a second course was convened at the University of Florida campus at Gainesville, while plans are now under way for a third course at the Inter-University Centre for Post-Graduate Studies at Dubrovnik, Yugoslavia, in the summer of 1974.

The considerable progress that has been made since the idea was first discussed is also reflected by this volume. A product of the two international courses, it represents an attempt to take ideas and views which are of vital importance to healthy relationships between people, between societies and between man and his natural environment out of the secure confinement of the classroom and to submit them to the public at large.

After an introductory piece on the equal status of the natural and social sciences, several authors trace the evolution of the man-environment relationship. Particular attention is given to contemporary processes and to some of their environmental manifestations; most authors also attempt to survey the extent to which the evidence produced is of relevance to current problems. Other contributions set out to assess the magnitude of the challenge to mankind today and in the immediate future. In this context suggestions are made as to the general direction in which change should proceed. The topical range of this section is dictated largely by the talents that could be drawn upon. We gratefully acknowledge the fact that Messrs. Bendavid, Burger, Du Boff and Syatauw, visiting or permanent staff members of the Institute of Social Studies, were willing to address themselves to international relations, politics, ideology, and international law, enabling some evident hiatuses to be filled. Many crucial topics have nevertheless had to remain untouched: for instance, a promised paper on the population problem has not been received; but incompleteness is inevitable in an area in which scientific investigation is still young.

However, we believe that the contributions included will further a better understanding of the interaction between man and his environment and facilitate communication across socio-political, cultural and disciplinary borders. Although the contributors were not given specific instructions with regard to their subject matter and general orientation, these objectives emerge clearly from most pieces. Brief prefaces have been added to help the reader relate the individual contributions. In addition to increasing the awareness of many problems that presently face mankind, several contributions to this volume also indicate ways in which some adverse trends may be halted or reversed and a situation created that may benefit the long-term progress of human society. The reader must judge of our success in achieving these aims. Since our primary intention has been to provide fuel for thought and to popularise the debate on societal and environmental issues, we hope that our readers will be provoked to express their reactions with as much vigour as did the participants of the Leiden and Florida courses.

The desire to erode some of the disciplinary and other boundaries that mankind has erected and which the world can do without is expressed in the somewhat peculiar title of this anthology. A joking remark in a slightly different context by a member of the faculty has not been without its consequence. For the connotations it conveys and some of the attributes it possesses, we have added the common English designation for an incorporated company to the title. The addition 'Ltd.' brings out the dimension of limits so pertinent to the main theme, of both man and his environment being limited in their potential and capacity. Furthermore, 'Ltd.' indicates the extent of co-responsibility and liability of man as an individual and as part of an aggregate. Even more important, it expresses the need to regard man and his environment not as components with discrete identities but as a corporate entity. The time has come to break through the artificial world of separations such as man and social sciences on the one hand and environment and natural sciences on the other. This practice and the specialisation it has produced might have facilitated our understanding of and speculation about the nature of things, but the fundamental question is whether such a dualism can ever yield genuine insight into crucial interrelationships. We believe not, and feel that only a monistic approach that unifies environment, man, and the plant and animal world into a single framework, will ultimately be able to do this. The abbreviation 'Ltd.' contains the dimension of ultimate legal personality and, last but not least, refers to the identity of interest needed to understand and to affect the dynamics of the single existent discrete identity, the Spaceship Earth.

The Hague,
September 1973

Hans G. T. van Raay,
Institute of Social Studies
Ariel E. Lugo,
University of Florida

1. All sciences are equal

D. VAN ARKEL-MERENS

The participants of the 'Man and Environment' Courses shared a deep concern for major societal and environmental issues and insisted on the need for a unified approach. However, experience has shown that mere preoccupation and keenness are far from sufficient; lack of a general apparatus entails the real danger of polarisation of the natural and social sciences. The author describes and assesses some of the difficulties that may emerge when students of different backgrounds are brought together. She also questions whether a unifying language is available and whether such a common denominator is really called for. An alternative to the monistic ecosystem approach is discussed in this context.

The Limits to Growth[1] is but one specimen of numerous frightening publications about the gloomy future of mankind, all of which deal with such questions as: Can we survive? How? Who are 'we'? Who will determine which conditions are to be considered 'human'? The present Reader tries to enumerate several angles of incidence; though often conflicting in their outcome, these all show a desire to develop a common conceptualisation of the situation that threatens the world.

A main problem in tackling mankind's gloomy prospects is to find the means whereby each scientific discipline may bring its expertise and techniques into fruitful harmony with those of other disciplines so that an attempt might be made to create an interdisciplinary apparatus or, if this proves impossible, to achieve at least a common understanding about the possible contribution of each discipline to the solution of the problems at hand.

Several attempts have been made to develop such a unified approach and the list of conferences, courses and working groups grows steadily. Very often it is believed that mere preoccupation with the problems will suffice to bring about a unified approach. The experiences gained in an interdisciplinary course on the theme 'Man and Environment' have proved this expectation to be naïve and optimistic.[2] The only instance of spontaneous generation known to this author is that of Pallas Athene, who sprang from Zeus' forehead, without previous conception or the care of a midwife. The inevitable misunderstanding was nevertheless propitious in that it stressed the necessity for utmost methodological care to be taken in any attempt to construct a general apparatus or approach.

Some clarification of the purpose of this article is needed here. In taking the over-simplification used during the course as an illustration of the difficulties met in an interdisciplinary approach, it should not be inferred that the author feels that one particular type of discipline should be blamed for the misunderstandings. Other examples could be easily provided. What should we think, for example, of the following reasoning used by a sociologist in a discussion with natural scientists: The concept of adaptation in science is a concept created and used by specialists stemming from the bourgeoisie. It is a value-oriented concept – as are all scientific concepts – and its application implicitly contains the aim to maintain the actual situation and the power position of the bourgeoisie. The same connotation is found when adaptation is translated by biologists into evolutionary concepts. Since adaptation as false consciousness of the bourgeoisie has no objective meaning, the idea of evolution in biology, based on adaptation, is bourgeois and therefore false science. The biologists present during such a discussion would feel not so much debunked as rightly flabbergasted and exasperated.

Examples of sociologists offering a comprehensive approach based on their own bias with an imperialistic disregard of principles from other disciplines, refusing to be methodologically corrected – behaviour known to exist among some sociologists –, could probably be found and could have served the purpose of this paper. The use of the course proceedings, however, provided the opportunity to follow a much more interesting, extended discussion in which there was less endeavour to wreck the argumentation stemming from other disciplines than one's own. If this paper seems rather critical of some course proceedings, it should be emphasised that its main aim is to illustrate the positive efforts and the attempt to reach constructive – though for the time being modest – conclusions in the field of conceptualisation, and also to achieve consistent procedures of interdisciplinary or multidisciplinary work.

Several quotations used are taken from discussion papers, written during the heat of discussion; they are not phrased for eternity or for a balanced publication. These quotations should not only be valued as such but also as part of a dialogue in an ongoing process to reconstruct relations between scientific branches, as an attempt to devise an inter- or multidisciplinary approach.

Each scientific discipline has its own concepts, its own tools and techniques, imagining that its chosen variables are the main and, as is often stated *expressis verbis*, the only ones of significance to the study of the problem at stake. A participant in the Leiden course gave the following apt description of this phenomenon:

The problem of multidisciplinary communication is strongly related to the question of professionalisation. For example: a [natural scientist] participant recommended that the social sciences use *more measurement*, thereby stating implicitly that a science not primarily based on exact measurement is not a 'real' science. This statement, of course, was *not* the result of a carefully prepared investigation [measurement of what? how? why? etc.] but the result of a process that goes under the name of 'professionalisation': we all once entered university after having chosen an academic subject more or less by chance. We then had a fairly narrow scientific training with the result that we think that our methods, scientific language and approaches are *the* scientific methods, etc. So we all look at reality through our own professional spectacles which are not 'objective' or 'neutral'. Furthermore, the result of this professionalisation process decides to a great degree what kind of variables and methods we choose for our research; this choice is *not* the result of thorough and unbiased investigation of all possible and relevant variables and methods. Each multidisciplinary group must have this fact in mind, otherwise its work cannot be fruitful.[3]

This quotation ventilates more than a widely felt irritation; it shows the necessity to look for procedures with which to build a common platform on which to investigate whether a common language (conceptualisation) can be constructed and whether we are able to use each other's specialised or expert knowledge. What kind of difficulties await us, which fallacies do we have to avoid while undertaking this effort? Let us examine a procedure that has a certain appeal to some scientists.

One way to accelerate the discovery of these principles [common principles valid for all who are involved in research, etc. no matter what disciplinary background] is through analogues from various fields which are at different stages in the development of knowledge about the systems of man and nature. While there is no question that many of the analogies will prove to be erroneous, their use may serve as a hypothesis to be proved or disproved by measurement and experimentation ... Care should be taken in making analogies from one field of knowledge to another as each system has unique properties that need to be studied using a particular set of theories and assumptions. While this is true, the fact remains that social as well as natural systems are made of the same material (matter) and matter always obeys physical laws which can be described and measured. Therefore, we should be able to find common principles of systems' structure and function that apply to natural and social systems alike.[4]

It is not clear whether this conclusion amounts to a hypothesis or a statement. Whatever the case, two interesting points arise. We shall return later to the question of whether such principles can be found and, if converted into laws, can be measured concretely and precisely. For the moment we are concerned with the interrelations between social systems and their environment. Considerable qualification seems needed. To quote Abma:

The behavioral adaptation of man to his environment is only partly determined through genetic inheritance. Man's biological inheritance makes certain demands on and puts some limits to his behavior, but there are no patterned biological solutions to satisfy his needs and wishes. Not even his organic drives result in uniform behavioral solutions.

Man is always born in a society and through this society he not only meets most of his needs and motivations but also acquires the standardized ways to satisfy his needs. It is through society that man adapts both to his own nature and to his environment.[5]

This view on interrelations was further elaborated by Lambooy:

It is quite natural to accept a certain conditioning of man by the environment. Certain types of environment had characteristics that 'invited' man to new creative acts. But one should not make the error of saying that human development is *determined* by nature. It is man with his culture who selects and creates within the range of possibilities that nature offers. Of course not all human acts and creations are the outcomes of a stochastic process rather than the results of explicit goal-seeking and optimising behavior.[6]

Comparison of these quotations shows that all recognise a certain conditioning of man by his environment, but there the agreement ends.

Apart from the tricky business of using analogies as a type of reasoning by which it is hoped to gain fruitful hypotheses, why is the statement so alluring about the sameness of matter of which social and natural systems are made? If the statement is correct and equally applicable to social and to natural systems, the gate to a unified approach should be wide open; those who care about the future and want to save what still can be saved could then hope to speedily have the required knowledge and tools at their disposal.

A proposal for such an unified approach stems from ecology and has been developed by H. T. Odum.[7] Phenomena are described in terms of the flow of energy caused by the application of the first and second law of thermodynamics. Biological principles constitute one of the basic elements in this approach; it would have farreaching consequences if it were – *quod non* – simply applied to the study of social systems.

Ecological systems are assumed to develop under normal conditions – that is to say without interfering factors – through successive stages of development into a final stage, called the steady state.[8] In the steady state the total input of energy, ultimately stemming from the sun, is used for the maintenance of the system (through storage and repair). The net productivity of energy is zero, but no auxiliary energy has to be put into the system to maintain it. By implication, the system would be self-maintaining and no exhaustion of resources would occur if interfering factors, including those induced by man, could be steered in the right direction. The following summary helps to clarify this in greater detail and at the same time points to another important implication:

> The process of ecosystem development is termed succession. Ramon Margalef, a distinguished Spanish ecologist, describes succession in the following words: 'Succession is viewed as the occupation of an area by organisms involved in an incessant process of interaction and reaction which in time results in changes both in the environment and the community, both undergoing continuous reciprocal influence and adjustment. The important point is that it is an orderly and directed change . . .' The levelling off of each characteristic at maturity indicates that, in general, there is no further significant time-related change except for continual internal repair. This continuation is called steady state, and thus we may call the end point of succession a steady state ecosystem.[9]

The great advantage of this approach is that every seemingly incongruous phenomenon can be translated into one common denominator: energy and its transformation, guided by the laws of thermodynamics. Thus the transformation can be measured,[10] its effects can be quantified, changes can be predicted and calculated, a cost-benefit analysis can be made of every change. Moreover, we know what changes we want because we know what lies ahead of us, and changes that keep us from reaching this steady state can be considered harmful. The fundamental question is now whether a similar approach can be adopted for the study of social systems.

> Processes of change in social systems are subdivided as changes which are powered from within the system and those which are powered by forces out of the system. In ecology these changes also occur and the process is known as succession . . . Ecologists have studied succession for many decades and have described changes that occur in developing systems regardless of their location or species composition. Thus the field becomes a forest, the number of species increases, the structural complexity increases, the net productivity of the system increases. It is possible that social systems experience similar trends through succession or through their process of social evolution. Thus the diversity of human occupations may increase, the complexity of the social structure may also increase, etc. If indeed analogies exist we then can quantify these processes and develop indexes and guidelines for the evaluation of social health. These indexes would be of value since the physical environment has predetermined the carrying capacity which, when exceeded, causes deterioration in the quality of life. With measures of maturity of social and natural systems we would be in a better position of evaluating not only man's relationships to his environment, but also the 'healthy' or 'unhealthy' status of the relationship.[11]

Without denying the desirability of such measures, it should be stressed that, according to Abma and others, the hypotheses that underlie the assumed analogy do not hold:

> The term 'institution', in its most general meaning, refers to standardised ways of doing things, of satisfying existing needs. Institutionalisation is the process by which activities which initially happened at random and unpredictably, get standardised or patterned and thus become predictable. However, the same need can be met in different ways. No two societies have exactly the same institutions to solve their economic, political, familial, religious or other problems. The human animal has no fixed behavior patterns and the sociocultural ways of acting differ from society to society and from time to time.[12]

Though the term social evolution involves social development and social differentiation, it thus does not refer to orderly and directed change towards a steady state society whose properties are determined and outlined in advance beyond the will of the actors within a social system.

In this context it is interesting to refer to an argument, repeatedly advocated, relating to the fact that the social sciences are young in comparison to the natural sciences and that, for that reason, it is likely that principles and laws will in time be detected which also operate in the natural sciences. Social sciences are indeed relatively young in terms of years, but this statement bears no relationship to their methodological maturity or immaturity, but only to the amount of research that has been, or remains to be done. Moreover, we cannot be sure that these sciences will ever find such principles or 'laws' (conceived as precise, measurable and logical statements) however assiduously research may be pursued. Apart from the fact that social laws do not lie around waiting to be detected by clever social scientists (no more than did physical laws, which are thought constructions), they are usually constructed on such an abstract level that they are completely void of meaning and therefore useless when applied to different societies, systems, situations and the like. The critical difficulty for the social sciences is that they have to cope with the human will and creativity. Man can be a conscious agent in his own reality, atoms are not. The human will and human creativity are more or less unpredictable in their effects, though certain probabilities can be foreseen.[13] To put it in another way: as laws are principally non-falsified statements (i.e. not identical with measured), logical statements of a non-quantitative character should not be considered as unscientific. Such logical statements are made in the social sciences. Since of necessity they deal with specific historical and cultural settings (Man as a conscious agent), their character is limited.

I venture to conclude that, however attractive the procedure of drawing analogies between the sciences – in the sense of creating hypotheses which have to be tested and might prove fruitful – may seem, if this procedure is not applied with utmost methodological care and if the original problem tends to be forgotten, the outcome will be disappointing and frustrating. To be more precise: it will represent a waste of energy. Social and natural sciences share a scientific methodology but they differ in their subject-matter, i.e. the questions they ask of reality. In fact their 'realities' differ.

Another proposal for a procedure in which all disciplines could participate seems less ambitious but, for the time being, more attractive.[14] This discards the possibility of an interdisciplinary approach, that is: a truly integrated approach all the way through. Instead, it advocates multidisciplinary and disciplinary consecutive steps. Initially, all disciplines should come together to define the problem and state the objectives; then each discipline should elaborate its own task. The results, stemming from research in individual fields, are brought together, after which inconsistencies in the proposed solutions are sorted out.

This approach can be applied to the problems outlined at the beginning of this article. Ecology can be respected for the clarity with which it has shown that man cannot continue to exhaust his resources, irrespective of how many economists say that price controls will guarantee reasonable consumption and production. These over-optimistic economists apparently forget that money cannot restore layers of oil, iron, ore and the like.[15] In other words, the very useful concept of the carrying capacity of the earth cannot be bypassed. Ecology also uses the intriguing concept of the steady state, the final stage to be reached when no-one or no force tampers with evolution. For the social sciences this may be translated into a normative or dialectical concept.[16] Ecology clearly outlines the carrying capacity of the earth, the processes of restoration, storage and maintenance of ecosystems, and indicates, classifies and elaborates on the various points of no return which Earthlings have reached or already passed. A host of limits which should not be violated are thus immediately brought to our attention when our common objective is survival.

This still does not answer the questions: how? under which conditions? who are 'we'? etc. It should be a principal task of the social sciences to design or elaborate a 'blueprint for survival'. This means a renewed and vigorous attempt to reinforce thinking about the future, that is: futurology, not only as an extrapolation of present-day trends, but a truly imaginative construct of what the future could or should be, with the consent of all involved.[17] That such a design of a steady state involves more than technocratic social engineering is self-evident. That the social sciences should occupy themselves with the analysis of times past and present also seems evident. They have to take into account belief systems, ideologies and political decisions as modes of human action. This is done with an eye to the future so that, within the framework of human experience and the constraints of the economic system, a humanly satisfying course can be set. That this course is a difficult one, full of pitfalls, is obvious but it should nevertheless be undertaken. It should be comprehensive and take into account all the limitations and feasibilities shown by science and its specialisations. Its motto should be a paraphrase on George Orwell's famous words: 'All sciences are equal and none is more equal than others.'

NOTES

1. D. H. Meadows et al, *The Limits to Growth*, New York, 1972.
2. Interdisciplinary interuniversity course 'Man and Environment' held at Leiden, The Netherlands, July-August 1972.
3. V. Kettnaker, course paper.
4. A. E. Lugo, discussion papers delivered during the course.
5. Lecture notes by E. Abma, used during the course.
7. H. T. Odum, *Environment, Power and Society*, New York, 1970.
8. The concept of the steady state is a basic principle developed in the field of thermodynamics and later applied by ecologists to the ecosystem.
9. S. C. Snedaker and A. E. Lugo, *The Ecology of the Okala National Forest* (forthcoming).
10. A constant wish to measure was expressed in discussions and writing throughout the course. For example: 'Power is defined [by a social scientist] as an actor's capacity to influence and limit another actor's choice of action in relation to the first actor's own goal. In ecology the word "power" has similar connotations but is defined more precisely as the rate at which energy flows.' A. E. Lugo, discussion paper.
11. *Ibidem.*
12. Lecture notes by E. Abma, used during the course.
13. For an elaboration of this argument and its complication when societal structures are taken into account, see G. van Benthem van den Bergh's contribution on 'Monopolisation, State Formation, and Colonialism'.
14. Course paper by H. P. Gallacher.

15. See Du Boff's contribution on 'Economic Ideology and the Environment'.
16. Course paper by Bj. Andersson, in which he elaborates on the methodological implications of this type of concept and how it should be applied.
17. Course paper by H. P. Gallacher. See also contributions by Tellegen and Burger.

2. Society and technology: 30,000 years in shorthand

D. VAN ARKEL

In this paper the evolution of (western) society and technology is traced. Though the biological basis of man's ability to deal with the natural environment is discussed, the perception of and attitudes toward the environment represent the central theme of the paper. Man's role as a toolmaker as related to a host of social, economic and cultural conditions is elaborated. Particular attention is devoted to problems of anomie, alienation and inequality and the need for individual solutions being socialised. Though from a different angle, the papers by Tellegen and van Raay enlarge upon some of the arguments raised.

The study of the complex relationship between man and his environment implies investigating how and to what extent he can control it in a manner beneficial to himself, to what extent he can control himself, and how forms of control vary with the types of environment, in terms of both modality and adequacy. As the latter could be described in terms of demographic, economic, cultural and other characteristics, criteria for measurement can only be established somewhat haphazardly. The range of man's success, however, is obviously marked; on the one hand by such low degree of overall control that chances of survival are almost entirely determined by the environment, and on the other hand by so great an over-extension of his grip that man can make his efforts self-destructive of their ends.

In praehistoric times man went through such a cycle; his success as a hunter in palaeolithic times resulted in so great an overkill of prey that the continued existence of many tribes was jeopardised or they were actually obliterated. The agricultural revolution started a new cycle. Thus at the dawn of history man was still very near to the one extreme, now he once more seems to face the other extreme. In between lies a period of consistent and in varying degrees successful effort to enhance the chances of survival – offset no doubt by equally successful effort at self-destruction – which seems to justify a historical approach to the problem. As man's successes were as a rule detrimental to other forms of life, it could also be asked to what extent he could disturb the equilibrium without causing too much harm to himself.

Since the measure of success – from an anthropocentric point of view – obviously depended on his capacity to devise the means of control, the angle of historical perspective is man as a toolmaker. His capacities as a toolmaker, however, are not merely dependent on his ingenuity, but also on a host of economic, social and cultural conditions. It is with these conditions, rather than with the history of technology itself, that this paper deals.[1]

Due to the development of his hands as extremely versatile tools and the concomitant and related rapid development of the brain – 'with each advance man's intelligence displaced his former methods of defence by tooth and claw and made him more dependent on his intelligence'[2] – man's place in general evolutionary processes became more and more specific. It is as a toolmaker that he is able to survive, and his success as toolmaker and user of tools depends on and stimulates his brain capacity. He is as much *Homo Sapiens* as *Homo Faber* and the one quality presupposes the other. This dual mutually interdependent specialisation had farreaching consequences. On the one hand it implied that evolutionary processes for the species man ran everywhere on parallel lines – instrumental and intellectual adaptation to the most diverse environments – and this, on the other hand, implied cultural diversification. Because of this kind of specialisation – an ever more organised brain coordinating in an ever more complex manner the senses and the movements of the hand or its extension the tool – he was biologically never wholly adapted to one particular environment as are most animals, but was in principle adaptable to almost every possible environment ranging from the Arctic to the Tropics, provided he 'completed' himself by devising the tools required by the situation. Even though such instrumental additions to his somatic endowments may, in the very initial stages in remote times, have been similar to that of the sea otter, which uses stones to crack shells, diversification of instruments and the multiplicity of their uses created tremendous differences. In very early palaeolithic times men, or rather hominids, began to use one stone in order to make another stone into an axe or knife. As skill increased over the millennia, these chains of instrumental inter-connectedness increased manifold and even during the palaeolithicum became very complicated: a stone made into a fist-axe could be used to cut wood, which in turn could be used for a handle-axe or a javelin. Some sort of 'rope', sinews, leather, or fibrous material which had to be somehow prepared, and complicated knots would have to be applied in both cases. The javelin would be fitted with a stone head, made by a bone-hammer, which was also used to make a splinter into a knife, a needle, a scraper, or a drill. It is difficult to conceive of these tools made by tools as not having existed as an idea before their execution. Some kind of forethought was necessary. Moreover, multiplicity of tools and their usages and purposes meant that man had to face an ever-increasing number of choices as to what instrument to use and how, and this implied an ever-increasing necessity to evaluate his situation. He had to make some sort of conscious interpretation of his sensory information in order to be able to make the right choices. This meant that for reasons of survival – the more he migrated to inhospitable climes, the more dependent he was on an ever-greater variety of tools – he was forced toward an ever-more-encompassing interpretation of his environmental situation; this implied that he was a subject who to some extent created his own reality, his own 'symbolic universe', to give meaning to his own actions in relation to what was acted upon. Since in this way he was obliged to establish for himself what was meaningful and relevant, he was forced to develop criteria with which to judge all sensory information.

From the point of view of philosophical anthropology, this biologically 'unfinished' state of man, which necessitated his completing himself in yet another sense than devising tools, created new problems. The necessity to interpret himself and his environment meant that, confronted with a mass and perhaps an overdose of information, he was forced to provide his own criteria for selection. This put him under a certain strain; failure to provide these criteria, which is identical to having no norms to guide his actions and decisions, leaves him disoriented, in a state of normlessness or 'anomie' which, since Durkheim, we know to be identical to a suicidal situation.

For sheer self-preservation, the problem has to be solved in a socialised form; otherwise it would leave the basic problem still unsolved. Man lives in a group, either because he is biologically determined to do so, or because of the necessity for cooperation, or because of the long period of children's dependency on their parents, or for any other reason. What matters is not so much the reason why, but rather the fact that group-life precludes a solitary solution to the problem of finding criteria for the interpretation of information. If each individual in a group had his own solution, the norms he would derive from it would in all probability make his behaviour incomprehensible to the others; what is more, the non-comprehended behaviour of all individuals would add enormously to the totality of information to be interpreted by each individual. This would lead to new individual norms and thus the process would go on *ad infinitum*, without ever reaching a more or less satisfactory solution; a situation of anomie would therefore persist. Consequently, individual solution is no solution.

A socialised solution, however, implies a certain (cultural) rigidity. All new members of the social units must be acclimatised by means of en- or acculturation, instruction or education. Not only does this presuppose the development of speech ('The evolution of the nervous structure underlying speech was established and relatively stable when the evolution of the mouth was still rapidly proceeding. Hence the extreme variability of its structure and capacity for sound production'),[3] but it also implies the growth of fairly complex belief systems of a mythological character. The very function of these myths would be the ordering of the universe, or reality as observed, by means of analogy. These belief systems are naturally dependent on the habitat of the social units concerned and by implication on the technology needed for survival. Paintings and sculptures of Lascaux, to mention just one example, bear testimony to extremely ancient forms of such ordering, with magical purposes, in hunter cultures.

As long as toolmaking of the palaeolithic period had survival value for food-gathering and hunting communities – decidedly limited because man, too successful, tended to overkill his prey – the world-picture was fairly unsophisticated, mainly involving such magical practices as effigy hunting and restorative offerings in order to guarantee a good hunt. Of necessity it became more complex after the agricultural revolution, sprung from the seeking of berries and fruits. In fact the very acts of planting, sowing, hoeing and watering cannot but be based on some (cosmological) interpretation of the ways and reasons why plants grow. More in particular this holds true for the great 'hydraulic societies', the great river-cultures such as were found in Mesopotamia, Egypt, the Indus Valley, and so on.

The high fertility of the well-watered valleys immensely enhanced the chances of survival, on condition that ways were found for centralised organisation and administration of irrigation and the drainage of superfluous water; on condition that means of barter (or military organisations) were developed in order to obtain the minerals and metals necessary for the making of tools; on condition that systems for the measurement of time were developed in order to be able to calculate when to plough or to sow; and on condition that methods for storage and transport were developed.

Where these challenges were met, very complex societies came into being. High yields allowed urban communities to emerge as centres of political organisation and of commerce where specialised artisans such as potters, metalworkers and wheelwrights formed their own 'guilds', of an esoteric character, carefully preserving their business secrets. Classes of priests and scribes arose whose function was not only to regulate man's relations with the gods but who also had the duty to make the calendar by observing the (divine) celestial bodies or by measuring the level of the Nile. (The extreme regularity of the rise and fall of the Nile waters is actually at the basis of our year of ± 365 days which was only later found to correspond to the solar movement.) These priests were also masters of the sacred script, necessary for administrative as well as for religious purposes. From the point of view of technology and social organisation, tremendous strides were made in these river valleys in a relatively short timespan, but they could not always keep pace with population growth. Sooner or later insurmountable organisational difficulties caused decay or stagnation to set in.

In these river cultures which evolved almost of necessity into large empires, the belief systems became ever more intricate. Complex social divisions and the various ascribed positions which had to be legitimised turned the original unsophisticated world pictures (in the sense that norms were derived from the ordening of concrete phenomena) into more and more complicated but more or less inflexible cosmologies, without changing the basic relations between conceptualisation and technology. This explains why the priests, as the initiated, as caretakers and interpreters of the belief system, had such key positions and such great political and social influence.

Diffusion of ideas and techniques by means of commerce or conquest on an ever wider scale would in the end lead to clashes between two or more incompatible cosmologies, clashes which in the long run could no longer be solved by syncretist solutions. (An example of such a syncretist solution could very well be the Kurnai culture as described by Ruth Benedict. This had a kinship system which caused all members to consider themselves related to each other, as father or mother, son or daughter, brother or sister, combined with an overall, absolute condemnation of any sort of incest. In all likelihood two cultures were interwoven. A specific ritual had to solve the inconsistency.)

It is submitted that such clashes twice took place in a manner which had farreaching consequences in relation to the problems of Man and Environment, to wit, the Jewish and the Greek reaction.

In the Greek city-states, where commerce was based on specialised agriculture for export (olive oil, wine, ceramic products for storage and transport, shipping and shipbuilding, etc.) and on imports of staple foods, and enhanced by the founding of colonies for surplus population, by new methods of warfare (iron weapons, the phalanx) and hence by slavery for mass production, the clash was severely felt. Entertaining commercial relations with all the great civilisations, the Greeks recognised the incompatibility of the diverse cosmologies, even though they borrowed many elements and techniques of the various civilisations. Among the things they learned were Babylonian astronomy, though perhaps not astrology (Thales), the method of constructing a rectangle by means of ropes with knots at distances of 3, 4, and 5 units which led to the theorem of Pythagoras, and Phoenician script.

The basic inconsistency between the various cosmologies, however, had to be solved. Members of the landowning and entrepreneurial classes, who had the leisure to think and as traders most frequently came into contact with the great civilisations, who perhaps felt the pinch most severely and were in a somewhat marginal position, stood up and said: 'We know how things are.' Whatever their mutual differences they based their views on the premiss of a universe answering to the rules of logic, which they began to develop. 'What Thales did was to leave Marduk out . . . It is an admirable beginning, the whole point of which is that it gathers together into a coherent picture a number of observed facts without letting Marduk in.'[4] This gave rise to Greek rationalist philosophy, an essential feature of which was the notion of the identity of being and thinking. At a crucial moment in the development of Greek thought, Parmenides asked how, if one accepted the logical structure of reality, one could accept change. Since something that is cannot at the same time not be, which one has to assume if change is accepted (if thing A changes into thing B, not identical with A, one has to assume a moment at which A is at the same time not-A), change cannot take place; what we perceive as change is a delusion of the senses which are utterly unreliable. True reality is unchangeable. This line of cogitation became very prominent in one branch of Greek thought which culminated in the idealistic philosophy of Plato and Aristotle and, at a later stage, greatly influenced medieval thought. It led to the notion of an unalterable true reality, ruled by the immaterial, unchangeable, self-thinking Thought, which accounts for the fact that everything that is is the way it is, because it has to be so, because it cannot possibly be otherwise.

Such a view of reality made philosophical speculation the true destiny of man, as the only way of obtaining insight; everything related to this world of change, this inferior world, as well as everything related to change or bringing about change, such as manual work, was of lower order. Manual work was thus considered contemptible, only fit for the slaves and the unenlightened. The true gentleman speculated but did not work. He believed that true insight into the order of the universe and man's position in it was to be achieved mainly by reasoning and not by observation and experimentation. In the long run this view became self-defeative, despite the Greek's remarkable contributions to technology which frequently had the character of toys. A society based on slavery, such as the Graeco-Roman civilisation, in the long run had less need for technological improvement but had to face increasing odds when slaves became scarcer.

An analogous yet very different solution to the problem of inconsistency between the various cosmologies was found by the Jews who, by reason of their geographical position, were exposed to conflicting ideas. Among them too, marginal men (though the reason for their marginality is less clear) in the form of the prophets stood up and, during the troubles that led to the Babylonian exile and thereafter, reinterpreted the world in terms of the Divine Will, of the Creator who had partially revealed Himself. Man, created in the image of God, was likewise endowed with a will, which should be in accordance with the Divine Will but is not always so. This led to notions of sin and atonement and to the sanctifying effect of manual work and technology. Although human toil was seen as the result of the Fall, related to sin, it was also conceived of as a means with which to restore the original order to some extent and was thus highly honoured. Laboriousness was a virtue, as is evident from the lives of the later Talmudic scholars who all prided themselves on also being craftsmen. This concept of labour, combined with the idea that Man remained what he always had been and was meant to be, the master of all creation, gave rise to the notion of the instrumental character of the earth and all it contained. Man could and should exploit the earth, the natural forces, the animals (within bounds) according to his will, but not his fellow human beings.

These two incompatible strands of thought – the Greek concept implying the basic inalterability of True Reality, and the Jewish concept in Christianised form posing the basic alterability under the impact of exertion of the human and the Divine will – met again in the re-emerging civilisation of medieval Latin Christianity.

In the west, conditions prevailed that were very different to those of the river valleys and the Mediterranean area. Regular rainfall throughout the year did not necessitate complex organisation or cooperation, and made in principle the one-family unit the basis of production or, for reasons of forest clearing, a small number of families. In practice, the feudal order demanded slightly larger units for reasons of defence.

A cluster of inventions involving the better use of horses (a more economical animal than the ox) of which there were for military purposes more than the economy could really stand, set off a chain reaction. The Chinese invention of the stirrup which gradually spread to the west, caused a military revolution, the shift from infantry to cavalry, to the knight who played so large a role in medieval culture. Collar-harness, horseshoe and bit, invented during the early Middle Ages, permitted more economic use of the horse. These inventions, in combination with the Germanic plough, created conditions for an agricultural technique more suited to the northern soils. In the 10th and 11th centuries they led to such increases in yield that European agriculture gradually ceased to be a subsistence economy. Gradually, a number of people could be freed for other tasks. This hesitant beginning to a division of labour slowly created conditions for a restoration of a money economy. Hoarded precious metals were again minted. (Throughout the Middle Ages, however, monetary development was hampered by a shortage of precious metals and a negative balance of trade, a problem finally solved by overseas expansion.)

The craftsmen and traders who emerged with the beginning of the division of labour gradually drifted to the towns, which as a rule became centres of non-agrarian production (there were exceptions, agrarian towns), thus bringing into being a very essential difference between town and country. Unlike the towns of the river valleys which were condensations of the surrounding rural areas, the western towns became autonomous, independent units consisting of autonomous sub-units, the guilds. They were almost *corpora aliena* in the vast rural areas, with no tribal or suchlike ties to the rural population and free of all feudal obligations. 'The air of a town liberates a man', was the saying. Relations with the rural population were purely economic in character.

It was primarily in these urban centres that the voluntaristic inheritance from Judaism in its Christian form again came to the fore in the shape of labour ethics. The medieval concept of labour was closely related to the Jewish concept. Manual labour is honorific; even though related to original sin, it ennobles a man, but the legitimate remuneration should never become an end in itself. Labour was seen as a means to a spiritual end. Whereas in the case of the Jews a certain amount of time had to be reserved for the study of the Law, the Christian concept prescribed that man should reserve sufficient time and effort for the performance of his Christian duties, for the imitation of Christ. However, monks should not spend all their time in prayer and meditation but should do some (manual) labour and should live off the fruits thereof. Labour should provide the means for a decent life, not more, for that led to the mortal sins of avarice or sloth. The less man worked to achieve freedom from want the better it was, for the sooner he was emancipated by means of the fruits of his labour from his bodily wants, protection against hunger and cold, the sooner he was free to fulfil his spiritual obligations. Hence the 'constant effort to diminish effort' as a characteristic and decisive feature of Latin christianity. That constant effort led to a perpetual search for labour-saving devices, to a generally prevailing technological habitus, once more based on the concept of legitimate instrumentalisation of the earth and of natural forces. As Christianity knew of no sacred mountains, sources, trees, animals and so on, everything might be exploited. Many inventions made elsewhere were only put to full use in the west, many were improved and many new ones added. Watermills for many purposes, lift locks, crank and shaft devices, steam bellows, trip-hammers, rag and chain pumps, windmills, cranes and spinning wheels, are examples of this pre-scientific technological development, based only on trial and error, which came to full bloom in the 16th century. As the gradually more intricate clocks of the later Middle Ages indicate, people delighted in machines for their own sake. These were far more than mere instruments to warn time-conscious citizens – the idea of using one's time well fitted into the whole concept of laboriousness. The clocks were ingenious pieces of machinery that indicated the movements of the sun, the moon and the planets according to the Ptolomaeic interpretation, and frequently had purely ornamental additions such as giants ringing bells or the twelve apostles appearing at the stroke of noon.

The effects of this technological revolution were immense. Western man could begin the adventure of overseas expansion – the era of Vasco da Gama (made possible by the advanced technique of founding small guns which, placed on the lower decks of the newly developed ocean-going ships, turned these into deadly weapons with which overseas territories could be terrorised) – with all the colonialist consequences which gave such a tremendous boost to the whole further development. Capitalism at home and abroad was promoted and became a twofold condition for the scientific revolution.

The more intricate and complex the machinery, the more costly it became. The net result of the technological development was therefore self-defeative of its own ends: i.e. guaranteeing that each worker is worthy of his hire, that he shall have a fair share of the work at a decent compensation, with a maximum of spare time. The later development led to the emergence of an entrepreneurial class, commercial and industrial, the new bourgeoisie, and hence to an ever-increasing class division and class conflict. The new rich classes, the Grassi (the Fat) as they were called in Italy, frequently grasped political power – the Medici for example – whereas at the other end of the scale a socially downgraded, impoverished group of formerly independent craftsmen came into being who virtually became wage-earners. The ensuing class warfare and social protest of these lower social orders usually took the form of chiliastic movements, emphasising apostolic poverty, prophesying the Second Coming and the immediate realisation of the promised millennium. These were movements of an extremely voluntaristic character, which the church for ecclesiological reasons could not but condemn as heretical. What better weapon could the established church use for the defence and legitimisation of the status quo, of the existing hierarchical order, against being jeopardised by these chiliastic and revolutionary popular movements, than Aristotelian rationalism, newly rediscovered via the Arabs, which vindicated the necessity of the existent order of things? (Aristotelian necessitarianism was still highly controversial in the 13th century, as is evident from the fact that Bishop Etienne Tempier in 1277 condemned it as not concordant with the sovereign Divine Will.) The mendicant urban orders entrusted with the Inquisition, in particular the Dominicans (Aquinas), became the chief promotors of Aristotelian philosophy, which acquired such prestige during the later Middle Ages that it was frequently accepted even if the evidence was contrary to its teachings. An interesting example is the Aristotelian interpretation of the movement of an arrow: pushed forward by the bowstring the arrow leaves a void where it once was, a void which because of the *horror vacui* is immediately filled with air which, running in, once more pushes the arrow forward. This would go on *ad infinitum* if the arrow, as an earthly thing, did not have the desire to go where it belongs, to the earth. Even though medieval philosophers were quite aware that the same reasoning would apply to a ribbon attached to the arrow, which consequently would have to point forward, and even though their eyes told them differently, it never occurred to them to reject the Aristotelian interpretation. They preferred a most complicated argument with which to explain the strange behaviour of the ribbon.

In the universities where they taught and dominated, the rationalism of these philosophers clashed with the somewhat secularised voluntarism of the entrepreneurial classes and the socially rising class of engineers who, though their voluntarism was not as extreme perhaps as that of the chiliastic movements, had inherited enough of the original labour ethics and the instrumental interpretation of the world to cause severe strain.

Thus the stage was set for the scientific revolution (and by implication for the new scientific technology of the modern period). Technology provided the means (the capacity to make the necessary instruments) and the problems (the questions of the engineers, usually of a mechanical nature which explains the primary interest in mechanics). The clash between voluntarism and rationalism provided the necessary philosophical setting: if the world is influenced and changed by inscrutable, Divine and unpredictable human will, one can no longer exclusively rely on reason to explain why things are as they are, one can no longer argue that they have to be so because the eternal unchanging order of the universe prevents them from being otherwise. Since one cannot completely rely on mere logical deduction from observation, conclusions must be tested by experiment: in other words, by the activity of the engineers. Thus modern science was born, as the offshoot of Greek rationalism and the Judeo-Christian voluntarism of the engineers and craftsmen. However successful experimental science became, however much it created conditions for unprecedented technological development and hence for economic growth and general welfare from a materialistic viewpoint, it was and remained a temporarily but never wholly adequate response to a new anomic situation. Once more, man was faced with such severe clashes and inconsistencies within his belief system that only with difficulty could he derive norms from it. There is a continuous effort to either emphasise the voluntaristic concept, as was the case in Reformist Europe (where early science was most developed), or the rationalistic concept, more notable in Counter-Reformation Europe (where mathematics made much progress), or to seek combinations in the form of the normative concept of history of the Enlightenment and kindred movements. There is also the irrational solution to the problem. It does not seem to be a coincidence that the period that witnessed the birth of modern science is also the period of the witchcraft delusion. It is a kind of hypostatisation of the innate conflict, a kind of reontologisation of the universe with an emancipated devil roaming at large to work evil. It reflects the loosening of social ties, the dissolving of medieval social cohesion, and the ensuing stress of early capitalist society. What holds true for the sixteenth century holds *a fortiori* true for the nineteenth and twentieth centuries. The combined onslaught of science and technology in the form of the Industrial Revolution created such uncertainty, atomised society to such a degree, so prevented calculability in the everyday life of the average citizen, that anomic stress assumed gigantic proportions. It found an outlet in such violent movements as antisemitism and kindred forms of racism, and in similar irrational 'isms' so typical of the nineteenth century, or in milder form in problems of communication or psychological strain.

It might be submitted that this anomic character of our society, the fact that it contains these inner stresses, has a lot to do with our environmental problems. Because of the rationalisation of our actions, the search for the scientifically determined way to achieve the best results with the greatest economy of means, because of the successes of the scientific approach, we perhaps tend to underestimate human values and to overestimate the technical solutions to our problems, thereby giving free rein to the technocrats. Emphasis on welfare, which we can more or less manage, has overshadowed wellbeing, and has led to over-exploitation of our natural resources. Thus, we not only have to reconsider our future but also the past.

Seemingly, we are not far removed from the problems that beset our early palaeolithic ancestors. Like them, we are faced with anomie and ensuing stress. Like them, we seem to be too successful. Like them, we tend to overkill our prey, the earth. Shall we, like them, find a solution? A solution which does justice to all those who do not profit from the environmentally problematic wealth of the industrialised world, to all those who are not responsible for present-day problems but are victimised all the more, the countless inhabitants of the developing countries? It is to be hoped that a sense of justice is the inheritance of 30,000 years of development of civilisation, as well as the key to present-day problems.

NOTES

1. This paper is a slightly adapted and immensely abbreviated version of a book that J. F. Glastra van Loon and I are writing. Apart from the adaptations, the ideas expressed are our joint property.
2. C. D. Darlington, *The Evolution of Man and Society*, London, 1969, p. 25.
3. *Ibidem*, p. 36.
4. *Ibidem*, p. 37.

3. Technology: its potential for solving environmental problems

ERNEST T. SMERDON
AND
ROBERT B. GAITHER

The optimist proclaims that we live in the best of all possible worlds; and the pessimist fears this is true.[1]

In this paper technology is viewed as an integral and vital part of man in the past, at present, and in the future. Weaknesses in projections employed in the report Limits to Growth are identified and the role of technology in a steady state society is discussed. The authors endeavour to relieve those who feel depressed by indicating the potential of future technologies for solving environmental problems. The reader is encouraged to compare their views with those of van Arkel, Du Boff, Gerber and Lugo.

INTRODUCTION

We live in a time when it's common to take a strong position on questions of future environmental conditions and how man's actions will influence the future. Perhaps it is also a time for optimism because the future is not predetermined and man has never before had greater opportunity to shape what will happen, especially when he acquires an understanding of the many aspects that comprise a social system and how they can be changed. This is one of the major goals of an interdisciplinary, international course on Man and Environment.

A common tendency, it appears, based on the surge of books and papers which has recently hit us with dire predictions concerning the future, is to look to only one side of the environment question. Technology has been blamed for so many of our environmental ills that pollution has even been declared to be inseparable from industry.[2] The report of the Club of Rome, *The Limits to Growth*, developed by a group at Massachusetts Institute of Technology (MIT), points to the possibility of a cataclysmic collapse of world civilization unless something is done about exponential growth and depletion of resources.[3] A host of other publications are filled with despair for the future, particularly if technological society is not somehow curtailed. This attitude is not justified.

In this essay we hope to put technology in proper perspective in relation to other aspects of society today and, in particular, in relation to future environmental problems. This can only be done by establishing a historical perspective for technology and squarely addressing the inseparableness of technology and man in the world today. What we say on this is expected to complement the excellent essay in this book on 'Society and Technology' by D. van Arkel.

We shall comment on fallacies of the numerous dire predictions of what a technological future may be like. We shall also look at the steady-state society concept and speculate upon how technology will fit in and complement such a society. No essay on the potential of technology for solving future environmental problems would be complete without looking at what some of these technologies might be. We suggest some future technologies which will help solve environmental problems. No grandiose scheme for solving man and environment problems will ever come to fruition unless the political realities are understood and continuously considered in any governmental framework intended to consider environmental matters. We hope all parties concerned with the environment will recognize this so very vital factor concerning government and politics.

A final introductory word on technology. It makes no more sense to defend an argument that technology is a cure-all than to broadly and indiscriminately declare all technology to be the instrument of mankind's demise. Technology by itself is neutral in an environmental sense – it neither causes pollution nor prevents pollution. It's how man chooses to use the technology that counts.

HISTORICAL PERSPECTIVE

Man and his technology are an interlocked couple that are difficult to view, much less study, separately. While attempts are often made to give each an isolated or localized place in history, few such attempts yield useful or realistic models upon which prescriptions for present and future actions can be based. Indeed, careful examination of the evidences of significant historical events reveals that technology is embedded in every step of man's progress from the savage to a civilized state. Moreover, technology is comprised of much more than a collection of devices that modern man uses in adjusting to and altering his surroundings. It is also a vital ingredient of man's culture and social structure.

Without ever intending to demean the many other important characteristics that distinguish man from the other animals, Benjamin Franklin identified the species of *Homo Sapiens* as 'the tool making animal'. Today, with the help of such well-developed sciences as physiology, anthropology and genetics, we know that man's earliest ancestors, who first appeared some 500,000 years ago, were physically quite ill-suited for survival. They possessed delicate skeletal frames and were covered with thin rather than armored skins; they had short arms and moved with difficulty except in an upright position; and perhaps more importantly they had no horns, sharp claws or overpowering strength to afford themselves any sort of advantage in combat situations with their natural enemies. But they did possess a remarkable dexterity and an unusual capacity to use their brains in ingenious and creative ways. They could combine information gained from past experience with an acute consciousness of current happenings and proceed with deliberation rather than blind instinct to make use of available forces and materials of nature to assist them in their struggle to survive.

In the habitats of these pre-man primates or members of the species *Homo Erectus* rather than today's *Homo Sapiens*, we find the implements and tools that they used to ensure their survival. And with these findings, we discover the beginnings of a course that clearly separated the further evolution of man from that of other living things. Like all other species that branched off from the main stem of simpler life forms, man continued to change and better adapt to his environment. Unlike the other distinct species whose evolution can be viewed as essentially passive in character, man evolved in a manner where he himself played an active role.

In totally passive evolution, the survival of mutations depends upon whether the errors in reproduction are more adaptable to, rather than being handicapped by, changes in the environment. Many species have displayed little evolutionary change over long periods of time, especially when confined to isolated and unchanging environments. This does not mean that mutations failed to appear but only that their occurrence during procreation more often provided offspring less, rather than more, adaptable to the local environment. Man, on the other hand, has displayed remarkable evolutionary changes as he proceeded from crude beginnings to his present form and state of intellectual development. There are many evidences today indicating that man was especially successful in adapting to his environment in an unconscious or passive sense, particularly when circumstances caused him to be isolated in severe environments. Witness, for example, the present short bulky frame of the Eskimo, allowing him to present considerably less surface area for heat loss than his lanky brothers in the tropics who possess high surface area to weight ratios, and who are therefore more ideally suited to survive in hot climates. But some of the most significant evolutionary changes in man including those that appeared prior to the beginnings of recorded history, some five thousand years ago, are those in which he played an active role, or more specifically, those which enhanced his ability to employ more and more technology in his life. It is often interesting to speculate on how different man would be today were he to have proceeded on his long evolutionary trek without technology. Certainly he would be different in physical form and mental capacity. Possibly, he would be unrecognizable as a self-determining animal for he would be incapable of altering his environment to suit his needs. More than likely he would not exist, having long since joined those species which became extinct when they failed to adapt to environmental changes over which they had no control.

Man has not stopped in his evolution. He continues to change today with every succeeding generation. True, within the short spans of a single lifetime containing but a few generations, we are unable to discern such major physical changes as the growth of an opposing thumb or an increase in the size and capacity of the brain which so distinctly improved man's dexterity, his technological capability and chances for survival. Even with the sharp focus provided by five thousand years of recorded history we find difficulty in finding startling changes in man. Yet these changes have been and are going on. Just as no child exactly resembles his parents or any other human being for that matter, man, with his technology, will be different in the future. Moreover, he will be actively contributing more and more to his own evolution.

Recorded history provides glaring evidence of the fact that technology is an integral and vital part of man. Indeed, history well bears out the fact that man's social and cultural development have always been intertwined with and in many cases dependent upon his technological advances. Some claim that as man proceeded from the stone age to his present state of civilization one of his most important social achievements came about when he replaced muscle power with prime mover engines. In 1769, James Watt so improved the steam engine that many identify him as the person most responsible for setting the stage for the abolition of slavery. In 1791, France abolished slavery; in 1833 England followed suit; and in 1865, the United States passed similar legislation. Certainly, one cannot disregard the fact that religious and humanitarian motives played important if not dominant roles in the achievement of this impressive social goal. The fact remains, however, that it is doubtful that the aforementioned series of dates could have occurred in reverse order. Even the most ardent of the anti-technology zealots would have to agree that the presence of a mechanical slave made much easier a society's decision to render illegal the maintenance of human beings in perpetual bondage. Others argue that man's improvement in food production, especially when he contrived the turning plow and effected the domestication of animals, is even more significant for then man was afforded the opportunity to change from a nomadic savage into a stable and cultural social being. Some give the lion's share of credit to man's improvement in communications, his discovery of writing, the printing press, paperback, and TV. Whatever the principal precursors of our present civilization, whether they are really some of these, or the development of metallurgy through the Bronze and Iron Ages, or the acceptance of Henry Ford's principles of mass production, or increases in the utilization of energy, it is significant to note that every one of them is related to, and in many cases dependent upon technological breakthroughs and engineering achievements.

Yet, there are others to whom such a view of social development relying upon technological change is unacceptable. The view that technology was the premium mobile or even a precursor of significant and difficult to achieve steps in the development of a civilized state is not shared by everyone. Some feel that technology has disturbed, confused, and in some cases, revolutionized great plans for achieving an orderly progress of man into a serene and 'natural' state of humanistic nobility. We cannot disregard criticisms and attacks on technology. Some have considerable merit. Henry Ford has been heralded as one of the first industrialists to exhibit concern for the worker and skilled craftsman as he elevated their positions and proceeded to make inexpensive conveniences available to virtually everyone. Albeit unconsciously, he also gave encouragement to others who used some of his principles to develop demeaning and mind-boggling occupations that not only divorced man from his natural environment but in some cases reduced him to a position of importance subordinate to the machines he worked with. Consider the wonderful achievements of Paul Muller who developed DDT and was awarded a Nobel Prize for his contributions to mankind. DDT has been credited with the saving of at least 25 million lives during the 1940s and preventing hundreds of millions of illnesses since then. Yet, there is a fear today that this chemical is also capable of severely altering animal growth patterns, endangering lives and so seriously altering the ecology that its use constitutes a threat to man's survival.

What many of the critics of technology have to say and what the examples above are expected to illustrate is not so much that review and criticisms of past achievements are justified but more that man, with all his wisdom and clever applications of technology, has been and continues to be imperfect. The history of man's achievements is a clear testament to the reality that few things can be said to be complete, ever done with once and for all time to come. History also shows us that with every hurdle passed over in the pursuit of that elusive and ever changing goal of progress, man, with his increasingly powerful technology, is confronted not only with new hurdles but some related to, if not resulting from, some of the great leaps forward that he has already accomplished.

Finally, history in supporting the conviction that technology has always been an inherent and vital part of man, the instrument most responsible for his survival in the past, also provides us with reasons for being optimistic about the future. Man's technology has always been powerful and dangerous. As the early cave man quickly found out, the improvements in life style made possible by proper applications of fire not only created problems that had to be attended to but gave rise to his having uncovered forces which, if not carefully controlled, could effect his own destruction. Our situation is quite similar today. Not only do we need to be careful in applying our technology, we need to continuously improve it and improve our controls of it. Thus, there is now and will always be challenges for new James Watts and Paul Mullers as our society of tool-making animals continues to find ways to survive and live in harmony with its surroundings.

TECHNOLOGY TODAY

The study of history allows us the opportunity to acquire insight and incorporate the stability of experience into plans for the future. But if such plans are to be truly useful we must also seek to understand the present, not just how it got that way but what it is really comprised of – stripped of prejudiced concepts and undistorted by wishful and romantic fantasies. Perhaps writings designed to shock readers with doomsday prophecies are helpful as long as they are not allowed to lead one onto a state of apathetic helplessness. Likewise, scenarios depicting the peace and serenity of Utopias in super-sophisticated technological as well as slow-moving pastoral settings can be of assistance in separating realities from fairytale images of where we are and wish to go. But the entirety of an inquiry into what our present society is comprised of requires an overriding dedication to honesty.

For the limited purposes we have before us here, we focus upon the extent to which our technology resides within our culture and life style. Let us begin by attempting to see how deeply we are involved with technology today. By simply looking around us, we note that every stitch of the clothes we wear, the vehicles we rely upon for the majority of our movement, the telephones we converse with, the food we eat, the water we drink, and much of the air we breathe are made, processed, and brought to us by a wide variety of well-engineered machines and systems. To some people, such a view of our present involvement with technology is an assessment of how much progress our society has made. It indicates that we have achieved a highly ordered state wherein even the very poor have access to the conveniences and life styles that used to be enjoyed by only a select few. To others, it is a disappointing, if not frightening admission that we are fast approaching a time when we shall be so completely swept up in our technology that our human values will simply cease to exist.

As we inquire further into this apparent conflict in human responses to an observation, we encounter more exacting questions such as how much of our culture, our value systems and life styles are affected by our technology and what roles do technologists play in effecting social and cultural change? Even if we correctly admit that everyone, whether she or he is a user, applier or creator of technological devices and systems, is a technologist, we need to know answers to deeper questions. Do those closest to the creation of new technologies comprise a neutral force working only in response to public demands? Do the users as well as the creators of technology use their judgment properly in assessing the effects that their inquiries, discoveries, decisions and applications have upon such important factors as ecology, culture and human relationships, or do they, and all of us, merely attend to fulfilling immediate demands for providing conveniences at the lowest possible prices?

Let us start by observing that scientists, engineers, appliers, and users of technology are not neutral discoverers of phenomena in nature nor are they innovators concerned only with developing curious novelties. In fact, they are all influenced by a multitude of factors including the desire to fulfil personal aspirations and a need to respond to demands from a public that is constrained by its economy from rejecting compromises. There is considerable justification for concluding that scientists and engineers are directed by the morals, aspirations and objectives of the society in which they live. Inventors within a nation at war contrive machines of defense and death; scientists in a society bent upon exploration and discovery work with submarines and space ships; engineers in tourist communities which have committed themselves to creating or preserving a particular ecological setting design sophisticated sewer systems and machines to prevent erosion. But the roles of these people as well as the appliers and users of technology are not passive. All have been using and are continuing to use their technologies to change and create new forms of music, art and other outward expressions of our culture as well as attempting to construct vehicles that move farther and faster and thereby effect changes in our concepts of time. Just as the industrial revolution made possible, by inventions of prime mover engines, a shift of demeaning physical effort from man to the machine, today's computer technology is effecting a shift of time-consuming, repetitive analysis from man to electronically-powered imitations of the brain. One need not look far to see examples of how this shift is already infused with the multitude of forces that is changing our culture. Because of our present utilization of computer technology, we can expect instant response of communication networks to individual demands. We can find wide ranges of choices available to us as we undertake tasks of analyzing exactly which is the optimum means by which a housing development or factory can exist in harmony with nearby forests and fields.

Admittedly, the fruits of technology available to us today cannot be accepted without an awareness that they contain risks of abuse and the potential for degrading other vital segments of our physical as well as cultural environment. We need to be careful.

Technology today is no more uniformly dispersed at similar levels of sophistication throughout the world than are the different levels of social development. The aborigines in Central Australia and the cavemen of New Guinea live in societal settings that appear incredibly crude when viewed from vantage points within the urban societies of Western Europe and America. Because leisure, learning and creative effort beyond seeking more effective ways to ensure the existence of tomorrow's diet are not among the choices for life styles, we find that the large majority of primitive people, whenever offered a free choice, elect to adopt and imitate the technology that so characterizes western civilization. Thus, we can see the beginnings of dramatic cultural changes occurring rapidly in locations where life styles have changed little in ten thousand years. Furthermore, we can expect increases in the drains upon natural resoures and energy supplies that we already recognize as serious.

In summary, we see technology today as an integral part of our life style in spite of the fact that there are some who would wish otherwise. That our technology today is beginning to be confronted with the necessity for adjustment to allow for conformity with both a finiteness of natural resources and an increasing public desire to avoid unnecessary degradation of the environment is perhaps not yet fully appreciated nor understood; but it is beginning to be recognized as important to survival. Today, we are also encountering situations calling for the rendering of difficult decisions about technology, such as how far we should go in developing central computerized storage facilities with wide public access and for use in general and specialized information retrieval in areas of medical, legal and personal matters, or how far we should go in allowing instruments to be used in overtly altering the structure of DNA. It is of importance to realize that these situations cannot be turned off or caused to disappear. We cannot retreat into the hills and practice medieval magic. Indeed, it may be our human condition today to be caught up in a multitude of paradoxes, but we also possess the capability for handling them while making enormous strides in the pursuit of a more perfect society abounding in a wealth of individual choices for life styles. To do so we need to make personal and collective decisions, continue to bend science and technology to our will and intelligently be concerned with our environment as well as our finite supplies of many materials and forces. In doing these things, it should not be our intention that order be imposed by small groups of specialists whether they be skilled technologists, or geneticists, or lawyers, or government bureaucrats, or sociologists. Order should be understood as a structure comprised of a vast number of interrelationships created by the constant activity of each of us in and with all of nature's elements rather than any predetermined plan. Man and his technology are a part of nature. Both are vital components of any plan for balance between living things.

FALLACY OF THE DOOMSAYER'S VIEW

It is unwise to criticize those who would warn us of impending disaster unless we can show how their analysis has gone astray. Some have termed Malthus one of the original 'prophets of doom' after he published *An Essay on the Principle of Population as it Affects the Future Improvement of Mankind.*[4] While the dismal predictions of Malthus may not have been met on a worldwide basis, the reasoning he used in making his prediction based on limits of resources to sustain an ever-growing population contributes heavily to the analyses held in high esteem today. Malthus did not recognize how one resource can be substituted for another, however.

The results of the MIT group of Meadows et al who authored the book *The Limits to Growth,*[3] are based on a concept similar to that of Malthus who wrote that '. . . the power of population is indefinitely greater than the power of the earth to produce subsistence for man . . .' But the MIT group had a more powerful tool than Malthus to analyze the future world situation – they had a mathematical model of the whole world. This model was an improved version of the world model developed by J. W. Forrester and reported in 1971.[5] The book, *The Limits of Growth*, was carefully reviewed by S. Fred Singer and many weaknesses in the analyses brought to light.[6] Singer does not question, nor can anyone, the warning that exponential growth of population or of consumption cannot indefinitely be maintained on a finite earth. One real question is how to judge the cut-off point.

A major weakness of the MIT study is that the relationships in the mathematical model are 'single-valued' and do not change with time.[7] The model does not provide for any feedback, so reasoning individuals and governments can make adjustments in their life-styles based on potential dangers as they perceive them. Yet, at the time the book was published there were already signs that a real concern for future environmental conditions was emerging among many groups. Witness the new laws and regulations concerning environmental pollution. There is even a changing emphasis in advertising by American corporations to show an environmental awareness. Clearly, there is a realization that what we do now and in the future must better consider the environment. Feedback is already occurring.

The recent book by John Maddox entitled *The Doomsday Syndrome* cites the danger in overemphasizing the environmental problems.[8] Maddox points out that overstating the case concerning environmental pollution could anesthetize by repetition of prophesies portending environmental dooms which are not coming to bear. There are many cases where pollution has lessened through recent years as a result of technology. Air pollution in Chicago, St. Louis, Philadelphia, London and several other cities has improved since the mid-1960s. A classic example is the improvement in air quality over the past couple of decades that has occurred in Pittsburgh. Pollution can and will be stopped or curtailed so that the discharge of pollutants are compatible with the natural assimilative capacity of the receiving body. There are many proposals to see that this is done. Some involve governmental action such as a value-added tax for products which tend to lead to pollution in their manufacture.[9] Environmental-conscious consumers will tend to shift away from the 'un-ecological' products because of cost and manufacturers will cease to produce them – or shift to a less polluting method of manufacture.

There is the concept, which Barry Commoner termed his fourth law of ecology, that 'nature knows best'. It follows, but erroneously, that all would be well if we left things to nature. How we view this concept depends mostly on our understanding of man's role in nature. Man is necessarily a part of the natural system and, as a reasoning animal, has always tried to make nature less harsh to himself. He must protect himself from cold, heat, floods, droughts, hail and even earthquakes, lest he not survive. Through technology man extends his abilities to cope with the hazards nature tends to thrust upon him. Yet, we would agree that there are natural systems that must be protected and man must always guard against any technology that is permitted to run rampant.

Some romanticists view nature as providing the answer to all environmental ills. Rene Dubose in his paper, 'Humanizing the Earth', points out that the idealized equilibrium state of nature is often only reached over extended time and then with traumatic shocks of repeated population crashes of animal species such as lemmings, muskrats or rabbits.[10] And he speaks of the behavioral disturbances which occur in the animals before death. Dubose concludes '. . . only the most starry-eyed Panglossian optimist could claim that nature knows best how to achieve population control'.

Dubose also cites the error in the claim that nature has no junk yards. Paleontology is built on the study of the waste and artifacts of primitive man. Also, the recycling of nature has never been complete. How else can we explain the accumulation of peat, coal, oil, shale and other deposits of organic origin? These materials were stabilized and accumulated without being recycled by nature. Dubose concludes that the burning of these stored fuels completes the cycle and thereby releases the impounded carbon and minerals for future plant growth – but there is the danger that the breakdown products may overload contemporary ecological systems.

The problem is to get at the business of better using technology to solve the environmental problems currently facing man. Man will not return to the lifestyle of generations back. Moreover, there is no reason at all to believe that technology in the future will be less important in improving the quality of man's life by reducing drudgery and providing better food, health, and more leisure time.

Sir Peter Medawar, Nobel laureate in medicine and physiology, summed it up well when he said:

> This kind of fatalism sounds very dated today but we should ask ourselves very seriously whether there is not a tendency nowadays to take the almost equally discreditable view that the environment has now deteriorated beyond anything we can do to remedy – that man has now to be punished for his abandonment of that nature which according to the scenario of a popular Arcadian daydream should provide for all our reasonable requirements and find a remedy in all our misfortunes. It is this daydream that lies at the root of today's rancorous criticism of science and the technologies by people who believe and seem almost to hope our environment is deteriorating to a level below which it cannot readily support human life.
>
> My own view is that these fears are greatly exaggerated... Insofar as any weapon can be blamed for any crime, science and technology are responsible for our present predicament but they also offer the only possible means of escaping the misfortunes for which they are responsible.[11]

TECHNOLOGY IN A STEADY-STATE SOCIETY

Perhaps the most important question related to a steady-state society concerns the energy required to sustain those technologies which the society desires. A steady-state society must be achieved at some future time – simply because exponential population growth cannot continue indefinitely. Lugo's definition of a steady-state society in his contribution to this reader implies a continuous energy flow, but no further growth. How would technology fit into such a system?

First, the frequently assumed relationship between technological development and growth deserves some comment. Growth here is population growth or other growth where the demand on resources increases. No growth in the above sense does not necessarily mean no economic growth, and certainly does not mean no improvement (growth) in quality of life, however society decides to measure the latter. In the steady-state future, we will have matured beyond our insatiable desire for economic security. Society will more and more equate increased quality of life with non-economic values. Leisure and esthetic values will become more important.

Several things will need to happen in this future steady-state society. Although we do not know when it should or will come, it will take a great deal of time to reach it. We do not even know what might be an ideal population for a developed country such as the United States. And certainly the less developed countries question whether curtailing their growth will forever destine them to a lower standard of living, relatively speaking. Witness some of the conclusions drawn at the 1972 UN Conference on the Human Environment in Stockholm by less developed countries. Singer has recently posed a good question: '. . . would we be better off or worse off in the US if we had arrested growth fifty years ago – or thirty years ago?'[6] This is certainly a proper question to ask when we speculate that the world would be better off with less population – considering commerce and all the things that go into the matrix of a society.

When a steady-state society is reached it will be because of the conscious efforts of a reasoning people, not because some computer model of the world decreed it. It will require new values, including those which have been identified by Lugo. Many of the technological inputs will of necessity be directed toward achieving stated societal goals in a non-polluting way. For example, the energy question will remain with us because there will continue to be need for energy to support activities such as maintaining viable communities and to produce food. More emphasis will be given to the durability and useful life of systems instead of planned obsolescence. New and improved technologies will be required.

The field of technological development of suitable substitutes will be very important. We will have an increasing need for substituting one material for another as those in current use become in short supply in much the same manner as aluminum is now widely substituted for copper in industrial electrical applications. Indeed, supplies of many things taken for granted today will not be plentiful in a steady-state society – otherwise the society would not have reached the steady-state. But most surely there will not be less emphasis on the ways in which technology can make life on earth pleasant in this new condition.

We daresay that this steady-state society into which we will evolve will be better than if society opted to accept overt steps backward and, in effect, put the labor back on the farm and to break up all cities, into small self-regulated communities. The recipe for survival published in the January 1972 issue of *The Ecologist* is a case in point.[12] Such a romantic existence will simply not come about because the people will not opt to return to an agrarian life, where agriculture has been made inefficient by design, so that human labor may be utilized. Nor will there be any need for such a shift.

SOME FUTURE TECHNOLOGIES

An essay on the potential of technology for solving future environmental problems should touch on some of the future technologies that might be involved. Space permits us to mention but a few technologies and give reference to others. The future technologies of specific interest here deal with environmental problems and often relate to natural resources – usually energy, food and mineral resources. A recent National Academy of Sciences report by the Committee on Resources and Man gives an excellent overview and points to some of the areas where technological opportunity exists.[13] This report provides an excellent survey of the world resource situation.

The question of where the energy to maintain a highly technological society will come from needs answering. The MIT group scenarios predict a collapse of society largely because of exhaustion of natural resources.[3, 5] This, of course, is a Malthusian view. Contrasted to this is the Ricardian or technological-optimist view that for every scarce material a substitute can be found, though at a somewhat higher cost.[14] In fact, Boyd has recalculated the Forrester scenarios with the Ricardian rather than Malthusian view using the admittedly optimistic, but realizable, assumption that technology can keep pollution under control.[15] He finds that the world will not collapse, but will achieve a completely acceptable steady-state.

The Ricardian view is not strictly valid in that it depends on an unlimited energy source – and of course this does not now exist. Weinberg is among those who have analyzed the energy situation, particularly in relation to nuclear power.[16] The use of nuclear energy most certainly implies a risk. But it is one demonstrated technology that can be used to provide power because eventually all non-renewable resources will be exhausted. Weinberg believes that in the very long run nuclear energy will be widely used with the uranium or thorium fuel for breeders coming from the granitic rocks.

To be sure there are environmental risks in nuclear breeder reactors that must have further evaluation. And there are other risks attached to future technologies that need careful evaluation. In fact, there is the developing science of technology assessment, and both the National Academy of Science and the National Academy of Engineering have recently addressed themselves to this problem.[17, 18] The report of the National Goals Staff of the Executive Branch of US Government entitled *Toward Balanced Growth: Quantity with Quality*, contains a chapter on technology assessment with an especial regard to the environment.[19] Technology assessment must be more carefully done and it must satisfy the concerns of all thoughtful citizens. Understanding this situation, the US Congress has established an Office of Technology Assessment to assure that all future technologies are evaluated and that the proper concerns of the public are not ignored.

On the international scene, technology assessment is also receiving impetus. The first International Congress on Technology Assessment was held in The Hague, May 27-June 2, 1973. Reasonable people in technology and otherwise want thorough assessment of the environmental dangers of any technology, but those who are 'anti-anything new' cannot be permitted to prevail. Remember how many skeptics there were of the first airplane?

There are many environmental energy sources that offer potential for establishing an unlimited supply of energy (possibly even to justify the Ricardian view). Among these are solar energy, energy resulting from thermal gradients in the earth and oceans, gravitational forces of tides and water flow. The power available from these sources is given in Table 1.[20] But of all these, the sun is the basic source of energy for earth. It is the only non-consumable source.

Table 1. *Environmental power sources*[20]

	Watts
Solar	1.73×10^{17}
Incident 30 percent	
Atmospheric 47 percent	
Hydrologic cycle 23 percent	
Earth	
Conducted to surface via rocks	32×10^{12}
Convection (hot springs and volcanoes)	0.3×10^{12}
Tides, tidal currents	3×10^{12}
Winds, waves, convection, currents	370×10^{12}
Water power	3×10^{12}

There is every reason to believe that solar power will become a significant source of energy in the future. For example, at 30 degrees north latitude on a typical March day, the integrated power from a horizontal surface over a 24-hour day yields an energy of 3.8 kw hours/m^2. This is far too much energy to be indefinitely ignored in a technological society that needs an ever-increasing energy supply. Hildebrandt and his colleagues have surveyed several mechanisms for solar energy conversion, and research by Farber and his colleagues is considering many others.[21, 22]

Other future technologies that may seem far-fetched at present, but offer real opportunity for a quantum leap in solving our energy problems of today and the future, are reviewed in a recent National Academy of Sciences report.[23] This report is concerned with some future technologies that will save water by posing less of a heat load on the water supplies. Such things as nuclear fusion, fuel cells, magnetohydrodynamics, efficient long distance power transmission through cryogenically cooled conductors, and others are discussed. Suffice here to say that some of these will be proven feasible, and that technology will help solve the energy problem in an environmentally acceptable way.

A final word on future technologies and energy. We have said nothing about conservation. This in itself offers the most readily available way to start an environmentally sound energy program. Attitudes of both people and governments will be important to start with, but more efficient machines and systems will also be required. The latter technological opportunity will most certainly be a part of future technological research.

Food production is an area where technological achievement has recently been impressive. Even though there are still people in many regions of the world who are hungry, much of this is more due to lack of infrastructure within and among the nations than it is to lack of worldwide potential to produce. To be sure, this circumstance does not make the problem less severe to those who are starving. But there is the technology now to grow far more food than is presently produced. In the United States, yields of such crops as wheat, rice, corn, cotton and soybeans far exceed the world averages. Yet wheat yields of over ten times the US average have already been obtained.[24] For rice and soybeans, yields of over four times the average have been obtained. For corn and cotton, the maximum yield has been over six times the US average.

The maximum potential yields will increase, but there is an upper limit. Also, there is a limit to the arable lands in the world, particularly in several of the densely populated countries. In Asia, less than three-tenths of a hectare is now cultivated per person. In Europe, the figure is little higher at about a third of a hectare per person, while in North America it is nearly one hectare of cultivated land per person. The cultivated hectares per person will most certainly continue to decline while the population grows. Increased technical input to agriculture then becomes a must for meeting food needs.

We recognize that as agriculture becomes more specialized, species diversity is decreased with the attendant increased risk of failure in the eyes of the ecologist. This real concern need not be viewed as an insurmountable problem, however. Once a highly specialized agriculture is adopted, a commitment must be made to provide the necessary production inputs to achieve a high yield. Especially bred high-producing crops require careful water management, fertilization, and control of pests and pathogens. The latter two may be with selective breeding of resistant varieties, biological or physical control, or chemical control with degradable chemical control measures. It is a truism that when we solve one problem we create another – or at least permit another problem of originally lesser importance to assume the number one position. Solving a disease problem to curtail an epidemic may result in a famine later if food supplies are marginal. But this does not make the original effort less noble. So it is when we use technology to augment food production.

Food factories should be included in any scenario on technological ways of meeting future needs. There is real potential in using protein from micro-organisms that possibly feed on waste materials as a nutritions base material for so-called synthetic foods. We also see food factories where especially bred agricultural crops are grown in controlled environmental systems using waste heat, carbon dioxide enrichment and sophisticated water, fertility and pest control systems. Vegetative protein will likely be used more to by-pass the less efficient animal protein production route. Still, the basic photo-synthetic reaction continues to be the basis for the production of food. Science and technology will continue to eliminate those things which curtail production to below the theoretical maximum.

When one speculates on the future, one can choose whether to adopt the Malthusian view or the technological-optimist view – and the future conditions can pretty well be perceived without the use of the computer. Our belief is that which view turns out to be correct is primarily dependent on which future man decides he wants to make correct. We see an increasingly challenging role for the technologist because the environmental and resource depletion constraints make his problems more difficult to solve. But they do not make them impossible to solve.

NOTES

1. Cabell, J. B., *The Silver Stallion*, Robert M. McBride and Co., New York, 1926.
2. Commoner, Barry, *The Closing Circle*, Alfred A. Knopf, New York, 1971.
3. Meadows, D. H., et al., *The Limits to Growth*, Universe Books, New York, 1972.
4. Malthus, T. R., *An Essay on the Principle of Population as it Affects the Future Improvement of Mankind,* 1798; Facsimile reprint in 1926 for J. Johnson, Macmillan and Co., London.
5. Forrester, J. W., *World Dynamics*, Wright-Allen Press, Cambridge, Massachusetts, 1971.
6. Singer, S. F., 'The Predicament of the Club of Rome. A review of *The Limits to Growth*', *Transactions*, American Geophysical Union, 53, 1972, 697-700.
7. There is no space here to analyze the MIT study, *The Limits to Growth*, but this has been done in the review by Singer and in the 'Postscript' in the book *The Doomsday Syndrome* by John Maddox (see following reference). Suffice here to say that the book has had inestimable value in simply reaffirming the dangers of exponential growth in population and use of resources. Four quotes from Singer and two from Maddox illustrate some of the weaknesses in the study:

   An analysis which allows for human behavior in the response to economic forces would show a large amount of rapid feedback. It would not show the inevitable overshoot and collapse associated with the MIT models which do not incorporate strong damping. (Singer)

   In technical language, he assumes that his relationships are 'single-valued' and do not change with time. For example, he assumes that whenever the average income hits a particular value then so will the birth rate, and he so instructs his computer. But let's see how this works in practice. If one looks at his computer runs, one finds that the world goes to hell shortly after the year 2000, as food-per-capita suddenly drops to a very low value and as pollution suddenly increases and kills those who are not starved. But look what happens to the birth rate. The computer only remembers that the birth rate goes up when income goes down. So bingo! The computer has increased the birth rate of these poor, starving, wretched people back up to 12 children or more; and of course, the death rate rises even more steeply. (Singer)

At first inspection, the book appears to be loaded with hard data ... But it is all window dressing; the data is never used. (Singer)

Clearly, every country presents a different situation; for Canada or for India the answers would be different, yet the MIT study deals with world averages. And in the process of averaging, they 'wipe out' the single most significant feature about the world today, namely the gap between the wealthy and poor nations. (Singer)

The first and most serious complaint against the Club of Rome study is that its authors have been forced to describe the world in oversimple terms. Their error is what the economists call aggregation. On pollution, for example, they have been compelled by the limitations of their equipment to describe the total population of the world by three numbers, with the result that their calculations are unable to take account of the way in which the pattern of population growth differs markedly between developing countries and advanced countries. On population, represented by a single number in the computer calculation, they are compelled to assume that this is at any time determined by the scale of industrial and agricultural output and are thus unable to make allowances for the way in which pollution of various forms might be drastically reduced, either by devoting industrial resources to the abatement of pollution or by changes in the pattern of industrial output and in particular the replacement of pollution industries by others. (Maddox)

The first publication suggests that the Club of Rome has given a great many hostages to fortune. And it is hard at this stage to know what to make of the claim, running through the Club of Rome report, that the study is meant only as an admonitory projection into the future, not a prediction. This, of course, is a familiar academic escape from responsibility. Yet, *The Limits to Growth* does at one point assert that: 'We can thus say with some confidence that, under the assumption of no major change in the present system, population and industrial growth will certainly stop within the next century, at the latest.' It is true that this sentence includes the familiar reservation of the extreme environmentalists, 'under the assumption of no major change in the present system', but in the circumstances the Club of Rome should not be surprised that *The Limits to Growth* has been publicly regarded as a prophecy. (Maddox)

8. Maddox, John, *The Doomsday Syndrome,* McGraw-Hill, New York, 1972.
9. McCleery, William, '*Rx* for the Environment: Ecological Capitalism', *University: A Princeton Quarterly*, Winter, 1973.
10. Dubose, René J., 'Humanizing the Earth', *Science*, 179, 1973, 769-772.
11. Medawar, Sir Peter, 'What's Human about Man is His Technology', *Smithsonian*, 4, 1973, 22-29.
12. 'A Blueprint for Survival', *The Ecologist*, 1972, Vol. 2.
13. Committee on Resources and Man, *Resources and Man*, National Academy of Science, W. H. Freeman and Company, San Francisco, 1969.
14. Weiner, Aaron, 'The Development of Israel's Water Resources', *American Scientist*, 60, 1972, 466-473.

15. Boyd, Robert, 'World Dynamics: A Note', *Science*, 177, 1972, 516-519.
16. Weinberg, Alvin M., 'Some Views of the Energy Crisis', *American Scientist*, 61, 1973, 59-60.
17. National Academy of Sciences, *Technology: Processes of Assessment and Choice*, US Government Printing Office, Washington, DC, 1969.
18. National Academy of Engineering, *A Study of Technology Assessment*, US Government Printing Office, Washington, DC, 1969.
19. National Goals Research Staff, *Toward Balanced Growth: Quantity with Quality*, US Government Printing Office, Washington, DC, 1970. The technology assessment movement in the US was started in the mid-1960s by the Congress within the Science, Research, and Development Subcommittee of the Science and Astronautics Committee of the House of Representatives. This movement has grown to the point that there now exists a real concern in both Congress and the Executive Branch of US Government. Public Law 92-484 was enacted on October 13, 1972, establishing an Office of Technology Assessment which reports to Congress. This is a very important step which charts the course for better assessment of those future technologies which will meet man's future needs and satisfy environmental concerns. The following is quoted from the Summary of the above reference:

    The Nation's infatuation with technology is at a turning point as profound as that of its relationship to the environment. Historically, we have tended to do that which was technically possible, if it were economically advantageous, on the simple ground that this represented 'progress'. However, as technology has increased with great rapidity, it has forced on us increasing unplanned social change and environmental problems we did not anticipate and do not want. At the same time, our notions of the complexity of social environmental problems have made us increasingly cautious with respect to the actions we plan to take. Our level of affluence has given us a longer time perspective within which to assess the consequences of our actions. As with so many other of the debates with which we have been concerned, the technology assessment movement – which embodies this new attitude toward technology – asks us to judge our actions by a wider range of criteria than we have used in the past.

    Formally, technology assessment is a term coined in the Congress to label a set of procedures to aid the Congress in making decisions for the orderly introduction of new technology and the evaluation of technology already in use. However, it is better viewed as a manifestation of a larger phenomenon of a decreasing willingness of both the public and its representatives to tolerate the undesirable side effects of things done in the name of progress. The public has protested effectively against the displacement of people by highways, aircraft noise, and the building of new power plants. Specific actions have indicated that we have the disposition to forego immediate economic benefits in order to avoid social and environmental costs which once would have been accepted with no more than pro forma consideration. The existence of formal technology assessment, now in both the congressional and executive branches, is to be taken as no more than a specific manifestation of the broader concern.

20. Roberts, Ralph, 'Energy Sources and Conversion Techniques', *American Scientist*, 61, 1973, 66-75.
21. Hildebrandt, A. F., et al., 'Large-scale Concentration and Conversion of Solar Energy', *Transactions American Geophysical Union*, 53, 1972, 684-692.
22. Farber, E. A., *Solar Energy: Conversion and Utilization. Building System Design*, Presstech Design Inc., Brooklyn, N.Y., 1972.
23. National Academy of Sciences, *Potential Technological Advances and Their Impact on Anticipated Water Requirements,* National Academy of Sciences, Washington, DC, 1971.
24. Hendricks, Sterling B., *Food from the Land. Resources and Man,* W. H. Freeman and Company, 1969.

4. Subsistence economies and the environment

HANS G. T. VAN RAAY

A review of the means of food collection and production in low-energy economies. The author assesses their relevance to the present-day situation in ecological and ideological terms. The observations passed on security and equality may be compared with comments by Van Arkel, Van Benthem van den Bergh, Burger, Du Boff in other contributions. Lugo also gives an energetic interpretation.

I

Man's struggle for existence and survival corresponds to that of other living beings in that it involves adjustment to the natural habitat, competition with his kind and other living beings for the more favourable habitats, and the capture and utilisation of energy. Man, like other organisms, could be compared to a solar engine that runs on the energy stored in plants and animals. But there is an important difference. To quote White: 'Man employs the organs of his body in the process of adjustment to and control over his environment, as do other animals. But in addition to these somatological mechanisms, man, and man alone, possesses an elaborate extra-somatic mechanism which he employs in the process of living. This extra-somatic mechanism, this traditional organisation of tools, customs, language, beliefs, etc. we have called culture.'[1] As much as the bodily organs, culture is a mechanism that serves the spiritual and material needs of man. Man's energy-capturing and utilising system thus has a somatic and an extra-somatic component. This accounts for his ability to establish hegemony over the environment however diverse it may be. To put it in energy terms, it has enabled him to harness energy at the expense of other organisms and to put it to his advantage.

This paper will examine the interaction of man and his environment in rural types of economy that for ages have supported mankind. The economies selected are all subsistent in nature, characterised by the fact that the more immediate needs such as food, clothing and shelter are satisfied in a direct manner. The focus on these activities has been prompted by several considerations. They represent once universal conditions of mankind but are also of importance today, both in terms of population and the area affected. An additional reason has been that they point to what the future may hold if 'civilised' man does not manage to avert a nuclear cataclysm or the ecological catastrophe that according to some is bound to occur if present trends continue. With two world wars within a time span of less than forty years still fresh in the memory and with growing concern about increasing signs of environmental deterioration and exhaustion of natural resources, it is sometimes wondered whether civilisation will end as it started.

After a few observations about domestication, some general characteristics will be reviewed of four rural occupancy systems, i.e. gathering, pastoralism, shifting agriculture, and intensive subsistence agriculture. The features described are predominantly of an economic nature, with due attention being given to the relationships with and consequences for the environmental setting in which they occur.[2] However, the selection may be somewhat biased since the author has been intensively exposed to gathering, pastoralism, and subsistence cultivation only as practised in the tropical and equatorial zones. The descriptive review of the four occupancy systems will be followed by an attempt to examine the relevance of some aspects of subsistence life to the present-day situation. This concluding section is clearly one-sided. Unlike the descriptive part of the paper which endeavours to give a balanced view of the four rural economies, it has a distinct positive slant. It cannot be stressed too strongly that the choice made does not derive from a romantic view of subsistence life, nor reflects any intention of idealising it. The conclusion is merely intended to highlight some features that seem pertinent to present efforts to determine a new direction in man-man and man-environment relationships.

DOMESTICATION

The domestication of plants and animals from about 6000 BC onwards is commonly referred to as a revolution in the history of mankind in view of the magnitude of the structural change that was brought about in the man-environment relationship. The food-production revolution allegedly heralded a new era in the development of man and turned him from a rare mammal into the most numerous and most dispersed. The change signified by the term revolution was indeed a radical one and was finally to initiate a farreaching transformation of the human environment, but the several innovations involved took a very long time to emerge and to spread out over the earth's surface. The full complex of domestication involves an extensive range of innovations. With regard to animals it is not only a matter of taming and training but also of breeding; the animal should reproduce in captivity before domestication is considered complete. Through selective breeding, man further cultivates the properties he values. Complete plant domestication also requires numerous steps of which seed collection and storage, clearing, planting, weeding, and harvesting are the more crucial. But a number of additional techniques are of great significance for increasing yields, such as plant breeding, manuring, fencing, fallowing, and irrigation. It is interesting to note that several gatherers applied one or more of these techniques as an initial step in their emergence from simple gathering. To quote Linton:

> ... in Australia, the natives made the discovery that if they threw peelings and shoots scraped off in preparing wild yams in a place where the soil was black, they would find a yam patch growing there when they returned to the camp site the following year. They replanted tops deliberately, but they never cultivated or fertilised yam patches. This haphazard planting was their only agricultural achievement.
>
> In British Columbia, on the other hand, the Indians did no planting except for the occasional scattering of tobacco seeds on burned-over ground by some of the southern tribes. However, they prized sweet clover and skunk cabbage as greens. The skunk cabbage is one of the first plants to appear in the spring ... women who discovered a good patch of clover or cabbage would fence it, weed it, and put up various ingenious scarecrows to keep the deer away. Other women would respect the patch as her property. However, it never occurred to anyone to try to plant or fertilise such patches.
>
> The use of fertilizer is one of the rarest agricultural techniques, yet it was used by the Indians ... The New England tribes put a herring in each hill of corn when they planted, then went off to hunt, leaving the corn to its own devices until they returned to harvest any which had survived weeds and insect pests.
>
> In the Rocky Mountain plateau the Paiutes neither planted nor cultivated, but they irrigated. They were fond of pig-weed, which they used as greens in the spring and as seeds in the autumn. The Paiutes built small dams at the heads of shallow valleys to impound the winter snow water. The pig-weed grew in the valleys below the dams and each band had an official irrigator who made the rounds of the pig-weed patches from time to time, and if they seemed to be getting too dry, would poke a hole in the dam, let some water run down over them, and then fill up the hole again.[3]

From these examples it can be seen that there has been no progressive evolution in agriculture in the sense of one technique following the other. Rather, it has been a cumulative process in which ecological differentiation, commonsense, chance discoveries and diffusion combined to produce several distinct agricultural management systems.

The increased human capacity to produce food that accompanied domestication is believed to have created a fertile soil for development in that two prerequisites of cultural progress were provided for, i.e.

the production of a surplus and the availability of leisure. It is indeed true that as a result of domestication the land could, on occasion, feed more people than were needed for its tillage and that as a consequence specialists in crafts and others who were agriculturally non-productive, such as administrators and scholars, could be supported. But rather than philosophising in broad general terms on the impact of domestication on man, his culture, and his environment, attention may be drawn to the several rural types of economy associated with domesticated plants and animals and their common root since studies of this nature facilitate our understanding of the issues at hand.

THE COMMON ROOT: GATHERING

It was by merely withdrawing items of value from nature's storehouse that early man supported himself. Several forms of the ancient way of life have persisted to remind us of our cultural ancestors, and it is by studying these relics that we shall try to shed light on what was once the prevailing method of existence in Eurasia, Africa, Australia and the Americas. Gathering has mainly survived in pockets within two major belts, i.e. the low and high latitudes. Most high-latitude examples are located in the subarctic parts of the northern hemisphere. The low-latitude distribution includes a greater diversity of environments, both north and south of the equator. Major areas of distribution are the arid interior of Australia and the deserts and semi-deserts of South Africa on the one hand, and the tropical rainforests of the Amazon and Congo Basins on the other. A great number of gathering communities are furthermore scattered over the heavily forested areas of the South Asiatic mainland and adjacent islands and archipelagos from India to New Guinea. Gathering is presently confined to the more inaccessible and inhospitable parts of the world, but the steady retreat caused by the encroachment of more advanced societies is going on at such a rate that before long all these 'cultural zoos' may have faded from the face of the earth.

A significant characteristic of food-gathering is that little attempt is made to increase the relative occurrence of certain plants and animals. I do not mean to say that there is no interference with nature's course. Whatever our views on the ceremonies performed to secure an abundant supply of foodstuffs, the gatherer genuinely believes in their effectiveness. Several instances could also be quoted of more effective interference as, for example, the protection of plant stands against animal attack by means of fencing. But there is no extensive collaboration with nature to facilitate the proliferation of more valued plants and animals, neither by seeding and breeding, nor by suppressing or extinguishing natural competitors.

This places the gatherer very much at the mercy of nature. Dependent as he is on nature's capacity to renew the sources of food and raw materials of the human population, consumption tends to vary greatly from day to day, from season to season, and from year to year. Though several examples could be quoted of gathering communities in the equatorial and tropical zones in particular which can secure a steady supply, periods of abundance often alternate with periods of severe shortage. Whenever the direct sustenance of life is at stake, and in some cases this is the rule rather than the exception, the gatherer has little opportunity to engage in other activities than those which meet immediate needs. In addition to repercussions on health and life expectation, it is sometimes also suggested that such conditions would not be conducive to cultural progress since all energy would be absorbed by food-searching activities, by improving the skills and material aids essential for the satisfaction of basic needs, and by securing the meagre resources against intruders. But it is clear that great qualities of resourcefulness tend to be displayed by those who live up to the challenge of a harsh environment, as is exemplified by forms of cooperation, hunting and fishing, and marvels of equipment. Also, those gathering communities which are capable of meeting their needs and wants with little effort are normally not more advanced. Without negating their possible impact on cultural progress, leisure and surplus should thus not be singled out as factors at work. Even in the case of the so-called simple gathering communities, the man-environment interplay is much too complex and diverse for any such generalisation to be of relevance. The designation 'simple' is not intended to convey a derogatory connotation. In the relative sense in which it is used here it is meant to imply that gathering societies are believed to share a number of attributes which are commonly considered indicative of low economic advancement. Closer examination of some of the more prominent economic attributes may substantiate this.

Gathering economies are more or less complete economies. They provide their practitioners with the food, clothing, shelter, and all other elements they have learned to enjoy. Each gathering unit produces practically everything that is consumed locally. Fulltime specialisation other than that based on sex is virtually lacking. Each unit and each sub-unit, if the localised community is made up of several sub-units, bends its efforts to directly providing for all its needs and wants, rather than aiming at the generation of surplus to be used for exchange purposes.

Though there is a lot of truth in the saying that 'Jack-of-all-trades is master of none', many gatherers have done remarkably well. The Eskimo boy learned to track game, prey the seal, snare fish, and also to make the igloo, kayak, harpoon etc., and his skills are unlikely to be contested. Another point directly relates to the present argument. By the very nature of their way of life, gathering communities are bound to be small and widely spaced. But despite the isolation this implies, basic inventions spread over wide areas. The speed at which this occurred is hard to trace but it happened and, as a consequence, the production efficiency of a great many gatherers was substantially increased. If the technique itself was not acquired or could not be applied for lack of the necessary raw materials, barter or trade would sometimes arise. Two cases in point are the trade in stone axes in New Guinea and the 'silent trade' in the Congo Basin. The New Guinea case is all the more interesting as shell money and 'markets' were some of the expedient conditions that evolved to facilitate the exchange. At present, the same channels are used for metal utensils, and it is not uncommon to come across iron axes in areas which have not previously been explored. The same holds true for the Pygmoids in the Congo Basin whose metal spearheads were obtained through exchange with the Bantu. But neither the Papuans nor the Pygmoids nor any other gathering communities produce the metal utensils they use. Two important conclusions can be derived from these observations. Firstly, gathering communities are not perfectly closed and self-sufficient. Secondly, gathering societies have made cultural progress in developing new techniques and material aids which facilitate a more effective adjustment to existing conditions; but however elaborate and ingenious the material equipment, gatherers do not command the ability to refine ores and produce metal objects.

Hence, we should not think of gathering economies as being technically backward and static entities which have shown no capacity for change. The body of accumulated knowledge which has passed from person to person and from generation to generation has tended to widen the gatherer's range and efficiency, resulting in a thorough exploitation of the environment and an extremely varied application of its limited resources. The equatorial gatherer knows all the edible fruits, roots and leaves and he supplements his diet with a great diversity of land and water animals. Most raw materials have a vegetal and animal origin and very few of the items collected are disposed of without being used for one purpose or another. If gathering is more exclusively based on animal life, as is the case in the higher latitudes, the application of animal products in satisfying all needs may have developed into a fine art. This definitely holds true of the Eskimo, credited with having realised one of the finest ancient material cultures.

But if we take the capacity of an economy to offer a decent living as a yardstick of its advancement, then we cannot but conclude that many gathering economies indeed take low place. In many cases, particularly in the dry and cold deserts of the world, they offer no more than a marginal existence which exposes the people to frequent hardship. Malnourishment, ill health, periodic famine and starvation, fear, insecurity, little leisure, all could be reduced to one and the same cause: the economy's incapacity to offer a living which is considered minimal by our standards and even by the gatherer's standard once he becomes aware of other opportunities. The gathering system can support very few people per land unit, and even then often only by condemning the people to a very low standard of living.

PASTORALISM

The only all-inclusive term for all types of livestock rearing is animal husbandry, of which pastoralism is a particular strain. The designation pastoralism, and synonyms such as herding and migratory herding, point to an essential characteristic: instead of having their movements restricted by fence or rope, the animals are controlled by herdsmen.

What else characterises pastoralism? First of all, a strong subsistence-orientation tends to prevail. The herd is the main source for satisfaction of human needs. Though day-to-day exchanges with sedentarists, for example, might be common, most needs are met by the herd. This undoubtedly helps to account for the full utilisation that is made of the livestock. The herd not only supplies most of the food consumed (meat, milk, cheese, and butter) but provides material for clothing and shelter (fibres, skins), fuel (droppings), and tools (bones). Finally, the animals are often used for transportation. Animals that through the ages have proved most satisfactory in these several roles are sheep, goats, cattle, camels, yaks, reindeers and horses.

Another typical feature of pastoralism is that the animals subsist on natural rather than cultivated fodder. This dependence on natural pasture, together with the fact that pastoralists do not normally store fodder, forces people to adjust to the seasonal variation in the quantity and quality of fodder by means of migration between ecologically complementary areas. Sometimes conditions are such that people live more or less in a state of perpetual wandering: nomadism. Others wander about as do the genuine nomads for part of the year, returning to their homesteads when conditions allow. This difference is closely related to the environment. Semi-nomadism is often to be found in areas with marked dry and rainy seasons, as on the fringes of the deserts.

It is striking that pastoralism as a dominant economy has developed only in the Old World. It is true that the guanaco was reared on the Andean plateau, but here animal raising was an auxiliary activity and formed an integral part of an agricultural and sedentary civilisation.[4] In the Old World, distribution is clearly associated with certain environments. Main areas of occurrence are the tundra and the fairly arid temperate and tropical grasslands and semi-deserts. The seclusion of pastoralism from forest country is no doubt related to the fact that herbivorous animals are not well suited to forest country where fodder is scarce and herding is difficult. Obviously, diseases are also a deterrent, particularly in the tropics.

The distributional pattern is also affected by other considerations. Pastoralism is an extensive undertaking that offers a hard and insecure life to its practitioners, and the fact that pastoralism is largely confined to areas that set limitations to cropping seems related to the fact that many pastoralists have in time yielded to the temptations of sedentary life. Yet several instances could be quoted of spatial competition between pastoralists and agriculturalists. Although not ignorant of the general methods of cultivation and the richer reward and comfort that may be obtained, many pastoralists continue to resist assimilation, sometimes to the distress of governments.

To appreciate this latter point, it should be realised that pastoralism is becoming increasingly precarious. Profitable caravan trade has largely been taken over by lorries. Traditional products such as wool, skins, dairy produce and meat, face more and more competition from external sources. Traditional moves are disrupted by the emergence of new political entities, the extension of agriculture and the reservation of land for public interest. Cultivators are no longer dependent, as they often were in the past. Finally, the role of public authorities should not be overlooked. Whenever land use competition arises there is frequently an inclination to appraise several resource uses and profitable options in a strictly economic fashion. It is true that in most cases it is less economic to convert natural plant growth into animal food before consumption than it is to modify that growth by cultivation so that it may be consumed directly. But several other interests are at stake; it could be argued with good reason that in several tropical areas the future of agriculture is very heavily dependent on the maintenance and better utilisation of livestock resources. There is another reason for concern regarding ill-considered attempts to settle the pastoralist. In many cases pastoralism represents the best way to utilise the resources of certain environments otherwise left idle, and its improvement rather than suppression should be considered.

SHIFTING AGRICULTURE

Shifting agriculture embraces a wide variety of agricultural systems which appear in the literature under various names, such as migratory cultivation, slash-and-burn cultivation, shifting field agriculture, field-forest rotation, and field-grass rotation. Whatever the differences in actual management, all systems have in common a manner of land rotation. Fields are used for a number of years and are then left fallow for a period of between one and thirty years. This often results in a shifting of settlements. Regular rotation also implies that the clearing of forest or grassland is an important feature of these economies. In this, fire plays an important role. Fire may do damage but also has beneficial effects; no other equally efficient means are available with which to undertake the hard task of preparing the land for cropping. In forest country, clearing is imperfect; standing and fallen treetrunks are left indiscriminately while certain trees may be spared because of the fruits they produce.

All tillage is done by hand and preparation of the soil is superficial, plots often supporting a great variety of crops which are irregularly spaced. Leading crops are maize, millet, rice, manioc, yams, peanuts, tobacco. Trees are often grown, such as banana, oilpalm, coconut, cocoa and breadfruit, which initiate regeneration of the 'forest'. Gathering has not disappeared from these economies and is often an important source of supplementary food. Shifting cultivators normally also engage in the rearing of fowls, pigs, goats, etc. Yet the demand for meat normally far exceeds the supply, resulting in a predominantly vegetal diet. Productivity per unit of land and of labour tends to be low, as is also the standard of living. The extensivity of land use makes shifting cultivation a large consumer of space. Measurements have shown that in many cases the carrying capacity corresponds to a potential of 30 persons to the square mile, although occasionally it falls to eight. Presently, shifting agriculture is mainly found in the tropics, major zones being tropical Africa, America and Asia, though in the latter case it tends to give way to more intensive agricultural systems along coasts and in the river valleys.

The idea has been advanced that shifting agriculture represents a kind of cultural climax in the tropics. Gourou, in particular, stresses this point; his reasoning as developed in *The Tropical World* is interesting as it entails some well-established biases. Without outside help, shifting agriculture would be the best that the people could achieve. Related to this viewpoint is that no high civilisations have been developed within the tropical realm. This may seem readily disputable with such examples on hand as the Maya and Inca civilisations, and those of Asia and West Africa. But Gourou suggests that in all these cases the spur to higher attainment came from outside the tropics. Two aspects of the tropical environment, in particular, are held responsible for the backwardness of the tropics: soil poverty and unhealthiness. Both are reducible to climate, which is therefore presented as the real cause. Tropical man, racked by disease, has only a highly vulnerable basis on which to make a living. He is a weakened man, living in an environment that sets wide limitations. Caught in a vicious circle, there is a ceiling to independent cultural development, a barrier that cannot be crossed without outside help.

The realisation that most parts of the world, including some of the most advanced, would still be backward if it were not for outside cultural injections, would be of little comfort to the inhabitant of the tropics if there were not reason to believe that there is something fundamentally wrong with Gourou's thesis. Although this extremely brief summary of part of his book may imperfectly and even erroneously reflect its contents, it is felt that the main thrust is unduly deterministic in nature. The author goes out of his way to perceive the evolution of civilisation in terms of a specific environment, but the inherent weaknesses of the tropical ecology that he advances seem invalidated by some of the evidence presently available. The limitations supposedly set to independent cultural development are equally hard to operationalise. In addition to the problem of defining levels of cultural advancement and the questionableness of the outcome of such an exercise, there is another fundamental complication. Limitations to independent cultural development are believed to prevail all over the world, but to argue that a cultural ceiling would be associated with a major ecological earth zone seems unacceptable. Such a view entails not only an overrating of the possible impact of the physical habitat but also, and more important, an underrating of man's resourcefulness and creativity.

Of equal interest is another assumption. Shifting cultivation is sometimes accused of being a robber economy since it makes use of available resources in such a manner as to destroy them. To assess this, it has to be recalled that the societies affected have rather simple material equipment (digging stick, hoe) and limited knowledge of the several natural processes; furthermore, they often occupy environments which, if not carefully managed, will rapidly deteriorate. Shifting cultivation appears then to be well-adapted to the cultural and natural situation. The farms may seem unsystematic and inefficient, but this haphazardness greatly facilitates soil conservation. In most cases shifting cultivation can be defended as the best means by which to maintain the production of annuals on the mature lateritic soils of the tropics. It is perhaps also the only means in that no other systems have so far been developed that have proven as successful as dry-land producers of annual crops. In some African countries the aim is no longer to replace the former system by another but rather to improve it.

However, it is understandable that shifting cultivation has earned the reputation of being a robber economy. Its weakness is its inability to support a considerable increase in population. It works well as long as a balance is maintained between man's needs and the spontaneous possibilities of nature to restore fertility. If this balance is upset by reduction of the fallow period, a spiral of deterioration is set in motion. Yields will drop, forcing the farmer to bring larger surfaces under cultivation. In turn, this will shorten fallow periods even more. In view of present developments, one aspect of which is rapid population increase, this inability of shifting cultivation to keep pace with population growth is indeed an important weakness.

INTENSIVE SUBSISTENCE AGRICULTURE

In terms of the sheer numbers of people involved, intensive subsistence cultivation is one of the most important economic activities on earth, approximately one-third of the world's population being estimated to depend upon it. It is particularly widespread in Asia in a belt from Japan to Pakistan, but also occurs in isolated pockets elsewhere in the world. Two important characteristics are implied in the phrase itself, i.e. intensive and subsistent. The intensity is mainly in the field of labour: there is a tremendous effort to obtain arable land by drainage and terracing, to maintain it, and to raise the productivity per hectare by irrigation and fertilisation. The system is based on muscle and sweat. With regard to subsistence-orientation, most of the yield tends to be consumed directly by the family and little surplus is generated for sale.

Related to these two main characteristics tends to be a host of others: high density of rural population, small and fragmented holdings, high productivity per land unit, low productivity per labour unit, multiple cropping, low standard of living, little trade, thin network of roads, relatively isolated villages, strong family loyalties and, finally, a heavy emphasis on high-yielding crops and animals. As to the latter, pigs, poultry, and fish, which thrive well as scavengers and are excellent convertors, are particularly important. Draft animals such as the water buffalo are common in some areas. Elsewhere, as is the case in India, a large cattle population is maintained that contributes little economically.

Though a variety of crops is typical of subsistence economies, one crop always has an outstanding place, i.e. the grain that comprises the basic food of the people. Of the grains, rice is most widespread. This is indeed a very useful crop: it can be grown on many soils, has a short vegetative cycle, is high-yielding, and produces food of high value. It has been said that rice allows the largest number of people not to starve on the smallest possible surface. Earlier, an example was given of the inclination to relate low advancement of civilisation to certain natural environments in a somewhat deterministic fashion. The type of economy presently under discussion supposedly could be associated with high civilisation, and gives us scope to further test this view. Intensive subsistence cultivation prefers certain soils and land forms, but is not confined to them. Ecological differentiation is no doubt important; much spatial variation within the realm of intensive subsistence cultivation can be related to variation in the physical setting.

Notably, regional variations in temperature and precipitation account for the distinct cropping zones that have emerged. Furthermore, few areas in the world repulse human occupance so much as the potential paddy (wet rice) areas. These disease-stricken, regularly flooded, tropical alluvial plains are rather hostile to human settlement and are often, as for example in tropical Africa, thinly inhabited. Their reclamation requires great skill and a tremendous collective effort, and only a well-organised community life can overcome the problems involved. The densely populated alluvial plains of Asia are therefore a cultural rather than a natural phenomenon. China and India, in particular, developed advanced cultures at a time when most other societies were still in a state of great simplicity. Aspects that denoted cultural advancement were: political unification of large areas, a good administrative apparatus, and such tautologies as a well-organised social system, law and order, script, literature, and achievements in philosophy. In the economic field, advancement appears from the development of an agricultural system that ensured a regular food supply and conserved natural resources. Early in history, the farmer of the Far East realised that in the process of cultivation the soil is robbed of its nutrients and that man could help restore soil fertility by recycling the waste products of plants, animals and humans into the soil.

A good economic base was thus established on which to maintain the advanced human structure superimposed upon the environment. Man established a certain mastership over the environment, of which sanitation and also population increase were important by-products. It is believed that the growth never assumed present spectacular proportions, but the long era of population increase finally brought about rural densities higher than in any other part of the world. Overall densities normally allow labour demand to be met at peak periods, but a substantial labour surplus prevails during most of the year in spite of the intensity of the system. Poverty, famine and dissatisfaction are signals that this system too has been put in jeopardy in the course of time. This is all the more significant as it concerns a part of the world that had such an early start in civilisation.

II

The above description of four rural traditions shows clearly that not all human groups have been equally efficient in monopolising increasing amounts of energy. The differences between gathering, pastoralism, shifting agriculture and intensive subsistence agriculture are quite important in this respect. If they were to be compared as a group to the urban, industrial cultures, still more significant differences would no doubt be obtained, but such a comparison might simultaneously produce evidence that greater efficiency and sophistication in energy-capturing devices is not yet to be equated with long-term human and environmental interest. At the same time, it would become apparent that there is much to be learned from the four traditional rural occupancy systems. Their relevance to the present-day situation has at least two dimensions, i.e. ecological and ideological.

ECOLOGICAL RELEVANCE

The four rural economies described have provided the majority of mankind with a solid base of subsistence for thousands of years. Admittedly, they have important weaknesses, as has become increasingly clear during the 20th century. Gathering, pastoralism and shifting agriculture cannot be intensified along traditional lines to any large extent without endangering the productive capacity of the environment and finally the environment itself. It is perhaps true that these activities have not yet matched the disastrous performance of some of the so-called advanced economies, but it is clear that they could easily do so. In line with members of more powerful technologies, gatherers, pastoralists, and shifting cultivators could threaten their economic base, but in contrast they are less capable of assisting nature to restore the losses it has suffered. As a consequence, they may have no alternative to extinction but to abandon their way of life or to abandon the area they occupy. The Eskimo experience subsequent upon their learning to use firearms is an obvious case in point; the settlement of pastoralists and the heavy rural out-migration recorded for many developing countries are more contemporary manifestations. In several cases, intensive subsistence agriculture seems also to have reached a point where it no longer can keep pace with an increasing rural population. Although not involving similar serious repercussions on the environment, further intensification tends to reduce the yield per head yet more by operation of the law of diminishing returns. But it should be realised that until recently these four subsistence endeavours predominantly entailed a use of land that was in harmony with its potential, thus conserving the productive capabilities of renewable resources.

The sort of strategy that subsistence farmers have adopted is equally instructive. This usually consists of insistence on security maximisation rather than on profit maximisation. Stronger still, subsistence farmers are prepared to minimise conceivable profits in any given year in order to maximise security, and this strategy is therefore sometimes referred to as a minimax strategy. The peasant knows what the environment may do but is incapable of foreseeing what it will do. In many parts of the world, for example, the local subsistence farmer is greatly influenced by variability of rainfall. Some crops do well in wet years, other in dry years. Through a long process of trial and error, the farmers have finally come up with a crop mix that maximises their chances to 'fill their bellies'. It has been suggested that the sort of solution obtained would be similar to the outcome if a game-theoretic approach were adopted which would formulate the situation in terms of a game with man playing against his environment. But it is obvious that the game may be one of life and death.[5]

It is understandable that the sensible farmer will hesitate to introduce changes in a production system that has for so long proved able to secure the life of himself and his dependents, however meagre this life might have been. In addition to its importance to rural planners, this caution has a much wider implication. In the game that 'advanced' societies have been playing with their environments, several have overplayed their hand and seem to have established an inflated relationship with their environment. Their continuous ignoring of the minimax strategy is all the more surprising in view of the fact that these societies not only know what nature can do, but at the same time have a fairly good idea of what it will do.

IDEOLOGICAL RELEVANCE

In passing, reference has been made to such features as cooperation, strong group loyalties, relative isolation, etc., but nothing has been said about social life in general and its possible relevance to modern society.[6] The socio-political limitations set by these rural types of life are as striking as the economic ones previously elaborated. Subsistence orientation favours small aggregates of population, although the size of the community and its social life is also affected by countervailing forces. Requirements of production efficiency and a feeling of insecurity occasioned by fear of intruders, in particular, militate against excessive fragmentation. Rather than dissolving into units, each of which would occupy part of the territory, groups which are associated with the territory as a whole may continue to operate as one unit. Obviously, this might imply a necessity for more frequent shifts of settlement. Whatever the case, success in the increasing search for and production of food and in the effective protection of interests, very much depends on the ability of the community to evoke a strong sense of loyalty and solidarity among its individual members and to form a tightly-knit fighting force whenever emergencies may arise. The community and the interests of its members orient the life and efforts of individuals. Also, the small and intimate group that makes up the community supports the individual if needed, feeds him in times of dependence, consoles, reassures, and inspires him in times of distress. The community and its associated territory is thus the real sphere of life.

This highly localised character of life should not be taken to imply that the prevailing systems of organisation are simple. Anthropological evidence attests to the contrary. The network of relations and rules of behaviour among, for example, the Papuan gatherers and cultivators of New Guinea, are of great complexity. But though social obligations and taboos might dog their steps at every turn, they are normally not incorporated in a hierarchically organised social structure that is topped by a ruling class of civic and religious leaders. Complex organisational structures involving a range of specialised functions are expensive, as we are also discovering, and could not be afforded by the Papuans. Moreover, specialised government functions are not really needed under the prevailing forms of social life. Localised units often coincide with kin groups and the face-to-face relations maintained by individual members and the consequent informal pressures are usually sufficiently effective. Inter-community relations also tend to be confirmed by the establishment of kinship ties and these are the customary channels for communication, even in the case of dispute. Admittedly, one individual may enjoy more prestige than another because of proven abilities, and individuals go to great pains to improve their relative social position, but no one can escape the need for mere subsistence endeavour. It is also interesting to note that if wealth differences emerge the affluent person's prestige tends to depend largely on his sharing the surplus with others. This he can do by displaying great generosity in his dealings with others, by 'overpaying' when entering into a transaction or, more conspicuously, by distributing most of his wealth on a particular occasion as during the 'pig festivals' in several parts of New Guinea. Most communities also have members who are believed to have special skills in dealing with the supernatural and on occasion warleaders may be appointed, but these do not normally perform their function on a fulltime basis nor become part of a hereditary class.

These observations derived from New Guinea evidence are believed to have much wider application. Strong egalitarian tendencies, as expressed in institutions that militate against sharp inequality in the distribution of wealth and in the absence of a rigid internal social differentiation, are believed to be typical of many subsistence communities all over the world. In particular, this is believed to apply to the basic community of all mankind, i.e. the gathering community. If this is true, and I think it is, it seems reasonable to assume that a significant change has occurred in the process of scale enlargement and increased organisational complexity of the community. The new communities that have in time emerged, including national and international ones, invariably confess to solidarity and equality; but in view of the present widespread tolerance and indifference to all sorts of serious disparity, it might be asked whether these ideals have not lost much of their force as guiding principles for social behaviour. Though the change that is assumed to have taken place thus amounts to one of degree only, it has yet been of great consequence. Domination and dependency, scarcity and sufficiency, wealth and poverty, abundance and misery, now exist side-by-side not only on the global level but also within societies; in addition to an overall increasing scarcity of certain resources, there are several signs of growing discrepancy. For those who view economies as being organised by an interplay of scarcity, differential accumulation of wealth, and rank differentiation, it is important to note that subsistence economies provide ample evidence of scarcity going hand-in-hand with a fairly even distribution of wealth and with a certain measure of equality. This is all the more interesting in view of the different degrees of scarcity involved between advanced and subsistence economies. In the first case it relates to the quality of life, to relative abundance, in the latter to the sustenance of life itself, to genuine scarcity. In addition to showing that the main slant of the conclusion should not be interpreted as an attempt to idealise subsistence communities, this condition poses the interesting question whether it is scarcity rather than abundance that makes people generous. Whatever the case, it seems unquestionable that modern society and economy would benefit from some deep soul-searching. If this review of basic communities of mankind has succeeded in reminding us of some of our roots as well as helping to identify some basic human needs, values and ideals, it has been a worthwhile undertaking.

NOTES

1. Leslie A. White, *The Evolution of Culture*, New York, 1959, p. 8.
2. Throughout the descriptive part of the paper I have borrowed extensively from several textbooks; numerous paragraphs are no more than summaries of lengthy descriptions by various authors. The following textbooks have been used: W. Allan, *The African Husbandman,* Edinburgh, 1964; J. W. Alexander, *Economic Geography*, Englewood Cliffs, 1963; G. Childe, *Man Makes Himself*, London, 1936; G. Childe, *What Happened in History*, Harmondsworth, 1942; C. Daryll Forde, *Habitat, Economy and Society*, London, 1957; R. Dumont, *Types of Rural Economy*, London, 1957; P. Gourou, *The Tropical World*, London, 1968, fourth edition; M. J. Herskovitch, *Economic Anthropology: a Study in Comparative Economics,* New York, 1952; R. Linton, *The Tree of Culture*, New York, 1955.
3. R. Linton, *The Tree of Culture*, pp. 90, 91.
4. C. Daryll Forde, *Habitat, Economy and Society*.
5. P. R. Gould, 'Man against this Environment: A Game Theoretic Framework', *Annals of the Association of American Geographers*, Vol. 53, 1963, pp. 290-297.
6. An elaboration of comments made by B. Anderson during the Man and Environment Course, Leiden, 1972.

5. Agricultural technology and food for a hungry world

JOHN F. GERBER

The author traces the origin of high-energy agricultural technology and discusses its merits and assumed demerits. The Green Revolution, defined as a movement from resource-based to technology-based agriculture, is defended and issue is taken in this context with the calculation of gains or losses merely through energy bookkeeping. Comparison with comments by Lugo is recommended. Reference may also be made to Van Raay's contribution for an account of so-called resource-based agriculture from a slightly different angle.

Food is the fuel for mankind; a form of energy uniquely adapted to his needs, a regulator of his activities, a guide of his trade, a part of his culture and the essential of his existence. Yet at least two-thirds of the world's population have less food than they need – they go to bed hungry. The land provides a place for plants to grow, to convert solar energy into the nutrient energy in plants that man and his animals can use. Land is a fixed quantity and not all of it is arable. It is estimated that there are about 3.2 billion hectares of arable land world-wide. Only one-half of it can presently be cultivated and crops are actually harvested from only about a half-billion hectares, because only a small part (7 percent) of the land has the proper mix of soil, temperature, topography, plant nutrients and rainfall to support agriculture.

In 1971, 4 billion people were fed by a half-billion hectares, albeit many fed poorly. At present rates of population growth, 8 billion people will have to be fed and clothed by the year 2000. There are several conclusions which can be drawn by these data: (1) all of the earth's people will be hungry by the year 2000; (2) more land will have to be brought under cultivation; (3) the growth of population will have to be controlled; or (4) agricultural productivity (yields) will have to be increased. Perhaps all of these factors will play an important role. Certainly, if population exceeds food supply this will be self-regulating in an effective but harsh manner. Implicit are even greater societal inequities than at present. Any consideration of man and his environment must consider the basic problems of food, shelter and clothing all closely tied to agriculture and silviculture.

It is an error to consider food and energy as being synonymous. Man and animals require not just food energy but a suite of carbohydrates, fats, proteins, vitamins and minerals. Globally protein is in critically short supply. Animal products are excellent sources of protein, vitamins, carbohydrates and minerals and are highly prized as food. Thermodynamically, it is tempting to suggest a solution to the caloric energy of hunger by eliminating animals in the agricultural food chain and feeding man directly from plant sources. This ignores nutritional requirements and the conversion by ruminants (cows, goats, sheep, etc.) of indigestible forages into protein, carbohydrates and fats and the high efficiency of conversion of feed to animal protein in fish, poultry and swine.

Every student of animal science knows more about the nutrition of animals than most scientists and physicians know about human nutrition. It is ironic that in an age when Linear Programming and high speed digital computers are used to prepare animal rations to meet the requirements for total digestible nutrients (not just total energy but usable energy), fats, carbohydrates, essential amino acids, minerals, vitamins and fiber and match these against available feeds to produce the best and lowest cost ration that we are still arguing man's food in energetic terms. Almost every pork producer in the mid-western US knows, if his pig feed contains too little or an unbalanced protein, his pigs will eat all his corn and still not grow to market weight. Yet on a global basis thousands of people eat as if they can live on corn, wheat or rice alone and scientists actually view their caloric need solely as examples of man's needs.

If proper nutrition affects animal performance so drastically what must it mean in human terms? Why do we know and do more about pig or poultry nutrition than about human nutrition? The answers lie obscured by our culture and social institutions. A part lies in the medical professions' attitude that subclinical malnutrition does not exist, a part in our reluctance to view the human as subject to the same biological laws as animals, and a part because agricultural food producers have been aggressive in applying science and technology. Obviously, we do not have to all eat beefsteak to be properly nourished, but the techniques of the animal nutritionist must be applied to the food supply before one can decide on the kinds and forms of energy which can best supply human needs.

Agriculture is an energy delivery system rather than an energy supply system. The food energy in agricultural products represents the channeling, concentrating and delivering of solar energy collected by plants. Along the way, much of the non-usable waste is discarded or recycled. This system has at least three and usually four characteristics. The quantity (yield) is combined with the quality (variety) and stability (reliability of crops or livestock) to achieve the best efficiency (mix) of products. These characteristics produced general farming – livestock and crops – that is practiced in some form in almost all agricultural systems. In the more technological systems where the risks of failure are shared and not thrust upon a single farmer, more efficiency in the total system can be obtained without so much diversity on each producing unit. Some non-agriculturally trained ecologists are alarmed at the lack of diversity on each production unit because of the lack of stability, but this view ignores the stability of whole agricultural sectors, overemphasizes the tenuous analogy between wild ecosystems and agricultural ecosystems, and minimizes the societal structures of interdependence between producer and consumer. Agriculture was in the diversity-stability phase in medieval times which was discarded on individual units because of low efficiency. Diversity has as its root total unitary self-sufficiency which is philosophically the antithesis of the world community – each doing what he can best do.

Agriculture began with the harvesting of plants and animals from wild or native populations. Wild populations are diverse and stable. The population oscillates around a mean value. This has been explained in terms of a limit to population or numbers in each ecological niche in a wild environment. This wild community guarantees survival but not necessarily highest productivity. For millions of years, man depended upon wild populations for his survival harvesting or hunting. The effect of harvesting was an immediate reduction in animals or plants which then returned to a new population equilibrium. If the births were equal to deaths the population was stable. It was not uncommon to over-harvest or under-harvest. Native predators kept populations under control when under-harvested; over-harvesting produced a scarcity of animals or plants and the hunter had to forage over a wider and wider area, expending more and more energy to obtain food and shelter. This limited population by periodic starvation, periods of feast and famine, not uncommon events in history.

When births exceed deaths the population grows, when births are less than deaths numbers decline and only if births and deaths are equal is the population stable. Man realized that it would be possible to increase food, animals and plants if predators and weeds could be controlled, undesirable species eliminated or controlled and plants sown rather than allowed to grow wild. Furthermore, if males instead of females were harvested, births and total animals increase. Population moved towards a new equilibrium limited by food supply, land, and to some extent by man himself.

Agriculture ensures the supply of food by reducing the oscillations of wild population and increasing the total food supply by controlling predators, collecting desirable plants and eliminating undesirable plants. This increases solar energy capture in harvestable and usable forms. The effect of management upon wild populations of plants and animals was not always predictable. Harvesting tends to reduce the number of older animals, lowers the mean age, producing herds that are more vigorous and often more disease-free. Similar effects can be seen with plants. Harvesting grasses by grazing leads to higher usable production than allowing plants to reach physiological maturity when dry matter production may be maximized but the production of digestible forages is reduced. Animal management results in an increase in births, a decrease in deaths by predators and diseases, with more animals available for harvest. If harvests equal births and births increase, the food supply remains stable even though more food is harvested.

It is doubtful that man as hunter ever took full advantage of management. However, these principles were used when herding animals began but they created the problem of protection of animals from predators and diseases. The result was a dynamic equilibrium sensitive to external factors that produced oscillations in the population number, i.e. the food supply. Hence, there was much effort to protect animals and plants.

Development of plant varieties, irrigation systems to prevent drought and methods of herding preceded earliest recorded history. Domestication of plants and animals began about 10,000 years ago. Farming and animal husbandry came first and herding following. No one knows how domestication began but very likely from raising wounded or young animals and from the appearance of desirable plants from spilled seeds. Domestication and agriculture appeared first in the Middle East, spread to the Black Sea, the fertile crescent, into eastern India and northern China. In the Americas agriculture was probably developed independently. Cereals, wheat and barley were developed in southwest Asia; rice and bananas later in southeast Asia. Sorghum and millet came from Africa and maize and potatoes from the Americas. Food animals were first domesticated in Asia and were later used to perform work. The development of animals as power sources led to cultivation of larger areas, the need to produce food for animals, and the development of animal-drawn tools. The need for stored foods favored the cereals with concentrated energy in dry, easily stored seeds and the development of salting, curing and drying of meats.

One of the early agricultural problems was declining soil fertility and erosion. The original farmer probably solved this problem by simply moving to new lands, but the establishment of villages made this difficult. Soil management practices to maintain fertility date back at least 2000 years. Fallowing was usually practiced, which controlled weeds, insects, disease, conserved soil moisture and allowed some accumulation of plant nutrients from decomposition and oxidation. Ashes, manure and compost were used to maintain fertility. There are latin writings by Cato the Censor on advice to farmers about growing grapes, olives and figs.

From Cato the Censor until the 15th or 16th century farming in Europe changed very little. Most of the common agricultural plants were known, but breeds of animals had not been developed. Fallow was practiced commonly and nitrogen-fixing legume plants were discovered and used. Agricultural practices in other parts of the world were highly developed and in some instances caused significant changes. The Aztecs of Mexico and the Incas in Peru both had flourishing agricultures when conquered by the Spaniards. The Bantu in Africa took over the Congo Basin largely because of crops (rice, bananas, taro, yams and sweet potatoes) brought from Indonesia. With these crops the Bantu conquered east Africa and moved cattle across the tsetse-fly belt and conquered south-central Africa. Declining agriculture (soil erosion and exhaustion), war and corruption had gotten so bad in China that by 1500 farmers were starving and the Ming dynasty finally fell in the 1600s. India at the same period was not suffering food shortages.

The development of breeds of livestock followed the construction of fences and enclosures so that farmers could control breeding about the 18th century. Plants selected for domestication had potential for high production of food energy – not necessarily high total energy production. Animals, especially cattle, were selected because they could convert cellulose (grasses and forages) to edible forms – meat and milk products. Feed conversion is highest in poultry, swine and fish. Theoretically one gram of fish can be produced with less than one gram of dry feed. One gram of poultry is routinely produced with less than two grams of feed. Plants vary in their ability to convert solar energy to plant tissue. It is related to the plant's ability to respond to a good environment, i.e. water, plant nutrients, lack of pests, warm temperatures, and sunlight. Selections of plants were made on their ability to withstand environmental stress (drought, low fertility, or pests) which often selectively removed the genes necessary for high solar energy capture.

Farming, growing plants and animals produced strong ties to the soil. In the hunting tribal system, hunting grounds and game became community property, although the hunter tended to claim the animals he killed. Plants were usually claimed by the person who sowed them or planted and cared for trees. This reduced mobility and made productive land valuable. The loss of good agricultural land became catastrophic. Transportation of food and labor required for seeding and harvest determined unit size. Large families were prized for labor, production of annual plants could be expanded rapidly, but tree crops required longer range planning and stability of labor, ownership and land. Herding was more mobile with less direct dependence upon single sites. Here are seen the beginnings to two very different kinds of agriculture; herding, a resource-based agriculture, harvesting what nature will provide with rudimentary management, and the more intensive in-place cultivation using what later became technology, i.e. the best techniques. Undoubtedly, the early encounters between these kinds of agriculture were violent and bloody. The herder concerned about restrictions of his grazing rights, the farmer protective of his land, labor, plants and soil. The latter developed strong ties to the soil he sought to nurture, conserve and protect. The herder harvested all he could and moved on.

Resource-based agriculture as opposed to technology is in a sense the most prevalent agriculture in the world. Forestry is almost entirely resource-based. The Green Revolution represents a movement from resource-based to technology-based agriculture. The main characteristics of resource-based agriculture are that it depends upon cultivation of large areas (extensive) rather than small areas, yields per acre are low, insect and disease control is meager, resource abuse is frequent (soil erosion, over-grazing, over-cutting of timber), and net return per hectare is low. Very little attempt is made to maintain or restore soil fertility other than by recycling natural wastes, and large-scale conservation schemes. Since such practices usually show no immediate return the farmer sees little immediacy in them and may not practice conservation.

Expanding food needs in resource-based agriculture are usually viewed in terms of expanding land needs. More solar energy can be harvested by harvesting more hectares. Since yields are low, the energy to bring new land into cultivation may exceed the increased yield. Yields further decline on new land as the first flush of plant nutrients are used and insects, diseases and weeds become established. There is a constant search for new areas adapted to new crops. Often this leads to a harvesting mentality with loss of the conservation ethic. Simply stated, it is 'harvest what you can and move on'. In the process much more may be destroyed than is harvested. Curiously, this system seems to have appeal to many who either claim resources are too limited for any other forms of agriculture or that the limit on population should be what we can continuously harvest. The Club of Rome study[1] implicitly considers this strategy as the only viable one.

In most resource-based agricultural systems there is a tremendous loss of harvested food because of low quality and insect and rodent damage. Quantity rather than quality is the goal. There is almost complete dependence upon natural systems, i.e. native pasture, forest, native soil fertility, common grains (unimproved varieties). Labor is traded for capital and since yields are low, labor productivity is low with the majority of the labor used in agriculture. Return to the farm-worker or farmer is minimal, thus, it is labor exploitative. Food prices in cities can only be kept within reason by low wages on the farm. Large farm families represent cheap farm labor which pushes up population. Natural occurrences, flood, drought, etc., have catastrophic consequences. People have pushed into marginal farming areas with no capital expenditure for control of floods and drought, both bring famine and floods bring death. Insects, such as locust, plagues and disease are much feared. Farmers choose diversity for survival. Auto-regulation is predominant at the expense of efficiency. Thermodynamic energists see efficiency in these systems because of small external energy subsidy, but ignore the loss of energy from erosion, soil deterioration, human life and quality of life.

Technology-based agriculture may be the best hope for feeding the world. Use of the best available techniques (seeds, feeds, varieties, pest control, fertilizer, etc.) can dramatically increase yield per hectare and productivity per man hour of agricultural worker. Technology should not be confused with mechanization which is largely the replacement of human labor with machines. Many countries with resource-based agriculture are alarmed at the implications of technology-based agriculture because they fear a loss of employment of labor in agriculture due to increased productivity per worker and mechanization. Since much of agricultural labor is menial, difficult and tedious, mechanization has great appeal to the human imagination as a way of freeing man from the bondage of hard work, but it is not technology as herein considered.

Technological agriculture is the judicious application of science to increase per unit yield and quality. One of the good early examples of agricultural technology was the work of Justus Liebig, a chemist.[2] During the medieval period in Europe rotations and animal waste recycling had been used as a means of maintaining but not increasing crop yields. In fact, yields showed a steady decline in most instances, because nature is inefficient and there was a steady loss of plant nutrients, especially calcium, phosphorus, potassium and nitrogen. Nitrogen increased if legumes were used to fix atmospheric nitrogen. Only on the very fertile, mineral rich soils, where weathering of primary and secondary minerals equal loss rates, were yields maintained. Liebig knew the amount of mineral nutrients removed by the crop. For example, one gram of wheat contained about 0.25 percent calcium, 1.7 percent phosphorus, and 2.35 percent potassium. If these elements were returned to the soil in this amount, he reasoned, yields should be maintained, which they were not, nor could he explain the difference in fertile and non-fertile soils. From this and much other work Liebig deduced a law of limiting factors. Simply stated, it says that the yield is limited by the nutrient in shortest supply. From this concept, the basis for plant nutrition and soil fertility was laid.

The use of fertilizers really did not cause significant increases in yields in the United States until after 1945. Botanists and plant physiologists held the view that if a plant could grow, reach sexual maturity and reproduce then nutrition was adequate, more plentiful nutrients led to luxury consumption and increased yields. Soil chemists knew that the soil colloids, clays and humus, had the capacity to retain huge amounts of plant nutrients and only slowly release them for plant growth. Not until nutrients were added in large quantities, much beyond harvest removal rates, were yields significantly increased. This concept of additions of lime and chemical fertilizer to increase rather than maintain fertility was developed and yields increased drastically. In the United States, corn (maize) yields went from 26 bushels per acre in 1940 to 37 in 1950, 55 in 1960, and 93 in 1971.

Concomitant with the developments in soil fertility were improvements in plant varieties. Plants had been bred to withstand stress (low fertility, drought, pests, etc.) rather than respond to increased fertility. Pest control systems were improved because fertility increased weed growth and made the crop a more luxuriant food source for insects and diseases.

Increasing the energy subsidy to crops by the use of fertilizers and pesticides increased yields. Each hectare of soil receives sunlight and rainfall independent of the yield. The amount of water used in evapotranspiration is partly dependent upon plant numbers and vigor, but mostly dependent upon climatic conditions. Since soil, light and rainfall are rather constant, anything which increases yield per hectare will increase the efficiency of water use and solar energy capture. Furthermore the labor required to plant and harvest a crop is about the same whether the yield is high or low. With these constant inputs, increased output can only yield increased efficiency. Fertilizers and especially nitrogen are available at a cost which virtually assures good return on investment. Weeds can be controlled with biochemicals (herbicides) which mimic the control of natural growth hormones and close spacing and vigorous crop growth shade weeds once the crop canopy is developed. Insects and disease control are large problems. Pesticide, agricultural chemicals, can provide protection from most pests, but unless properly managed pests become increasingly difficult to control. If one pesticide is used exclusively a population of resistant pests may result because all the surviving adults produce mostly resistant offspring.

The use of technological energy subsidies (fertilizers, pesticides, improved varieties, irrigation) increases yields and output per agricultural worker. This is the basis for the Green Revolution. The increase in yields due to technology has been challenged in recent years[3] mostly on the basis that the increased yield in energetic terms is less than the energetic input and that technology produces a secondary effect of societal disruptions – agricultural unemployment, concentration of wealth, changed cultural patterns and environmental degradation. Examples used are often selected for a specific point rather than examined globally. A part of the energetic argument is irrelevant because man can utilize energy only in the form of food. If technology represents the conversion of energy from fossil fuel to food it may be a good trade. What happens when fossil fuels are exhausted? Where then do we get energy to mine chemical fertilizer and fix nitrogen from the atmosphere? No one knows the answer. Perhaps from nuclear fusion or fission, solar energy, geothermal energy, ocean tides, etc. The pessimistic view is that there will simply not be much energy for man's use. Such arguments have a simplistic appeal, but ignore the historic reality of development of energy sources and view the technical and environmental problems as unsolvable. A more concrete solution to this problem can be obtained by energy yield from energy inputs of fertilizer, pesticides, and cultivation. Several authors have approached this problem[4] from the vantage point of assigning a dollar value to each unit of energy input and output. On this basis, using a value of 10,000 Kcal per dollar the return per hectare for corn, wheat, cotton, soybeans and oranges can be calculated (Table 1). If one assumes that producers invest until the area of diminishing returns is reached then energy returns from technological agriculture are high.

Table 1. Energy gain from agricultural crops calculated on basis of dollar cost and yield and estimated on an energetic basis

CROP	Yield Kg/ha	ENERGY Yield Kcal	Cost Kcal	Net Gain Kcal	Amplification
Maize:					
High Technology	9419				
Dollars*		3.7 × 10⁶	1.24 × 10⁶	2.4 × 10⁶	2.98
Energy**		37.5 × 10⁶	2.67 × 10⁶	34.8 × 10⁶	14.0
Normal Technology	6279				
Dollars		2.5 × 10⁶	1 × 10⁶	1.5 × 10⁶	2.5
Energy		25 × 10⁶	2.0 × 10⁶	23 × 10⁶	12.5
Low Technology	2093				
Dollars		.83 × 10⁶	0.62 × 10⁶	0.21 × 10⁶	1.33
Energy		8.33 × 10⁶	0.67 × 10⁶	7.66 × 10⁶	12.5
Wheat:					
Normal Technology	2660				
Dollars		1.97 × 10⁶	.61 × 10⁶	1.36 × 10⁶	3.23
Energy		10.8 × 10⁶	1.2 × 10⁶	9.6 × 10⁶	9.0
Soybeans:					
Normal Technology	1882				
Dollars		2.22 × 10⁶	0.86 × 10⁶	1.36 × 10⁶	2.58
Energy		14.1 × 10⁶	1.1 × 10⁶	13 × 10⁶	12.8
Oranges:					
Normal Technology	2309				
Dollars		15.83 × 10⁶	3.5 × 10⁶	12.33 × 10⁶	4.52
Energy		9.2 × 10⁶	7.2 × 10⁶	2.0 × 10⁶	1.27

* at 10,000 Kcal/dollar (see Odum, *Environment, Power and Society*).
** Maize 3980 Kcal/kg,
Wheat 4060 Kcal/kg,
Soybean 7492 Kcal/kg

Another method of calculating the gain from energy subsidies is to do a total energy budget. On the one hand are all the inputs, on the other the outputs – the difference being the net gain or loss. The ratio of output to input is the amplification from agriculture. The difficulty is in the bookkeeping or balance method. A corn yield of 6200 Kg hectare is the equivalent of 25×10^6 Kcal in the grain harvested. The energetic value of the fuel, machinery, fertilizers, herbicides and man labor to produce this is more difficult to estimate. If one uses the USDA data[5] 11 man hours were required to produce 6200 Kg of corn. Fuel energy used in machinery is about 6.5×10^5 Kcal with about equivalent amounts required for fertilizer, production of machinery and pesticides. Thus, for an energetic investment of 2×10^6 Kcal, 25×10^6 Kcal is harvested for a net gain of 23.0×10^6 Kcal/hectare or an amplification factor of 10. This contrasts with a recent report by Perelman[6] that more energy is spent in fossil fuel in agriculture than the total food energy consumed in the United States. Without going into a point-by-point critique of Perelman's paper the fuel consumption in primary agricultural production is too high by at least two fold. Much of the primary production is converted to animal protein with a caloric content on a fresh weight basis in meat of not more than 1:10 (meat: feed). In addition, a sizeable amount of the agricultural product in the United States is exported and perhaps most importantly cotton, hides, wool and other fibers do not appear in the food supply even though they have a high caloric content. Clearly, productivity and gains of energy must be calculated on a careful basis. If all fertilizer and pesticide subsidies are removed and maize yields returned to the 1930 US levels, the energy gain would be about 5.2×10^6 Kcal/hectare and the amplification factor would remain about 10, but most importantly a 75 percent reduction in corn supplies would occur and a loss of 18×10^6 Kcal in solar energy captured even though the same amount of machinery, fossil fuel for cultivation and man hours were invested.

Increasing the capture of solar energy by food plants is the main environmental problem. If an additional 1 percent of the sun's energy could be captured by plants, the food supply would double. The strategy of agricultural technology is to remove or minimize environmental factors which limit plant growth and thus restrict solar energy capture. Plant breeders should select plants which have high efficiency of solar energy capture and are genetically resistant to insects and diseases. Such plants will require large amounts of nitrogen, phosphate and potassium (unless they are legumes which 'fix' nitrogen from the atmosphere).

The solar constant, the amount of energy received perpendicular to the sun's rays outside the atmosphere, is about 2 g.cal/cm^2 min. The amount of this energy which reaches the surface on the earth depends upon the latitude, the time and clouds, water vapor and haze in the atmosphere. Typically 50 percent falls on clouds, 25 percent is reflected, 10 percent absorbed by the clouds and 15 percent transmitted to the surface. Of the remaining 50 percent, 25 percent passes directly to the surface, 15 percent is scattered by the atmosphere (10 percent back to space and 5 percent to the surface), and another 10 percent is directly absorbed by the gases in the atmosphere. A total of about 45 percent reaches the earth's surface.

Over half of the solar energy which reaches the surface is used in evaporation of water from lakes, soil and plants, about one-fourth is used to heat the air. The remainder is lost directly as radiation from the surface. The solar energy absorbed by plants is mostly used in transpiration and heating the plant. This energy determines the amount of water needed by the plant for survival. It is largely a passive process over which the plant has little control. Restricting water increases plant temperature, changes stomatal openings, reduces in CO_2 exchange and photosynthesis, increases respiration, and lowers the net production and eventually causes death.

Over 50 percent of the solar energy has a wavelength greater than .680 μ. Five to 10 percent of a wave length is too short to be used in photosynthesis. Since photosynthesis is dependent upon solar radiation shorter than .680 μ, only 35 to 40 percent is useable. Some light is reflected from the leaf, some transmitted and the efficiency of utilization of the remainder influenced by wave length. Solar energy is linked to photosynthesis by a transient photochemical reaction with an efficiency of perhaps 10 percent. Only 25 percent to 30 percent of the energy is available for photosynthesis, and with 10 percent efficiency 2 or 3 percent probably represents the maximum solar energy which can ever be captured by photosynthesis; however, this would represent a two to six-fold increase in total yields.

Agricultural mechanization began with the use of animals to power cultivation instruments. While many primitive societies used animals not all used them to draw cultivation equipment. The first tools were crude wooden plows usually pulled by oxen. The land was leveled or smoothed by harrows and the seed sown by hand. Grains were cut by scythes and thrashed with flails. Often the concept of a machine was known long before it was used. For example, the Chinese had used a grain drill for seeding about 2800 BC, but grain drills did not come into general use until after 1200 when Jethro Tull made and patented a grain drill. The iron plow probably came from Holland; however, the first factories for making iron plows were set up in England in 1730. The real transition from hand to mechanical farming occurred with the invention of the grain reaper in 1833 by Obed Hussey and in 1834 by Cyrus McCormick. Today the mechanization of agriculture is not complete but well advanced in the technological societies. Most of the staple food crops are completely mechanized. The fiber crops and many of the speciality crops such as fruits, vegetables and flowers are rapidly becoming mechanized. These machines are interesting, fascinating devices which perform highly specialized, intricate jobs efficiently and effectively. They are expensive to manufacture and require skilled operators. Operation is difficult being very much like the operation of heavy earth moving machinery.

Machines and tractors are available today which can plow 20-25 hectares per day, harvest 10-20 hectares of cereal grains or maize per day, or pick an equal amount of cotton. More intricate machines have been developed which can harvest celery, pick tomatoes, pick cherries or oranges, harvest grapes, potatoes or blackberries, blueberries and raspberries.

Mechanization with large machines capable of greatly increasing labor productivity can most easily be adopted in large, level fields, where little land, labor, time or energy is wasted in turning and realigning equipment. To be efficient and effective plants should be standardized. They need to be sufficiently alike so the machine can cultivate, sow, or harvest without loss of quantity or quality. Success of mechanization depends upon uniform seeds and plants which are ripe and ready for harvesting at the same time. Hybrid maize is a good example of a crop adapted and developed for mechanical harvesting.

Mechanization has changed the rural scene and the efficiency of farmers. In 1917, there were 26 million horses and mules on US farms and essentially no tractors. In 1970, there were 4.8 million tractors and 3.0 million horses, many of these for recreational purposes. In the same timespan output per man hour rose over 400 percent, farm output 100 percent and man hours of farm work declined 50 percent. Most of the change occurred after 1945. At the same time crop yield rose 60 to 70 percent. Crops produced per hour of labour rose 450 percent. The production per man hour showed an almost exponential rise in most crops except fruits and nuts.

Production per man hour of livestock shows a similar though smaller increase. Production per man hour rose over 100 percent. The greatest gains in mechanization in animal production occurred with poultry, the least with meat animals. Since 1960, however, there have been very large gains made in the mechanization of meat animal production. The result of mechanization can best be demonstrated by the people fed per agricultural worker. In 1940, one US farm worker produced enough food for 11 people, in 1960 for 25, and in 1971 for 51.

Mechanization requires capital resources, which results in larger, more efficient farms. Farm size in the USA increased 50 percent between 1940-1960; total capital increased 65 percent between 1940-1960. Investment in machinery and equipment increased 225 percent. At the same time (1960),[7] farmers in the US used 6.5 million tons of finished steel, 45 million tons of chemicals, 18 billion gallons of crude petroleum, 285 million pounds of raw rubber, and 22 billion kilowatt hours of electricity. The average capital invested per farm worker in 1960 exceeded $50,000 which was about three times the average for workers in US industry. The US farmer spends more than 65 cents of every dollar of income on operating expenses. The total value of production items purchased by US farmers in 1970 was 44 billion dollars.[8]

The result of mechanization has been a movement of the population from the farm to the city. Each year about 20,000 farm youths are needed to replace retiring farmers, but each year 200,000 farm boys reach the age of 20. The result is that only about 1 in 10 can farm. An additional 15,000 people are needed in agricultural research, education and technology. Most of the farm youths will have to find employment outside agriculture.

The consumer has been the primary beneficiary of agricultural technology and mechanization. Americans (US) spend 16.5 percent of their income for food. By comparison people in the British Isles spend 25 percent, Italians and Japanese about 35 percent, the Soviet Union about 45 percent and in India about 80 percent.[9]

The agricultural producers receive only about 5 percent of money spent, the other 11.5 percent goes to processing, marketing and distribution. Since 1960 there has been even more rapid growth and mechanization in agriculture. Output per man hour increased 74 percent from 1960-1970. Cash farm income increased from $33.5 to $47.4 billion, a rise of 41 percent. In Florida the rise was even more spectacular. Farm income increased 298 percent from 1948-1970. Florida's cash farm income was 1.4 billion dollars in 1971. In order to achieve mechanization agriculture has had to depend heavily upon science and technology provided largely through the agricultural research service of the US Department of Agriculture, and from the Agricultural Experiment Stations located with the Land Grant Universities. Crops had to be developed which were amenable to harvest. Animal and plant health and disease and pest control had to permit them to be crowded and mechanized. Plant and animal nutrition had to be improved and developed so that high yields per acre and per animal could be maintained to pay for the high capital and operating cost of machines. Monocultures are especially fitted to mechanization because the number of harvesting and handling machines are reduced, the size of fields can be increased and labor and machine efficiency increased.

Mechanized agriculture can produce environmental problems, especially soil erosion and consequent depletion. On the other hand, it can make positive contributions to soil fertility maintenance. High yields provide more organic residue to the soil. Deep tillage, contour farming and terracing contribute to water and soil conservation. Green manure crops and minimum tillage can be more correctly and easily handled with mechanized agriculture.

The high agricultural efficiency achieved in the US and western Europe could not have been achieved without machines and mechanization. This has lowered the cost of food and slightly increased the return to farmers. Farmers and farm laborers have benefited by a reduction in heavy, strenuous labor. Farming remains hard labor by industrial standards. The per hour production efficiency has been greater in agriculture than in most of industry. There has been a displacement of labor and people from the land because of mechanization, or mechanization has resulted from a loss of labor to industrial jobs in the cities. This relationship is not exactly clear. Mechanization has increased the capital invested in farming until it is higher per worker than in other industries. Labor has essentially been replaced by science, technology and capital. In countries with little capital and much labor, mechanization of agriculture might be less important than in the technological countries if science and technology are used in agriculture. There will be less subsidy to agriculture from machines and more from labor. This system ties the cost of food very closely to the wages of agricultural labor. It has been used to help achieve industrialization in countries such as Japan and the USSR, but agricultural labor has borne the brunt of the cost of such schemes.

Technology and Mechanization used together offer the greatest gains in total food production but produce some of the greatest environmental challenges. If one accepts the concept of limited energy resources, i.e. fossil fuels, then technology and especially mechanization represent an accelerated rate of energy depletion. Other environmental quality problems are produced by intensive agriculture. Animal feedlots, where large numbers (10-50 thousand) are collected for labor and management efficiency, cause animal waste disposal problems. Excessive use of fertilizers, especially nitrates, can cause water quality problems. The case against excessive pesticide usage has been stated elsewhere and perhaps overstated. Soil erosion and depletion continue to be major environmental problems caused by the loss of the soil resource and by silt pollution of surface waters. Phosphorus from fertilizers is tightly held by soil particles. The largest loss of phosphorus from soil is by erosion. Soil conservation practices on a world-wide basis have generally been a failure. In the USA, 3×10^9 tons of soil were lost in 1934, 4×10^9 tons in 1971. A part of the reason is that the farmer who will not benefit from the long-term benefits has been expected to pay the major costs.

There have been numerous suggestions[10] that agriculture abandon those practices which produce environmental pollution. While there is some merit in this argument, it largely ignores the loss of productivity from soil, labor and machinery and the increase in land required. It also largely ignores the problems of pest control and quality. Instead there is the implication, and in some cases the open contention[11] that yields would increase and pest damage decrease if technology were reduced. This defies reason and logic, and implies that the scientific research upon which modern agriculture is based was done without any real comprehension of the agricultural ecosystem or was done by scientists who were colossally stupid. Obviously, this was not the case.

The deleterious effects of agricultural technology upon the environment can be largely prevented or reduced to a permissible level. Animal wastes can be recycled through the soil-plant system. The nutrients removed by the plant and soil, and water pollution prevented. Human sewage can be treated and the effluent and sewage sludge recycled in agricultural systems in a similar way.

The loss of fertilizer nutrients to ground and surface water is an undesirable loss from the standpoint of both the farmer and the rest of society. To prevent their entry into ground water by curtailing their use is 'cutting off one's nose to spite one's face' because we need more not less food in the world. What we need is better management to prevent soil erosion and fertilizer leaching. There are slowly soluble fertilizers available which may reduce leaching.

Pesticides represent a serious problem because in many cases there are no good alternatives. Each year pest losses exceed 20 billion dollars in the US. Chemical pesticides help reduce these losses, but produce secondary problems of pollution and human safety. Pesticides were carefully monitored for mammalian safety and until we became aware of the biological magnification of the chlorinated hydrocarbons such as DDT appeared that pesticides were used very safely.

Agriculture became too dependent upon pesticides. There are several promising avenues open to reduce the need for persistent pesticides and in some cases any pesticides. Biological control, the use of insects and diseases to control pests, is one promising technique. There are about 10 economic insects in the US controlled biologically.[12] Genetic resistance to insects and disease is a second promising avenue. Pest management by a combination of bio-controls, plant host resistance, specific pesticides which decompose quickly, careful timing and use of cultural practices to remove secondary host, denying breeding areas, etc., is perhaps the most immediate way of maintaining pest control with less pesticide.

The control of weeds, especially aquatic weeds, in the tropics is virtually impossible even with herbicides. These weeds interfere with irrigation, drainage, navigation, fisheries, mosquito control and maintenance of water quality. Plant nutrients in water encourage their growth, but weed control by removal or elimination of the nutrients is almost impossible. Biocontrols, insects, diseases, animals (fish, snails, manatees, hippopotamus, geese, etc.) have shown promise as control measures. The weeds can also be used for animal feed but the quality is generally low.

World hunger and food supply are a fundamental consideration of man and his environment. Without going into social and political problems of population growth and control, there are some things which can be done to alleviate world hunger. The Green Revolution has been described elsewhere,[13] but some consideration needs to be given to its implications. Basically it is a strategy to increase food supply by increasing yield, because most of the good land is in cultivation, increasing cultivated land is risky, costly, and most farmers are unwilling to accept the risks of moving to new areas unless there are strong incentives. About the only way to significantly increase yields (2-10 times) is to implement science and technology. Small gains are really rather meaningless in countries short of food. This strategy requires switching from resource-based to a technology-based agriculture. It requires new high yielding varieties, high fertilization rates, irrigation, but not necessarily mechanization. The development of the Green Revolution was due largely to Ford and Rockefeller Foundations, FAO and US-AID. The use of high yield varieties (HYV),[14] especially in India and southeast Asia, has made dramatic increases in total cereal grain production. Twenty-two percent of the acreage is now in HYV wheat and 13 percent in HYV rice. India appears to be at least temporarily self-sufficient in food grain production. Grain production in regions where the HYV seeds are used has risen 31 percent for rice and 47 percent for wheat from the period 1965-1971.

The possibility of inexpensive, plentiful food on a world-wide basis has been ruled out by many people with little knowledge of agriculture and no experience in food production. The Green Revolution has even been held up as a failure because the more aggressive farmers utilize it quickly and profit from it first, but local food production increased. To claim it has failed is like claiming that education fails because the better educated, more intelligent members of society profit from it first and probably most.

According to FAO reports,[15] North America, Western Europe and Australia are well-nourished with enough energy and protein in the diet to meet requirements. Much of the rest of the world is undernourished. Included in the list of undernourished areas are: Japan, Latin America, Near East, East Africa, West Africa, North Africa, India, Pakistan, and Central Africa. This list is not complete, but it points out the critical need in many parts of the world for food. The question is how to meet this need? Industrial nations can obviously meet the need through trade. Non-industrial nations can only meet it on a sustained basis by local food production. It would seem that one of the first goals of a more equitable world should be an adequate diet for everyone.

Is such a diet possible? The Green Revolution and the technological agriculture of the United States both indicate that it is, and at a resource cost which the world can afford. In the United States less than 5 percent of the population produces more food than the rest can consume and as a result the US produces more food for export than any other nation. Food is cheap in the United States. Inexpensive food is more important to people with low incomes. If the world food needs are to be met food will have to be plentiful and low cost.

The effects of technological agriculture upon society raises moral and ethical questions beyond the immediate problems raised by science and technology. If yields can be increased, human nutrition improved, hard human labor reduced and the general welfare improved, can technology be morally and ethically discouraged? Can one view the societal problems, less need for agricultural labor, more and cheaper food which will encourage growth of cities, better nutrition with longer lifespan and reduced mortality as valid reasons for withholding technology? These problems and the many more produced by agricultural technology are not the exclusive problems of the agricultural sector. Population control, marketing, storing and distributing food and price structure are problems with which all of society must deal. In the USA technology has produced environmental problems. We are learning how to cope with these problems and hopefully how to avoid them in other parts of the world.

Some final thoughts about the concept of a finite world with finite resources, which is an old and not a technological idea. Resource allocation in the world has been based upon economics. Science and technology have been called upon from time to time to inventory total resources and have done so with reasonable accuracy, but have rarely foreseen innovations with drastically changed resource use such as oil for coal and uranium for fossil fuels. In fact, inventories of fuels 30 years ago would not have included uranium.

In industrial societies population trends have changed drastically in the past decade. Industrial and agricultural production has risen as has per capita consumption. For several reasons, including no doubt the protestant ethic and in the US the puritan ethic, this consumption has been questioned on ethical and moral as well as scientific grounds. The opponents to increased consumption view it as wrong because it will deplete the world's resources and it will be ecologically and esthetically damaging. A view also held is that it deprives or deters development in the poor nations of the world. This last view is probably based more upon moral, ethical and emotional rationalization than upon scientific fact.

There is an increasing disparity in consumption between nations and individuals within nations. Science, technology and industrialization are blamed in about that order for the increasing disparity. There is probably some basis in fact for this view. Because of the increasing complexity of technology more scientific specialization and research have been devoted to the complex problems in industrial countries than to the mundane but highly relevant problems of poor countries. However, the significant discoveries of science and technology which have had profound effect upon the poor countries have in most cases come from the industrial countries.

There have been attempts from time to time to analyze the future effects of technology and industrial growth upon a global[16] and regional basis. Almost without exception these analyses show that the wealthy nations become wealthier. These studies are interesting and in some quarters frightening because in almost all cases they show a general worsening of world conditions in the future, based largely upon continued exponential growth, dwindling world resources, and too large world populations.

Most models makes no comment about the areas of the world where the pressures will first be felt, but in all probability they will be felt most intensively in poor countries with large populations. While growth and technology have undoubtedly produced disparity between the technological and non-technological societies, it has largely been the efforts of these societies through organizations such as the UN and via the increased communication technology that have aroused sympathetic world opinion. While the relationship between ethics, morality and esthetics is indirect, it is much harder to conceal acts of government and industry in a technological world. Moreover, the individual is becoming increasingly aware of his power over public opinion if properly used and applied.

The consequences of technology and growth may be interpreted as restricting individual and collective choice. A high degree of individualism in a dense population can create havoc with the collective good. Land taken for roads, buildings and industry is really usable for other purposes. The high rate of obsolescence in technological societies allows the individual to choose again in a short time and gives him a chance to quickly discard poor choices. The potential for freeing the individual life from tedium has not yet been fully realized. It should be possible in the future to tailor many goods to individual tastes, needs and wants with computer-controlled machines without losing the efficiency of mass production. If the gains of automation in production are equitably divided in society much more time should be available for creative efforts. To dismiss or decry automation and technology because of the conviction that the gains will not accrue to society generally is extremely shortsighted.

One should remember that the dynamic response of any system

depends upon its design. The general design of the world is for a finite but long life. The important features of the Limits to Growth Model[17] are that even though the constraints are relaxed (unlimited natural resources, pollution control, birth control, etc.) the same dynamic behavior occurs with a varied time scale. Such dynamic occurrences have appeared in the past and resulted in famines, wars, labor strife and revolution. Avoidance of a repeat of past performances and future disaster is a challenge to man. Models are not precise or even really predictive for time scales. Thus the time element is really most uncertain. A model's main appeal is that it allows us to critically examine the future effects of strategy in pollution control, resource use, food production and population trends. To look upon it as the harbinger of the disaster which will occur as the result of unethical exploitation and growth from science and technology is to get caught up in a trivial argument such as estimating the end of the world on a theological basis.

While runaway growth can have disastrous results, too great restraints on growth could have even worse results, especially if growth were restricted in the wrong areas of the world. Restricting growth of science, technology and agricultural industry in technological societies might make the latter much less willing to share. If their populations became stable there is the real possibility that the technological power and natural resources control could become entrenched in the hands of fewer and fewer people who would be increasingly less inclined to share it with the rest of an overpopulated, underfed and restive world: a world which showed little inclination to solve its social problems. Conceivably, the technological societies could use their power and wealth to ensure for themselves their corner of the world and protection of their resource sources.

Thus, from a technological view, a free flow of science, technology, goods and resources directed at meeting world needs in all areas offers more chances of food production in the well-fed parts of the world. There is much more incentive to protect the supply, reduce the cost, increase the quality and diversity and ensure the success and participation of food producers in the economic, social and economic benefits of that society. This has occurred in the US as farm price stabilization programs, rural electrification, equity in schools, roads and services.

The real restraints which should be put upon agriculture, industry and technology are limitations upon pollution, resource efficiency and use, recycling and other environmental and social insults. These same restraints should be applied to government.

The problem of population control in the non-technological societies is perhaps the most important problem on a global basis. Too many times it is politely avoided because it is offensive, unpopular or viewed as socially and culturally unacceptable. Such actions are hypercritical from the scientific and technological viewpoint because they ignore the clear implications of resource dilution beyond the power of regeneration without a cataclysmic occurrence such as war, disease or famine. Such societies perhaps need not have as their goal the life style of the present industrial societies, but they must employ science and technology which is based upon natural and not social laws if they wish to gain freedom of action in the world community.

NOTES

1. D. H. Meadows, D. L. Meadows, J. Randers & W. W. Beherns, *The Limits to Growth*, New York, Universe Books, 1972.
2. 'Soil', *Yearbook of Agriculture*, USDA, Washington DC, 1957.
3. H. T. Odum, *Environment, Power and Society*, New York, Wiley Interscience, 1971, and M. J. Perelman, 'Farming with Petroleum', *Environment* 14,8, 1972, 8.13.
4. Odum, *Environment, Power and Society*, and Perelman, 'Farming with Petroleum'.
5. Fact Sheet on Fuel No. 3, 'How to Conserve Fuel and Dollars in Farm Operation', Washington DC, USDA, 6/8/1973, mimeographed; Fact Sheet on Fuel No. 4, 'Energy Estimates for Crop Production', Washington DC, USDA, 6/26/1973, mimeographed; US Bureau of the Census, *Statistical Abstract of the United States*, Washington DC, 1972, 93rd edition.
6. Perelman, 'Farming with Petroleum'.
7. 'Power to Produce', *Yearbook of Agriculture*, Washington DC, USDA, 1960.
8. *Agricultural Statistics*, Washington DC, USDA, 1972.
9. *The Biosphere*, A Scientific American Book; San Francisco, W. H. Freeman & Co., 1970.
10. D. Chapman, 'An End to Chemical Farming?' *Environment* 14,5, 1973, 10-18; Odum, *Environment, Power and Society*; Perelman, 'Farming with Petroleum'.
11. Chapman, 'An End to Chemical Farming?'; Perelman, 'Farming with Petroleum'.
12. R. I. Sailer, 'A Look at USDA's Biological Control of Insect Pest, 1888 to Present', *Agricultural Science Review* 10,4, 1972, 15-27.
13. L. R. Brown, *The Seeds of Change: the 'Green Revolution' and Development in the 1970s*, New York, Praeger, 1970.
14. Diane Tindall, 'Five Years Later. War on Hunger', An Agency for International Development report, 1972.

15. Food and Agriculture Organization, *Provisional Indicative World Plan for Agricultural Development,* Rome, UN-FAO, 1970.
16. A. B. Makhijani and A. J. Lichtenberg, 'Energy and Wellbeing', *Environment* 14,5, 1972, 10-18; D. H. Meadows et al, *The Limits to Growth*; Odum, *Environment, Power and Society.*
17. Meadows et al, *The Limits to Growth.*

REFERENCES

1. *Agricultural Statistics*, Washington DC, USDA, 1972.
2. Brown, L. R., *The Seeds of Change: the 'Green Revolution' and Development in the 1970s,* New York, Praeger, 1970.
3. Chapman, D., 'An End to Chemical Farming?', *Environment* 14,5, 1973, 10-18.
4. Fact Sheet on Fuel No. 3, 'How to Conserve Fuel and Dollars in Farm Operation', Washington DC, USDA, 6/8/1973, mimeo.
5. Fact Sheet on Fuel No. 4, 'Energy Estimates for Crop Production', Washington DC, USDA, 6/26/1973, mimeo.
6. Makhijani, A. B. and A. J. Lichtenberg, 'Energy and Wellbeing', *Environment* 14, 5, 1972, 10-18.
7. Meadows, D. H., D. L. Meadows, J. Randers and W. W. Beherns III, *The Limits to Growth*, New York, Universe Books, 1972.
8. Odum, H. T., *Environment, Power and Society*, New York, Wiley Interscience, 1971.
9. Perelman, M. J., 'Farming with Petroleum', *Environment* 14, 8, 1972, 8-13.
10. 'Power to Produce', *Yearbook of Agriculture*, Washington DC, USDA, 1960.
11. Sailer, R. I., 'A Look at USDA's Biological Control of Insect Pest, 1888 to Present', *Agricultural Science Review* 10, 4, 1972, 15-27.
12. 'Soil', *Yearbook of Agriculture*, Washington DC, USDA, 1957.
13. *The Biosphere*, A Scientific American Book; San Francisco, W. H. Freeman & Co., 1970.
14. Tindall, Diane, 'Five Years Later. War on Hunger', an Agency for International Development report, 1972.
15. Food and Agriculture Organization, *Provisional Indicative World Plan for Agricultural Development*, Rome, UN-FAO, 1970
16. US Bureau of the Census, *Statistical Abstract of the United States*, Washington DC, 1972, 93rd edition.
17. US Bureau of the Census, *Statistical Abstract of the United States*, Washington DC, 1966, 87th edition.

6. Monopolisation, state formation and colonialism

G. VAN BENTHEM VAN DEN BERGH

'Both the environmental and population crises are the largely unintended result of the exploitation of technological, economic and political power. Their solutions must also be found in this same difficult arena. This task is unprecedented in human history, in its size, complexity and urgency.'

Barry Commoner

The author presents convincing arguments to dispel the idea that social change is chaotic and intractable. The emphasis placed upon the need for a systematic approach to the whole field of social science will no doubt appeal to those interested in developing a frame of reference that will offer scope for interdisciplinary work. Equally pertinent to the general theme appears the discussion of competition. The argument developed by the author may indicate that competition is indeed a basic property of social and biological systems alike and a principal structuring force of their patterns and behaviour. In this context reference should also be made to contributions by Lugo, Du Boff, Syatauw, Burger, and Tellegen, Hilhorst and Lambooy. For evidence of scarcity and egalitarian tendencies occurring simultaneously, the chapter by van Raay may be noted.

I. PROBLEMS OF ORIENTATION

The subjects I have been asked to discuss are very general and wide in scope. They include the main dynamics of social change: what we might perhaps call the internal and external expansionism of societies. We may even say that they describe world history – if we regard that as having started with the expansion of Western Europe, because it has been through that process that mankind has forcefully been made into the present interdependent whole. The world still shows its historical origins in the fact that it is dominated by the few states that have emerged victoriously from the centuries-long struggle through which the chances to achieve military and economic superiority were increasingly monopolised.

How interdependent the world has become is perhaps demonstrated most clearly by the environmental crisis. But this increasing interdependence is not yet matched by a decision-centre at world level to regulate and coordinate it. What have developed are the so-called nation states, but these are *competing decision centres*, attack and defence units perceiving each other as a potential threat to their own survival and as an actual threat to their own power, economic development and prestige.[1] Not only that: the interdependence of present world society is far from symmetrical. The industrial societies benefit much more from it than the still predominantly agrarian societies of Africa, Asia and Latin America. Their economies have been subordinated to the needs of the industrialising societies of Western Europe and the

United States; in fact, to those societies that have at the same time contributed most to the emergence of the environmental crisis with which we are now faced. If a different direction of industrial and technological development (including the industrialisation of agriculture) is of paramount importance for remedying the environmental crisis, it may be clear that the uneven distribution of industrial development in the present world, corresponding with the historical patterns of colonial expansion and rule, constitute a very serious obstacle.

The environmental crisis is not the only problem with which world society is faced. According to Barry Commoner's convincing diagnosis in *The Closing Circle*, the specific direction of technological development in advanced industrial countries is chiefly responsible for the destruction of the environment. If this is so, the environmental crisis is not only linked with the continuing arms race and the threat of nuclear war, but also with the problem of 'underdevelopment', of hunger, poverty and oppression – in general of the degrading conditions in which the majority of mankind has to live.

These problems have not only their origin in common – the specific direction of technological development fostered by expansionist societies – but also the fact that it is much easier to find out what should be done to remedy them than it is to discover whether and how what should be done in fact can be done. 'Reasonable' people – such as the readers of this publication – will be able to come to an agreement at least about the broad direction of necessary changes. It is in no way beyond human ingenuity to find from an ecological perspective more specific solutions for the problem at issue. But as Barry Commoner writes:

> ... there is a sharp contrast between the logic of the ecology and the state of the real world in which environmental problems are embedded ... What is real in our lives and *in contrast to the reasonable logic of ecology, chaotic and intractable* [my italics, vdB], is the apparently hopeless inertia of the economic and political system; its fantastic agility in sliding away from the basic issues which logic reveals; the selfish manoeuvring of those in power, and their willingness to use, often unwittingly, and sometimes cynically, even environmental deterioration as a step toward more political power; the frustration of the individual citizen confronted by this power and evasion; the confusion that we all feel in seeking a way out of the environmental morass. To bring environmental logic into contact with the real world we need to relate it to the overall social, political, and economic forces that govern both our daily lives and the course of history.[2]

Chaotic and intractable, that is how the 'real world', the power relations within and between states, the economic and political 'systems', appear from the perspective of the necessity to order human relations more 'reasonably' according to our present knowledge of the functioning of ecosystems. And indeed, scientific understanding of the 'overall social, political and economic forces that govern both our daily lives and the course of history' is very limited. The way in which most people think about social relations and processes is determined by the need to order the social universe on the basis of identification with a particular group, of a specific we-perspective which makes it possible to assign responsibility to others: if all people would think and act as we do – or as we would like them to do – the world would be alright. Because they do not the world is as bad as it is. Not we – not our nation, class or profession is to blame, but the others. Someone or something (capitalism, communism, imperialism, human nature) must be the cause of wars, poverty, alienation, destruction of the environment – of what *they* are doing to *us*. Because social relations are so full of violence, exploitation and suffering, because people cannot help feeling threatened by other people, it is very difficult not to see social relations from such an involved, we-they perspective, where the basic question is 'Who is to blame for this?' But adequate understanding of social reality demands that it should be viewed not in terms of friends and enemies, of blame and guilt, but in a more detached manner as a changing configuration of interdependent, struggling and cooperating, human beings, that may appear 'chaotic and intractable' from the perspective of a conscious attempt to order it differently within a short time-span, but that is not without a structure that can be better understood.

Norbert Elias has most illuminatingly described the difficulties inherent in achieving the more realistic orientation in a constantly changing world that people need to better cope with the problems at issue:

> ... the growth of men's comprehension of natural forces and of the use made of them for human ends is associated with specific changes in human relationships; it goes hand in hand with the growing interdependence of growing numbers of people. The gradual acceleration in the increment of knowledge and use of non-human forces, bound up with specific changes in human relations as it is, has helped, in turn, to accelerate the process of change in the latter. The network of human activities tends to become increasingly complex, far-flung and closely knit. More and more groups, and with them more and more individuals, tend to become dependent on each other for their security and the satisfaction of their needs in ways which, for the greater part, surpass the comprehension of those involved. It is as if first thousands, then millions, then more and more millions walked through this world with their hands and feet chained together by invisible ties. No one is in charge. No one stands outside. Some want to go this,

> others that way. They fall upon each other and, vanquishing or defeated, still remain chained to each other. No one can regulate the movements of the whole unless a great part of them are able to understand, to see, as it were, from outside, the whole patterns they form together. And they are not able to visualise themselves as part of these larger patterns because, being hemmed in and moved uncomprehendingly hither and thither in ways which none of them intended, they cannot help being preoccupied with the urgent, narrow and parochial problems which each of them has to face. They can only look at whatever happens to them from their narrow location within the system. They are too deeply involved to look at themselves from without. Thus what is formed of nothing but human beings acts upon each of them, and is experienced by many as an alien external force not unlike the forces of nature.
>
> Thus vulnerable and insecure as men are under these conditions, they cannot stand back and look at the course of events calmly like more detached observers. Again, it is, on the other hand, difficult for men in that situation to control more fully their own strong feelings with regard to events which, they feel, may deeply affect their lives, and to approach them with greater detachment, as long as their ability to control the course of events is small; and it is, on the other hand, difficult for them to extend their understanding and control of these events as long as they cannot approach them with greater detachment and gain greater control over themselves.[3]

As long as people have so little control over the course of events, it is not surprising that so much of what is presented as 'objective' social science, is in fact connected with ideological debates. Lack of adequate knowledge and continuous feelings of insecurity combine in influencing, explicitly or implicitly, the development of the social sciences.[4] It is often very difficult to separate the 'ideological' and the 'scientific' elements in the theories presented by social scientists. Not only the ideological perspectives of *de facto* or potential ruling groups, but also the needs of ruling groups for specific kinds of knowledge and information have influenced the development of the social sciences, in particular its fragmentation into supposedly autonomous disciplines and specialisations. The consequence of this development has been that a static, short-term perspective has become predominant in the social sciences.[5] To this should be added the powerful attraction of the method of the natural sciences for the social sciences, the imitation of which has led to what Barry Commoner has called reductionism: 'the view that effective understanding of a complex system can be achieved by investigating the properties of its isolated parts'.[6] It is in this connection interesting to reflect on the fact that René Dubos has called his own approach to the analysis of the interdependence between man en nature *holism*, a concept that the influential philosopher of science Karl Popper considers to be characteristic of a pre-scientific stage (in the development of thought).[7] But to study the interrelations between the 'whole' and 'the parts' is just as necessary for the social sciences as it is for ecology.

By way of conclusion of this section we may thus say that it is not only the complex character of their subject-matter but also the social pressures to which they are subjected, that can explain why social scientists have contributed so little to improving our understanding of the structure of social change or development, to the question why societies have changed and are changing in the way in which they do. But it is precisely such more adequate orientation that is necessary if these processes are to be brought under control to a greater extent than is now the case; if they are to be steered in directions less destructive for men and for ecosystems, that constitute the environment of which men are a part, whether they want to or not.

II. MONOPOLISATION

Long-term social processes are blind, unplanned, uncontrolled – even though in recent decades it has become possible within specific organisations, in particular state bureaucracies and large corporations, to plan the direction of change within their sphere of control to a much greater extent than before. But only up to a certain degree: if the American government could in the early 1960s have foreseen the consequences of its involvement in continuing the colonial war in Vietnam (which perhaps it could have, if its perspective had been more detached), it may very well have terminated the war in time, before being drawn into committing war crimes and 'ecocyde' on the Vietnamese countryside. Notwithstanding the enormous power surplus that the United States has over North Vietnam and the National Liberation Front of South Vietnam, it has not been able to control the course of the war: that process results from the moves and counter-moves of both parties, and to a large extent also depends on the development of the total configuration of international power relations, in particular the relations between the United States, China and the Soviet Union.

This example may illustrate what I mean when I say that social processes are blind, unplanned, uncontrolled. The increasing concentration of power within multinational corporations and the ruling bureaucratic institutions of industrialised nation-states – though even there change is often 'surprising', unexpected and therefore unsettling and even threatening – makes many people believe that social change is planned and controlled to a much greater degree than is, in fact, the case. But if long-term social processes are blind, unplanned, uncontrolled, how can they be studied and understood? Is not Barry Commoner right, when he calls them chaotic and intractable? The answer is that social processes have a structure; social configurations (in social science language usually called social 'systems') which are processes, even though they appear to persist unchanged over long periods of time, have a structure. And if that structure would be better understood by the people who form it, their chances to control its direction might become greater.

In what follows I shall begin with some general remarks and then move to the specific examples I was asked to discuss. My aim is to further clarify what I mean by the 'structure' of social change through a summary description of some of the processes that have resulted in the present power configuration in world society. I can do no more than present the rough outlines of a framework for analysis.

The structure of social change (or development) results from (or: is connected with) the development of productive technology,[8] which I cannot discuss here, and from the struggles (which force people to cooperate) between individuals, families, tribes, states, classes, corporations, political parties, etc., who compete for scarce chances, for material resources such as land, tools and commodities, but also for social positions, for power, privilege, status. Most chances available to men in societies are scarce in relation to needs. It is often postulated, that the development of technology has decreased scarcity (the age of 'abundance'), but it may well be that if we take the whole of world society into consideration instead of only the industrialised societies, scarcity has increased rather than decreased, particularly if we include social positions. But that is a hypothesis I only put forward for further discussion and analysis.

As long as there is scarcity there must either be competition or controlled distribution.[9] The latter has to a limited degree been achieved within particular so-called welfare states. A good criterion for the level of development of state societies may be the degree to which it has achieved such controlled distribution – which implies equal distribution if competition is to be mitigated – not only of goods, but also of social positions. It might be added that this criterion corresponds with the ideal image of a 'nation', as a people living together harmoniously guided by common norms and values.

All participants in a competitive process – whether individuals or organised groups – plan in the sense that they try to achieve their aims by more or less conscious strategies, but their strategies lead them into conflict with the strategies of others in a process of move and countermove that none of the participants can plan or control and the outcomes of which may be wanted by none of them. But the degree of control over a specific process that a particular individual or group can have varies with the degree of asymmetry of the power relations between the participants. The greater the number of participants and the more equal they are in strength, the less control each of them has over the process as a whole. In economics the situation in which no participant in the market has any control at all is called perfect competition – a situation that in fact has never existed, but upon which the models of capitalist economics and the justification of capitalism as the most 'rational' system of production have been based.[10]

The more unequal in strength and the smaller the number of participants, the greater the degree of control which the strongest participant in the process will have over the course of the process itself. Take a game of chess: an expert player not only has the power to win the game, but if he has an inexperienced opponent, he may even be able to completely control the course (structure) of the game itself. But if he plays simultaneously against a large number of opponents, his degree of control over the course of the games he plays becomes less and he may even lose from players who he would defeat in a normal bipolar game. Competitive processes tend to lead to increasing monopolisation of chances in the hands of few individuals or groups (states, corporations, social classes, ethnic groups). Norbert Elias has called this the monopoly mechanism:

> When within a larger social unit, many smaller units which form the larger unit because of their interdependence, have relatively equal strength and are therefore able to compete with one another – unhampered by already present monopolies – for the chances to acquire mastery over social goods, mainly means of subsistence and production, then there is a very great probability that some will win and submit the others. As a consequence, gradually ever fewer units will have ever greater chances, so that more and more social units have to stop competing and become directly or indirectly dependent upon a smaller and smaller number of strong units.[11]

This is of course a very general formulation, that only expresses the general tendency of competitive processes. It may therefore help to illustrate the structure of monopolisation processes by a contemporary example: that of professional soccer competition. At the point of transition from amateur status the clubs are still more or less equal in strength. But the clubs winning in the first few years will start to attract larger crowds and acquire bigger receipts. They can start to hire good players from less successful clubs during the transfer period; they can provide better trainers and other facilities for the players; they can increase the salaries of their players, etc. These chances, that are not available to less successful clubs, increase their strength even more. If they win the national championship, they are able to participate in international competitions, which give them again increased receipts and added prestige. Gradually a few 'star' teams emerge against which the rest of the soccer league has practically no chance to win. They accumulate chances to such an extent that they acquire monopoly power. This situation implies serious financial difficulties for the rest of the league: they either have to merge with other clubs, drop out altogether from the competition (in the Netherlands the second league disappeared after a few years), or become dependent on 'aid' from the local business community or town government. In soccer competition the monopolisation process can of course not become complete: the league has to remain in existence and the second-rate clubs must at least be able to offer some credible resistance to the star teams, if the purpose of soccer competition – to provide excitement to the spectators – is not to be undermined.

I believe that an understanding of monopolisation processes as unplanned processes with a particular structure and particular consequences is a first step to a more realistic understanding of the 'overall social, political and economic forces that govern both our daily lives and the course of history'. Examples of monopolisation processes are the formation of states and empires ('great powers'); the formation of 'developed' versus 'underdeveloped' societies; the formation of 'multinational' corporations and the process of increasing concentration of 'capital' in general.[12] It may be clear that these examples indeed have to do with 'overall social, political and economic forces'. In the next section I will discuss one of my examples – the process of state formation – in greater detail and attempt to connect that process with colonialism and its consequences.

III. STATE FORMATION AND COLONIALISM

The process of state formation in Western Europe should be seen in terms of the formation of monopoly power and the subsequent struggle for control over established monopolies. That process cannot be separated from colonialism: 'internal' and 'external' expansionism are interconnected; in other words, there is a continuity between 'state' and 'empire' formation in the history of the West. There are also – as yet insufficiently analysed – structural similarities between the competitive struggles among feudal lords, that led to the formation of states as we now know them and the competitive struggles between states, that are still with us. There is continuity between the strategies that Machiavelli recommended to Medieval Princes, that Metternich pursued after the Congress of Vienna, and that Henry Kissinger advises to President Nixon. In order to understand the structure of power relations between and within states in the present world, it is therefore necessary to understand the long-term process of state formation in Western Europe and its consequences for the rest of the world. I should also stress that state formation and the development of the capitalist mode of production are interconnected, though not in the sense that states are simply part of the 'superstructure' emerging from the 'needs' of capitalism, as is often suggested.[13] But I am unable to discuss here the difficult theoretical problems to which the relations between state formation and the development of capitalism give rise; problems which result perhaps more from the unfortunate separation between economics, sociology and political science and the partly self-imposed, partly forced upon position of Marxism as an alternative social science, than from difficulties inherent in the subject matter.

Most people tend to take the nation states as they exist today more or less for granted. It is even believed that what are presently regarded as 'nations' have always been there as the 'natural' units of people belonging together in one state. But that is far from the case. With but few exceptions, nations have followed 'states' instead of the other way round. How then did states emerge?

A short answer to this question is impossible, and I am therefore forced to simplify excessively.[14] Around the year 1000 Europe was divided into small, more or less self-sufficient and autonomous units, ruled by warriors. These 'feudal' lords tried to expand the territories which they controlled, but had only limited possibilities to do so because the social units over which they ruled were not yet sufficiently interdependent. Only military conquest was possible. But in order to be successful it was necessary to acquire support from other feudal lords: these then had to be rewarded with land. Effective central control over large territories was impossible because agriculture yielded only a small surplus: there were few roads, little trade and very limited money circulation. The decentralising tendencies were therefore impossible to overcome. Vassals soon became independent lords. But – for reasons that are discussed in the paper by D. van Arkel – interdependence started to increase, and in a particular manner. In Western Europe, in contrast to earlier 'empires' based on slavery,[15] towns emerged as autonomous units separate from the feudal order, the inhabitants of which were 'free', that is, not subject to control by the feudal lords. Thus a twofold power structure emerged that became in a later period the basis for the continuing expansion of the power of what have come to be called the 'absolutist' monarchs, or better: the dynastic states. We see a similar process of state formation all over Europe: not because someone planned it that way, but because the competitive struggles for control over territory between feudal lords had the structure of a monopolisation process. More and more of them were forced out of the competition and relegated to a permanently dependent position. It did not occur in all European countries at the same time: England and France became states at an earlier time than Germany and Italy – latecomers also as industrial and colonial powers.[16]

Why were ruling dynasties (the succession of kings belonging to a particular family) able to acquire such a great power surplus over the other groups in their societies (the landed aristocracy, the urban bourgeoisie)? Basic to the explanation are the functions that kings fulfilled for the towns (and the fact that the towns competed among themselves instead of forming stable alliances): the towns needed protection against external attack, they needed safe trade routes, and the ruling groups within the town sometimes needed royal troops in order to suppress revolts. The towns were thus prepared to pay taxes to the king so that these services could be provided. Gradually the monarchs acquired the monopolies of violence and taxation: taxes pay for the maintenance of regular armies, police forces and central bureaucracies. And in turn the state bureaucracy, supported by the 'strong arm' of government, assures that taxes are being paid. Of course, the process was much more complicated and less 'linear' than it may seem from this brief account. It took four to five centuries before the dynasties that emerged victoriously were able to eliminate their competitors through strategic marriages, buying of land, and warfare. Because of increased money circulation and their monopoly of taxation the kings no longer had to pay for military services in land: they could pay in money. Gradually what had been an independent warrior aristocracy was thus transformed into a court aristocracy, more and more dependent on privileges that the king provided. Thus, the king could use in turn the town bourgeoisie in order to balance the power of the aristocracy (in France, for example, the kings recruited the state bureaucracy from the bourgeoisie and prohibited the aristocracy from engaging in trade and commerce) and the aristocracy to balance the power of the bourgeoisie. What specific form the process of state formation has taken in different European countries has been primarily based on the development of that triangular struggle between king, aristocracy and bourgeoisie.

In dynastic states the central monopolies of violence and taxation combined with and considerably reinforced by a third monopoly, that of the conduct of external (inter-state) relations, were still private monopolies of the king: no separation was made between the royal household and the state budget. Tax revenues benefited in particular the groups upon which the king was dependent for the increase and maintenance of his own power position: the state bourgeoisie and the court aristocracy which, though competing, yet had a common interest in the maintenance of hereditary privileges as an institution. But the way in which tax revenues were used caused rising dissatisfaction among the commercial, banking and manufacturing bourgeoisie who were forced to struggle for a degree of control over the state monopolies commensurate with their increasing social power. Seen in a longer-term perspective it was mainly this struggle that led to the French revolution, through which the delicate power balance between king, court aristocracy and state bourgeoisie was destroyed and the hereditary privileges of the state bourgeoisie abolished. But the French revolution only compressed into a short period what was accomplished in other European countries in a more gradual process: the transformation of private royal monopolies into 'public' monopolies, for whose control whole social classes struggled and which were administered increasingly by elected governments receiving fixed salaries. If ministers or civil servants used tax revenues for private purposes or received money for their services this was increasingly considered as 'corruption'. How 'corrupt' were the European monarchs only a few centuries ago!

The industrial revolution changed the nature of interdependencies between higher and lower social strata. In the eighteenth century kings and aristocrats could still regard the people over whom they ruled as 'subjects', as only being there to fulfil functions for them. But when technological skills became increasingly important for industrial production, reciprocity of dependence between social classes became greater. At the same time another process continued: once a monopoly is established (whether the 'political' monopolies of violence and taxation, or the 'economic' monopolies of large corporations) the individual or group controlling it becomes more and more dependent on his/its dependents for the administration of the monopolised chances. Therefore the power of the dependents as a group (class) gradually increases. Because of this gradual reduction of the unevenness of reciprocal dependence between higher and lower social classes, ruling elites and political parties increasingly had to justify themselves as governing for the 'public interest', for all the people living within the state. The industrial revolution thus transformed dynastic states gradually into nation states. We can begin to speak of 'nations' when the distance between ruler and ruled becomes less great, when state monopolies are to some extent controlled by and used for the governed. In the eighteenth century the word 'nation' was still a term of opposition: used to stress that the people were there not for the state, but the state was there for the nation. Again, this process of nation-state (or perhaps better, state-nation) formation has been very slow, with many ups and downs, and it is by no means completed.

With the increasing strength of the working class, through the formation of trade unions and socialist parties, the liberal states of the nineteenth century were transformed into the welfare states of the twentieth century. The working class, in the nineteenth century still struggling to be represented in the political system, becomes 'integrated' in the state. And in the process the state apparatus becomes increasingly powerful and begins to perform more and more functions. These centralising tendencies occur even in a country like the United States, where the national political ideology is very much opposed to it. The class struggle inherent in the development of capitalism, combined with the increasing need for central coordination in societies with a highly developed division of labour, continuously strengthens state power. The 'internationalism' of nineteenth century socialist parties was unable to counteract this process, as was most clearly demonstrated by the fact that the German socialist party voted for the war credits in 1914.

The formation of states in Western Europe as large, internally pacified territories, has been important for the development of capitalism. The existence of stable monopolies of violence made it possible for a process of purely economic (market) competition to take place. If entrepreneurs had had to maintain private armies to protect their factories from attempts at destruction by competitors and the roads, railways and canals over which their products were transported, the industrial revolution could hardly have occurred.[17]

The West European states have always been expansionist. The very beginnings of colonialism were made possible by the financial support of monarchs hoping to acquire precious metals. In the early period of colonial conquest kings also attempted to maintain trade monopolies over the territories they controlled. Colonial expansion thus provided not only the capitalist bourgeoisie with increased surplus with which they could finance new activities, but also the kings and later the nation-state. Only the aristocracy did not profit from colonial expansion: the inflow of precious metals contributed to increasing inflation, and this impoverished the aristocracy which received its income from fixed land rents. In later phases the competition between states and the competition between capitalist entrepreneurs reinforced each other and therefore intensified the struggle for control over (and penetration into) territories outside Europe. Competitive processes force the participants to adopt expansionist strategies, as was already recognised by the Romans who called these strategies *praevenire*: be there before your opponent. This dynamic is also expressed in the saying about an American pioneer: he did not want all the land, he just wanted the land next to his. Or in the more abstract formulation of the German philosopher Fichte: 'whose power does not increase, while that of others does, in fact decreases'. That expansionist logic is the main driving force behind Western-European (and American) colonialism, though, of course, in each phase of the development of capitalism new forces making for colonial expansionism were added (trade, mining, raw materials, markets for finished products, investments).[18]

The consequence of colonialism has been a process of what one could call *dependent* state formation in colonised territories. These became states not because of autonomous developments, but because large territories had been unified and pacified by colonial administrations and colonial armies. But the colonial monopolists also became increasingly dependent upon the original inhabitants of these territories 'for the administration of monopolised chances'. They were forced to educate a westernised 'middle class' for the subordinate positions in army, police and colonial bureaucracy. But this new social stratum had also very restricted chances to rise in the hierarchy: it was not allowed to become really assimilated to the white ruling class. It thus came gradually to identify not with the colonial metropolis, as had been expected by the colonial rulers, but with the administrative unit created by the colonial power as its 'nation' and potential power base. From this westernised but discriminated 'second class' state bourgeoisie emerged the nationalist movements leading the struggle for independence, again not for the political units existing before the colonial powers arrived, but for the territories which these powers integrated as units of rule. Because of their increased power, in many cases based on successful mobilisation of large parts of the population, and because the European colonial powers were weakened by the world wars resulting from their continuing competition, direct colonial rule could no longer be continued and the 'new states' of Asia and Africa came into being. But not only have these states in their administrative and formal political structures been closely modelled upon their former metropolitan powers, they remained in a subordinate position within the vertically-structured network of the world division of labour. It is therefore still very easy for outside powers (whether states or multinational corporations) to achieve their own ends ('friendly' governments, favourable investment climate, etc.) by supporting particular groups in the struggle for control over the state monopolies. In many cases, that struggle has resulted in the take-over of the state by the carriers of the monopoly of violence, the military. Because of the need for financial and military support of the elaborate bureaucracies of the new states, their ruling groups with but few exceptions remain strongly dependent upon America, Western Europe and Japan.

A framework for the analysis of the present distribution of power in world society has been put forward by Johan Galtung,[19] who distinguishes between Centre nations (US, Europe, Japan) and Periphery nations (the Third World). Within these nations he again distinguishes between centres (elites) and peripheries (masses).[20] These are linked together as shown in Figure 1.

The most important element in this structure is that the centre in Centre nations has a bridgehead in the Periphery nations: their centre.[21] The arrangement as a whole favours the periphery of Centre nations – there is more disharmony of interest between centre and periphery

Figure 1

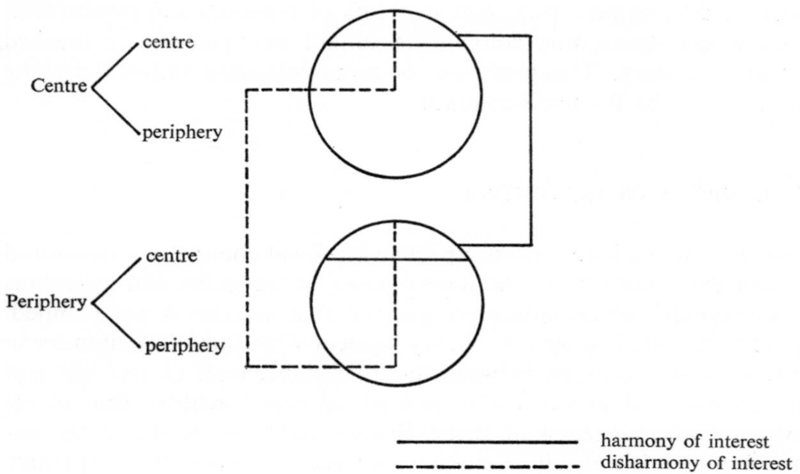

in Periphery nations than in Centre nations. And for that reason there is disharmony of interest between the peripheries in Centre and Periphery nations: 'The two centres are tied together and the Centre periphery is tied to its centre: that is the whole essence of the situation.' This structure of power relations is based upon a vertical division of labour and a pattern of exchange relations which not only makes it possible for Centre nations to extract goods, capital and labour from Periphery nations, but also allows them to keep for themselves economic activities with higher degrees of processing from which all kinds of favourable spin-off effects result. The most important of these can be observed in the spread of education and technological skills over the population in Centre nations and the lack of it in Periphery nations, including the difference in levels of unemployment. In Galtung's framework the combined effects of dependent state formation and dependent capitalist economic development in the Third World are represented. What has been said before about the state formation process in Western Europe and America contributes to the explanation of the disharmony of interests (or lack of identification) between the periphery of the Centre and the periphery of the Periphery. The increasing integration of the working class into the political systems of what have become 'welfare states' explains the lack of identification and cooperation of subordinate classes across national boundaries. This type of analysis, which does not treat states as closed systems interacting with each other but also looks at development processes in terms of transnational power relations, demonstrates that colonialism cannot be treated as a finished period in history. The processes of monopolisation initiated by the expansion of the West still continue.

IV. COMPETITION AND CONTROL

If we take such a long-term perspective on social change as a structured process that results from the interweaving of the plans and intentions of individuals and organised groups, but that as such is not planned, willed or intended by anyone, it may be clear why Barry Commoner can write about the contrast between the 'reasonable logic of ecology' and the 'chaotic and intractable' character of social reality. But as we have seen, the processes of social change that have produced the environmental crisis result from the coercive dynamics of competitive processes which, though they change in character – for example, once states are formed, competition is no longer over the establishment of monopolies of violence and taxation but over control of these monopolies – nevertheless continue in new forms. The Stockholm Conference of the UN was interpreted by many representatives of poor countries as an attempt to preserve the international division of labour and power by invoking 'a general interest' in the survival of the human species. But without the creation of an international mechanism for redistribution of the scarce benefits of technological advance, the measures necessary for solving the environmental crisis could in practice amount to additional handicaps for the poor in the international competitive process into which they were forced to enter. To stop 'economic growth', or rather to change its direction increasingly to services that human beings fulfil for each other, as is deemed necessary from an ecological perspective, therefore requires a greater degree of control over the competitive processes between states, corporations and social classes than has been so far achieved. Winners want to preserve their position, losers want to catch-up. But we presently seem to be in a situation similar to that of the soccer league in which the clubs with monopoly positions acquire an interest in supporting the clubs that are permanently losing, because the league must remain in existence if the clubs are to survive. However, in practice the clubs with monopoly positions usually rely on others (local governments, business firms, the national association) for the necessary measures.

To rely on the 'enlightened self-interest' of those who have acquired monopoly positions in competitive processes (the great powers, the large multinational corporations, the ruling classes within states) is to overlook the coercive dynamics of competitive processes. These require simultaneous and controlled changes in policy. Otherwise, those participants that act first on the basis of enlightened self-interest will disproportionally lose. The same logic always proves to be an effective argument against unilateral disarmament: if we disarm and the others will not follow our example . . . Similarly, it is always pointed out that government measures of environmental control should not 'falsify' international competition by increasing the costs for national firms. The crucial question therefore remains: how to achieve a greater degree of control over those competitive processes that even though they benefit small groups of people are destructive not only for the majority of mankind but also for nature?

Many solutions for the environmental crisis – as for the other two crucial problems of the present interdependent world: the threat of nuclear war and the increasing inequalities in life chances – are offered on an *as if* basis. They are argued as if governments in fact were in control, as if it were only a matter of their choosing the right kind of planning and policy-making. That presumption may have as its unintended consequence that the people for whom the plans are made are seen as disturbing elements who do not understand what is good for them, a view that may lead in turn to increased reliance on coercion and repression by the state.

The main purposes of this paper have therefore been to point to the need for a more realistic and more widespread understanding of the problems of competition and control in social change and, hopefully, to show through the analysis of state formation processes that such understanding is possible.

NOTES

1. The latter competitive dynamic remains even where states have formed institutional frameworks for permanent cooperation, such as EEC, OECD, Comecon, OPEC, etc.
2. Barry Commoner, *The Closing Circle*, New York, 1971, p. 294.
3. Norbert Elias, 'Problems of Involvement and Detachment', *British Journal of Sociology*, 1956, pp. 226-252.
4. See e.g. Alvin Gouldner, *The Coming Crisis of Western Sociology*, London,

1971; István Mészáros, 'Ideology and Social Science' in *The Socialist Register 1972,* pp. 35-83; Norbert Elias, Einleitung to *Ueber den Prozess der Zivilisation*, Bern and München, 1969, pp. vii-lxx; William E. Connolly, *Political Science and Ideology*, New York, 1967.

5. For a more detailed analysis of the origins of the static perspective on the social sciences see G. van Benthem van den Bergh, 'The Structure of Development: an invitation to the sociology of Norbert Elias', Institute of Social Studies, Occasional Papers No. 13, October 1971.
6. Commoner, *The Closing Circle*, p. 189.
7. René Dubos, *Man Adapting*, New Haven, 1965; Karl Popper, *The Poverty of Historicism*, London, 1961. Popper is mainly concerned with showing the impossibility of holistic planning, which he rightly believes to lead to extreme coercion by the state, and to which he opposes a strategy for piecemeal planning. I would maintain, however, that piecemeal planning can only be successful on the basis of more adequate knowledge of the overall ('whole') process of social development.
8. See Darcy Ribiero, *The Civilisational Process*, Washington, 1968; Marshall D. Sahlins and Elman R. Service, *Evolution and Culture*, Ann Arbor, 1960; V. Gordon Childe, *What Happened in History*, Pelican ed., Harmondsworth, 1964.
9. I am aware of the fact that scarcity is a relative category: it may be decreased not only through making more chances available ('growth'), but also through change in what people perceive as their needs, for example through a more realistic understanding of the effects of the structure of competitive processes based on the particular perception of needs prevalent in industrialised societies. Competition can only be mitigated, not completely eliminated. Rivalries between human beings will always exist. The question is whether it will be possible to eliminate destructive kinds of competition.
10. See K. W. Rotschild (ed.), *Power in Economics,* Harmondsworth, 1971; esp. Introduction, pp. 7-19.
11. Elias, *Ueber den Prozess der Zivilisation*, Part II, pp. 142-159.
12. That process is not confined to 'capitalist' societies. In 1963 Yugoslavia had 232 banks, in 1966 112, in 1970 55, and in 1972 only 15 were left. R. M. Boonzaayer Flaes, *Yugoslavian Experience of Worker Self-management* (Proceedings of the First International Conference on Self-Management and Participation, December 1972, Dubrovnik; forthcoming).
13. For example: 'Capitalism unified the nation state . . .,' David Horowitz, *Imperialism and Revolution*, p. 42, a statement based on the following passage from the *Communist Manifesto*: 'Independent, or but loosely connected provinces, with separate interest, laws, governments and systems of taxation, become lumped together into one nation, with one government, one code of laws, one national class-interest, one frontier and one customs tariff.' Similarly: 'A successful capitalist society needs a strong and centralised state to provide the conditions for unimpeded trade within a good-sized national market . . .' Harry Magdoff, 'Imperialism: A Historical Survey' in *Monthly Review,* 24, 1, May 1972, p. 5.
14. The only existing sociological theory of state formation processes, on which

the following account is based, is to be found in the work of Norbert Elias, *Ueber den Prozess der Zivilisation*, and *Die Höfische Gesellschaft*, Neuwied and Berlin, 1969. In political science the state is treated as a given, a static entity, not as a process.

15. See Ribiero, *The Civilisational Process*, pp. 53-81; S. N. Eisenstadt, 'Empires', *International Encyclopedia of the Social Sciences*, Vol. V, pp. 41-48.
16. That fascism came to power precisely in these countries may be related to their position as latecomers in these three respects.
17. This does not mean that the state does not also fulfil other functions for the development of capitalism. Robin Murray lists as the six most important functions performed at present: (1) guaranteeing of property rights; (2) economic liberalisation: the establishment of the conditions for free, competitive exchange; (3) economic orchestration: the regulation of business cycles and economic planning; (4) input provision at low cost: labour (education, wage control), land (public utilities), capital (national banking system, special credits), technology (financing of research and development, particularly in connection with the military), economic infrastructure (energy, communications); (5) intervention for social consensus: prevention of pollution, wide regional disparities, regulation of conditions of work and sale, social security; (6) management of external relations.
    Robin Murray, 'The Internationalisation of Capital and the Nation State', *New Left Review*, 1971, pp. 83-109.
18. On the dynamics of colonialism see further: Geoffrey Barraclough, *An Introduction to Contemporary History*, London, 1964, esp. Ch. II; Ernest Mandel, *Marxist Economic Theory*, London, 1971, esp. chapter on 'Imperialism', pp. 441-485; and Harry Magdoff, 'Imperialism'.
19. Johan Galtung, 'A Structural Theory of Imperialism', *Journal of Peace Research*, 1971, pp. 81-117, and *The European Community: A Superpower in the Making*, Oslo and London, 1972.
20. In Galtung's view the terms centre and periphery are defined in more complex terms than 'elites' and 'masses', but in the course of his argument they do come to mean this.
21. That is the reason why the term 'internal colonialism' has been introduced.

7. Population redistribution and migration

A.C. KUIJSTEN

The author devotes much attention to the problem of population implosion, which refers to the increased spatial concentration of people. The contribution by Hilhorst and Lambooy may be consulted for a somewhat different perspective. The author brings to the fore the interesting question of human adaptation to a new environment following population migration. The ideas expressed in this respect might also have implications for adaptation to environmental change caused by pollution, resource depletion and degradation.

Population growth is considered one of the biggest problems, if not the biggest problem, of our contemporary world. The well-known report *The Limits to Growth* offered by the team of Dennis L. Meadows to the so-called Club of Rome, chose exponential population growth as a point of departure for its forecasts of future use of food, natural resources and energy and their polluting effects in sketching the highlights of the modern, technological version of Doomsday.

An important aspect of the world-wide problem of population growth is its distributional component. On the one hand, the population is already unevenly distributed over space, globally as well as nationally, purely numerically as well as in relation to its animate and inanimate resources, and further population growth will undoubtedly worsen this situation of imbalance. On the other hand, population redistribution can offer at least a part of the solution to the immense social and environmental problems that will arise if population growth itself cannot be checked within a short period of time.

Philip Hauser, in his Presidential Address to the 63rd Annual Meeting of the American Sociological Association on August 28 1968,[1] stated that contemporary society, whether observed globally, nationally or locally is realistically characterised as 'the chaotic society' and is best understood as 'the anachronistic society' because of its manifest confusion and disorder caused by what Hauser calls the 'social morphological revolution'.

This social morphological revolution, closely related to other revolutions – agricultural, commercial, scientific, technological, and industrial – is the product of three developments energised by and in interaction with a fourth: the three developments are population explosion, population implosion, and population diversification; the fourth and interrelated development is the acceleration in the tempo of technological and social change.[2]

Several technological changes, in many respects responsible for the contemporary environmental crisis, have been or will be discussed in this volume. One of the themes of this paper is what Hauser called population implosion: 'the increasing concentration of the world's peoples on a small proportion of the earth's surface – the phenomenon of urbanisation and metropolitanisation'.[3]

The scope of this process is world-wide: the Statement and Conclusions of the recently held UN Symposium on the Impact of Urbanisation on Man's Environment formulates it as follows: 'There can hardly be one country in the world that is now coping adequately with the problems of urban life and growth in both a human and an ecological sense. The urban crisis is global, affecting both the industrial nations and those somewhere on the road towards industrialisation, but the burden of population increase and new waves of migration from the countryside is most acute and overwhelming in the poorer developing lands.'[4] This statement pays attention to the global character of this process of concentration of population as well as to existing regional differences in the way it takes course and the problems it creates.

On the global level the trend is clear: in 1800 only 2.4 percent of the world's population resided in places of 20,000 and more inhabitants, and only 1.7 percent in places of 100,000 or more. By 1960, however, 27.1 percent of the world's people were located in places of 20,000 and more, and 19.9 percent in places of 100,000 or more.[5] Projections of the world urban population indicate that by the end of this century 42 percent of the world's people may be resident in places of 20,000 or more, and more than a fourth in cities of 100,000 and more.[6] Intensity and acceleration of the process are clearly demonstrated in these simple figures and, as Kingsley Davis stated, 'there is no apparent reason why it [= the world] should not become as urbanised as the most urban countries today – with perhaps 85-90 percent of the population living in cities and towns of 5,000 or more and practicing urban occupations.'[7]

With this last quotation in mind, it must immediately be clear that even in discussing the problem on a global level, the trends and prospects revealed by several authors not only depend on how urbanisation really develops empirically, but also on their definition of what is urban and what is non-urban! On the level of continents, countries and regions, especially from a comparative point of view, these differences in definition are all the more important: not only do students of urbanisation define their subject matter in different ways, but national Statistical Bureaux use definitions that are not easily comparable and change their definitions from time to time.

The main criteria used are size, density, function, and possible combinations of these three; sometimes an administrative criterion is added, if only for the sake of statistical convenience ('municipality' instead of 'place' or 'town' as entity of observation). The global trends mentioned above use the criterion of population size, indicating three different possible size-levels in four sentences, but David, in his prospect of the future level, immediately adds to it the functional criterion of 'practicing urban occupations', leaving it to the reader to imagine what it is that makes an occupation urban.

In another article Davis defines urbanisation, or rather its growth, as 'the proportion of the total population concentrated in urban settlements, or else a rise in this proportion',[8] but on a following page he states, in discussing the phenomenon of urbanisation, that 'in a sense the slowing down of urbanisation [in societies advanced enough to be highly urbanised] is thus more apparent than real: an increasing proportion of urbanites simply live in the country and are classified as rural.'[9] In rather inconsistent arguments like these, Louis Wirth's more sociological definition of urbanism 'as a way of life' clearly plays its trick. The two different questions of what makes a place urban in a physical ecological or functional sense, and what makes a person 'mentally urban' are too easily confused.

The statistical consequences of trying to avoid the possibilities of such a confusion of personal and ecological characteristics can be seen at the other end of the scale, in defining what is rural. In 1964 the US Bureau of the Census changed its definition of rural from a mere residential criterion to that of 'farm families': those families actually earning their living from agriculture. The 20.5 million 'rural' Americans in the 1960 Census decreased to 12.9 million 'farm families' in 1964 as a result of this more functional definition of non-urban population.[10] Such a change in definition is of course only relevant when it is possible to distinguish a category of people who earn their living purely from agriculture or from services rendered to the agricultural business of others.[11] While Davis chooses proportional figures as his point of departure in discussing trends in urbanisation, Epstein considers such proportional figures only significant for 'certain limited purposes, e.g. as a measure of demographic change, but in other respects the results they give are not always very helpful, particularly in the African context.'[12] Epstein illustrates his point by comparing Nigeria and Zambia: taking the size-category of 100,000 or more inhabitants as a criterion, Nigeria would have an index of urbanisation of 4.3 and Zambia, with its Copperbelt region as a large modern and industrial urban complex, would have an index of 0. Nigeria traditionally has several so-called Yoruba towns with a population of over 100,000 which stayed 'fairly homogeneous' between 1921 and 1952 (Yoruba country in that period showed the lowest 'rate of urban growth' of Nigeria), while in Zambia during the same period about 250,000 Africans moved into the Copperbelt towns.

Although Epstein's example is a little unfair in my opinion, in as far as he takes a very high size-standard of urbanity, I think he is right in the general point he suggests that it may be more relevant to consider urbanisation as involving a process of movement and change; its essence is that it creates the possibility of discontinuity with some pre-existing set of conditions. Urbanisation is a social-structural fact related to, but not necessarily linked up with 'urbanism, which is the way of life in towns themselves'. Urbanisation is not a unidimensional phenomenon, it has demographic, social-structural and cultural aspects.

It is the combined effect of all these various, less statistical and more situational and processual aspects, that determines the real or possible impact of urbanisation on man's environment. The statistical form of the process of urbanisation is less important than its socio-cultural contents.

Moreover, the urbanisation process – statistically speaking, but no less in its situational and processual aspects – cannot be regarded as something on its own, separated from what is going on in the non-urbanising part of a country. Urbanisation is not a social but a societal process, interwoven with other societal processes such as economic development, industrialisation, structural and cultural changes on a macro level; as McGee argued in one of the most lucid articles on this subject in recent years, it is perhaps more dependent on and responsive to these other societal processes than it generates them.[13]

This last point is of great significance to the evaluation of contemporary and expected urbanisation trends in developing countries, also from an ecological point of view. Experts on economic development, Americans in particular, are perhaps too apt to consider contemporary trends in urbanisation in newly developing countries as a mere replication of what happened about a century ago in Western Europe and in the United States.[14] They see the cities as 'beachheads', centres of modernisation acting as catalysts for economic growth, the centres from which the benefits of modernisation flow outwards to revitalise the stagnating agricultural sector. Their point of view is biased by the ideological overtone 'that the strength of these newly developing countries is lying primarily in their cities because as capitalist structures they have the capacity for economic growth which has characterised the developed capitalist nations, most notably the United States.'[15]

This point of view is further illustrated by Hoselitz, who states: 'in the town or city – and only in the town or city – a labour force can be found that is finally committed to industry and does not tend to float back regularly to the land, and this fact makes the labour contract more impersonal, functionally specific, and tends to endow it with universalistic criteria in the selection of individuals for industrial jobs.'[16] After joining to this, the argument of the greater variety of skills and occupational specialties, Hoselitz simply concludes: 'All these factors appear to be commonplace, but together they explain why in under-developed countries industries tend to concentrate in a limited number of cities, why these cities often grow to a very great size, and why many countries entering the path of industrialisation have vast agricultural regions with very few industrial islands in them.'[17]

Apart from the questionability of the universal validity of Hoselitz' remark on the relatively low degree of floating back to the countryside of rural-urban migrants, sharply contrasting to Epstein's generalisation (based on the observation that in many African towns the cultural break with the village has been less radical than, for example, in 19th-century Western Europe) that 'it is the *circulation* of labour rather than its migration which has become its characteristic feature,'[18] a more serious criticism of the arguments of scholars such as Friedmann, Hirschman and Hoselitz could be that they implicitly see the typical Western shape of industrialisation – regarded here merely as the organisational 'translation' of the indeed typically urban feature of functional variety and diversification – as the only possible and thus necessary organisational vehicle of future economic development of the Third World. The ecological impact of large-scale industrialisation annex urbanisation in the Western countries – the Rotterdam area, the Ruhr area, London, etc. – should be a clear warning signal. Of course, the authors of the concluding report on *The Impact of Urbanisation on Man's Environment* are right in stating that 'recommendations that curtail or restrict economic progress and dampen the rising expectations of the people of developing countries for a better life would be unacceptable to most Governments of these countries.'[19] (I would even add ethically objectionable.) However, the meaning of such general remarks completely depends on how one likes to operationalise 'economic progress'. It is too easy a solution to advise governments of developing countries to locate their large-scale industrial plants at sites where they do the least harm to environment, without in the first place answering whether it is advisable at all to industrialise in a way that is technologically and organisationally the same as was done in Europe a century ago. In arguments like these the Western frame of reference is assumed to be present in the minds of Government leaders of developing countries. And to a certain degree such an assumption may be right: to those leaders it is indeed easier to see New York City as the World Capital of wealth and welfare than to consider Robert Redfield's Tepotzlan in Yucatan, Mexico, as an attractive alternative. In regarding the only fundamental alternative to the capitalist pattern of economic growth, Communism, such leaders must conclude that at least the Soviet Union tried to reach its economic goals successfully through the same vehicle of large-scale industrialisation combined with urbanisation. Future environmental problems of urban growth are partly dependent on the choice made by Government leaders, national and local, on such fundamental issues.

Urban population growth has generally three main components:

a. natural increase of the urban population;
b. its migration balance; and
c. administrative enlargements of the urban municipal territory.

The increase in the degree of urbanisation of a country – in the proportional sense as defined by Davis – has a fourth component: the entry of places previously classified as rural into the ranks of urban places, as a result of the effect of the three aforementioned components on the population growth of those rural settlements.

Quantitatively, the factor of administrative enlargement in general is the least important. The importance of the component of entry into the urban size-ranks varies from region to region, dependent partly on the definitional size level of urbanity that is used, partly on the typical shape of the size-class hierarchy of the total settlement pattern of the region. The two remaining components are generally the most important: natural increase and migration.

Davis[20] has pointed out that migration can be held responsible for the urbanisation process as it unrolled in the Western world, especially in the second half of the 19th century, whereas in today's developing countries the growth of urbanisation is induced much more by the high rates of natural increase of urban populations. This point is true in its most generalised form, and can be regarded as another reason not to consider contemporary processes of urbanisation in newly developing countries as mere replications of what happened in Europe and Northern America a hundred years ago; nevertheless, there are so many exceptions to this rule that it has very little predictive power.

Migration and natural increase are not independent of each other in their effect on total urban population growth, as appears immediately from the example that Davis uses to illustrate his point: only 20 percent of the rapid growth of Costa Rica's towns and cities was attributable to urbanisation per se [i.e. rural-urban migration]; 44 percent was attributable solely to the country's general population increase [i.e. the growth of the urban population holding the proportion of urbanisation constant], the remainder to the joint operation of both factors.'[21] Davis omits here the simple fact that the joint operation of both factors in this case still attributes 36 percent to the total urban population growth.

Therefore, the argument completely depends on whether one likes to add this 36 percent of what could be called 'the natural increase effect of migration' to the general natural increase component or to the migration component, the latter being very difficult for statistical reasons. The natural increase of a town that has grown rapidly in the recent past by net migration gains can be very high because of the contribution to it by those recent migrants, who in general belong to the younger age-brackets, assuming the sex-distribution of those migrants to be fairly equal. The migration and natural increase components being partly interdependent, in their *relative* contribution to total urban growth they also depend on the phase in which the urbanisation process is at a specific moment. Davis has described the typical way of the urbanisation process as one that is to be represented by a curve in the shape of an attenuated S.[22] In the Western world, migration was the most important growth component in the first stages of the urbanisation process, where the first bend of the S-shaped curve ushered a period of attenuation. In the latter phases of the process, when the proportion urban has reached a level of over 50, a second bend makes the curve flatten off to a level of proportion urban that is characteristic of contemporary highly developed countries.

In this situation the migration component becomes less significant because the rural-urban migration stream is counterbalanced more and more by the counterstream of the sub-urbanisation process: at this very advanced stage the entire concept of urbanisation indeed becomes ambiguous, as Davis correctly states.[23] As far as urban population growth is concerned, its main component will be natural increase and not migration, even to the extent that urban places only grow because natural increase is just capable of compensating migratory losses. Take, for instance, the Soviet Union. According to official Soviet statistics, urbanisation at the All-Union level rose from 18 percent in 1913, via 32 percent in 1939 and 48 percent in 1959, to 56 percent at the January 15, 1970 All-Union Census, with the Baltic Republics of Latvia and Estonia, the RSFSR and the Transcaucasian Republic of Armenia above this mean.[24] Thus, the Soviet Union has not yet reached the last phase of the S-curve. Indeed, net migration still played an important role in urban growth between 1959 and 1970, but its importance is now decreasing: the total growth of the urban population between 1959 and 1970 of 36 million people can be attributed for 40.5 percent to natural increase of the urban population itself, for 15.0 percent to the elevation to urban status of settlements that were still rural in 1959, and 44.4 percent to the net result of migratory movements between countryside and urban settlements.[25] Although according to these figures migration is still important, its role had already diminished as compared to the period 1926-1939, the years of agricultural collectivisation (as a push-factor) and large-scale industrialisation (as a pull-factor), when natural increase contributed only 18.5 percent, the transformation of villages into cities and so-called workers' settlements 19.5 percent, and migration as much as 62.1 percent to total urban growth, which was then 113 percent in 13 years![26]

The way in which migration can diminish in influence is shown by an analysis of growth components of Dutch municipalities of over 25,000 inhabitants.[27] As period of observation I chose the 11 years from January 1, 1957-December 31, 1967, in order to make the results comparable to the 11-year period of the above-mentioned Soviet figures. The results of this analysis are given in Table 1.

While the total population of the Netherlands grew during the 11-year period from 10,957,000 to 12,661,100, the population living in municipalities of 25,000 inhabitants or more rose from 5,904,382 to 7,269,735, implying a slight proportional increase from 53.9 to 57.4 percent. However, the size-class of 25,000-100,000 inhabitants showed a total population growth of 39.0 percent in the same period, increasing its proportional share from 21.8 percent to 26.3 percent of the total population, while the size-class of 100,000 and more had a population increase of only 12.3 percent and saw its proportional share decrease from 32.0 tot 31.1 percent. But while in the size-class of 25,000-

Table 1. Growth Components of Dutch Municipalities 1957-1967

Size-class of Municipality	*Population 1-1-1957*	*Natural Increase 1957-1967*	*Net Migration 1957-1967*	*Adminis-trative Corrections*	*Entry into or Exit from size-class*	*Territorial Enlargement*	*Population 31-12-1967*
25,000-100,000	2,393,652	407,946	+105,424	123	386,749	32,307	3,326,201
100,000 & over	3,510,730	368,251	—251,304	9	301,982	13,866	3,943,534
Total	5,904,382	776,197	—145,880	**132**	688,731	46,173	7,269,735
25,000-100,000		43.7 %	11.3 %		41.5 %	3.5 %	
100,000 & over		84.8 %	—58.1 %		69.8 %	3.2 %	
Total		56.8 %	—10.7 %		50.4 %	3.4 %	

100,000 inhabitants migration still contributed a modest 11.3 percent to its total growth, and the component of entry into the size-class even contributed 41.5 percent despite the fact that in this period three municipalities (Apeldoorn, Hilversum and Leiden) with a total population of 301,982 at the moment of their size-class alteration moved into the category of over 100,000 inhabitants, this last category suffered a net population loss by migration equal to 58.1 percent of its total population growth! The Dutch case therefore shows a typical pattern of deconcentration and suburbanisation of population, in contrast to the Soviet case in almost the same period. The conclusion to be drawn – and of course it is not a new one – is that migration plays an important role in the process of urbanisation all over the world, but its proportional share differs in highly developed countries to that in contemporary newly developing countries and is partly dependent on the phase of the urbanisation process along the S-curve.

In the latter conclusion, migration must of course be understood as the net result of rural-urban and urban-rural migratory streams, but there are several other kinds that are also relevant to the problem of population distribution and redistribution. The next thing to do is to define migration accordingly. The most general definition possible is a permanent or semi-permanent change of residence', with no restriction as to the distance of the move or the voluntary or involuntary nature of the act. Such a definition can be used only when the level of analysis is the individual one: as soon as migration is analysed in the aggregate, the amount of migration expressed either by an absolute number or by a ratio expressing that absolute number as a percentage of the total population affected has to include a temporal and spatial restriction. A change of residence from an address in the inner part of the city to its outskirts is generally not included in statistics on internal migration, defined as movement from one municipality or comparable autonomous administrative entity to another. However, such a change of residence is sometimes over a much longer distance and may mean a much sharper disruption in social relations for the people involved than the intermunicipal move of a rural agricultural labourer to a neighbouring rural place. The inclusion of temporal and spatial restrictions in the definition of migration has its consequences for the trends that are or are not noticed, but does not imply denial of the environmental impact of those trends that are not noticed. The rate of intermunicipal migration, for example, can be increased by a process of suburbanisation of middle-class people that is stimulated by municipal authorities in order to acquire moderately cheap replacement housing for working class people who have to more intramunicipally because of slum clearance.

To put it more generally, international migration, seasonal movements within national boundaries, recurrent commuting between dwelling and working places, and similar shifts which do not immediately alter the internal distribution of population, nevertheless have a bearing upon the course of internal migration.[28] Changes in the internal distribution aimed at changing the relative share of some of these shifts within the totality of movements can have their consequences, positive or negative, for the environmental situation. These consequences should not be evaluated without looking at the consequences of the existing pattern of population distribution: the wish to change and the necessity to change this pattern through stimulation of internal migration or by other means depends upon its evaluation. In such an evaluation urbanistic or anti-urbanistic ideologies sometimes play their part. Social science is not as yet able to give a distinct answer to the question: is concentration of population better than deconcentration? On the contrary, two currents in the evaluation of population concentration can be distinguished in sociological theory. One current has a positive attitude towards urbanisation. This so-called *structuralistic* current bases its arguments mainly on economic considerations: a high density of population, together with a large population size, is a necessary precondition for a diversion of labour carried through as far as possible to the best advantage for every individual and thus for society as a whole. 'Economies of scale', 'agglomeration effect', 'external economies' and 'catalysts of social change' are key-words in these arguments which have played their part in theories on the urbanisation of developing countries. But the economic mechanisms for which these key-words stand and the economic ideas connected with them, also play their part in highly developed countries such as the Netherlands, where Government has not been very successful in attracting industry to so-called problem-areas, despite the pool of unemployed manpower available there and despite the various systems of premiums on investments created by the Government. Population concentration is considered advantageous, and so people and investments go to places where concentration already exists. The negative effects of such concentration – high land and building prices for industrial plants as well as for housing, long commuting times from home to work, congestion, pollution – were until recently taken for granted as unfortunate but inevitable side-effects of a development that in itself is good.

The other current, while not denying the positive effects of concentration mentioned by the structuralists, lays more stress on the negative social effects of population concentration. In this, the so-called *behavioristic* trend, we look in vain for economic arguments; the effects of concentration have been described by Louis Wirth: 'the social organisation of a city is to a large extent conditioned by the variables number, density, and degree of heterogeneity of its population, which means great importance of secondary rather than primary contacts, less integrated social organisation, pecuniary nexus, greater independence of specialists, less dependence on particular individuals, impersonal, transitory, superficial, segmental and utilitarian social contacts, and exaggerated importance of time.'[29]

No wonder that such a view of the social-structural characteristics of city life (which in many respects is quite correct) leads easily to a more normative 'vice-and-misery' ideology that sees urban places as monkey rocks, that lays stress on the aggression-stimulating effects of high density, and on the nervous tension bred by the frustration that is created. This view ultimately culminates in the argument that suggests a strong analogy between the future state of urbanised man and the results of Calhoun's experiments with rats which showed a high correlation between density of population and the mortality of adult males, miscarriages among females, perinatal mortality, sexual deviances in males combined with attempts at cannibalism, and various behavioral deviances varying from frenetic over-activity to pathological apathy.[30]

An interesting facet of all this is that at both ends of the distributional continuum we are led to the same conclusion: economically and socially, complete dispersion of the population is undesirable. No wonder, then, that most redistribution policies aim at a solution somewhere in between the two extremes. A general characteristic of recent population redistribution policies in West European countries is that, while they aim at decentralisation of population as between regions, e.g. levelling-off of population densities, within the regions their aim is usually the concentration of population.[31] The 'concentrated deconcentration' model presently advocated in the Netherlands is a good case in point.

Another common factor of these policies, namely, that they are more concerned with internal migration than with regional differences in the rate of natural increase, in a way that tries to influence trends of internal migration rather than actually to redistribute the present population, makes internal migration the most acceptable policy instrument. In itself this is quite realistic: after a long period of rural-urban migration, highly age-selective in that generally the younger people move away while reverse movements, if any, are usually of older people returning to their rural places of origin, the structural effect of the whole urbanisation process on the rural population is such that it would be highly unrealistic to expect a levelling-off of population densities by some natural process of birth-and-death differentials alone.[32] But the feasibility of such policies depends completely on the degree of realism with which targets for internal migration are determined.

In the Netherlands, for example, the aim laid down in the *Second Report on Physical Planning* was to obtain, under reinforced dispersal goal-conditions, a population of 3 million in the three northern provinces by the year 2000.[33] However, during the last few years, natural increase and internal migration have not been in correspondence with these distributional goals. It has been calculated that if this 'natural' development does not change, the objective can only be reached if an additional positive net migration into the northern provinces, representing an additional negative net migration from the rest of the country, of 59,000 people per five years, is created by redistribution policies.[34] For several reasons, this figure is an underestimation of the redistributing task that Dutch politicians have taken upon themselves.

The task is even less feasible than mere numbers can suggest, implying as it does the creation of work opportunities in the northern region – already characterised by relatively high unemployment rates – for at least 20,000 people in a period of five years, to say nothing of the social and cultural amenities necessary to attract people from the densely populated areas. Obviously, the effectiveness of policies intended to influence population redistribution is greatly dependent on various other measures, for example in the fields of employment, vocational training and regional industrial development, and on the way in which these are coordinated and adjusted to general economic and social needs.[35] In capitalist societies Governments can only act as stimulating agencies in these matters, and so we are confronted with the deplorable situation that several successive systems of investment premiums in the Netherlands have not caused the expected distributional effects. Now that the Dutch Government has proposed the introduction of an investment tax in the Western part of the country, captains of industry have suddenly declared that 'history has shown that business does not like taxation but prefers to respond to premiums as stimuli', which rather casts doubt on the integrity of major industry in this matter.

It would seem, therefore, that communist societies with their directed economies are much more capable of implementing redistribution policies. It has been stated that 'in modern conditions paramount importance is assigned to those functions of migration which are connected with increasing economic efficiency of public production'[36] – which is considered to prevail over the more individual functions of creating channels for job mobility and social mobility, and even over the societal function of improving the system of settlements. In the Soviet Union, migration is regulated from above, directly and indirectly. Direct measures include various forms of publicly organised migration; indirect measures include the creation of advantageous living, economic and social conditions in developing areas which suffer from labour shortage, i.e. higher wages, low-priced consumer goods, better housing and cultural-consumer facilities, additional holidays, preferential treatment at entrance examinations to higher educational institutions, etc.

These measures have proved necessary because even socialist societies have not been able to escape the general 'law' that publicly organised forms of migration are efficient only if living conditions in the arrival areas secure a high degree of adaptation by the migrants. However, the creation of these facilities apparently lags behind economic developments. During the 1960s, the Soviet Government has been confronted by a tremendous stream of uncontrolled migration from those regions in Siberia and the northern parts of the European territory which are characterised by manpower shortages, to those regions in the southern part of the European territory and to the Central Asian Republics which are characterised by a surplus of labour, both in the urban and rural sectors.[37]

Perevedentsev suggests in this connection that it might be advisable 'to establish and maintain certain relationships between the living standards of the urban populations of different regions, between urban and rural populations within regions, between various occupational and skill groups of workers within the urban and rural populations, and between new settlers and old residents.'[38] He bases his argument on the opinion that the basic principles for interregional and intraregional regulation of the standard of living must be 'the establishment of a higher living standard for personnel of the same occupation and skill levels where there is a shortage of labour resources as compared to places with a surplus of labour; fewer differences in the living standards of urban and rural populations in regions having a surplus rural population; the creation of conditions for new settlers so that they can achieve the necessary level of wellbeing within a relatively short period of time.'[39] Such a solution may seem auspicious, but the fact that skilled workers and experts with high school or university degrees are leaving the developing areas in large numbers[40] should warn Perevedentsev that decisions whether or not to migrate are not made 'by bread alone'.

In the developing countries, where urban places are growing rapidly due to their high rates of natural increase, and urbanisation is growing somewhat less rapidly because migration, though sometimes considerable in absolute numbers, cannot keep up with urban natural increase, such an economic base of internal migration seems to be much weaker.

Economic reality, particularly the employment aspect, is apparently less important than is optimistic expectation. A general characteristic of the migration system is that each act involves an *origin*, a *destination*, and an *intervening set* of obstacles.[41] While knowledge about the origin side in rural-urban migration may be based on hard economic reality, knowledge about the destination side is sometimes completely inadequate. Through the process of 'social mobilisation,'[42] i.e. a breaking-down of local frames of reference, people become slightly more educated, they have more contact with mass communication media and with government agencies; consequently, the local agrarian pattern of aspirations and needs has to compete disadvantageously with the pattern that prevails in industrialised countries. Of course, the situation in urban slums and shantytowns does not come up to the expectations of the migrants, but they have no alternative because local governments are not even capable of providing dwelling space for their own populations with their high rate of natural increase. Thus arises the phenomenon of the 'autonomous urban settlement': urban settlement that, whatever its duration or expectations, takes place independently of the authorities charged with the external or institutional control of local building and planning.[43]

Apart from assimilation problems in a sociological sense, especially under environmental conditions such as prevail in slums and shantytowns, there is the much bigger problem of adaptation, a notion that encompasses the sociological meaning of assimilation, including social participation, acculturation, and social and psychological adjustment, but also covers the process of physiological and biological adjustment.[44] How does the individual build up immunity to new diseases found in the cities? How does the body mechanism react to air and water pollutants, sound levels and time schedules that may differ from the area of origin? Myers gives us an example of possible causes of maladaptation in working out the case of mental illness. A number of studies have noted that reported rates of mental illness are higher for migrant populations than for native urbanites in a large number of cities and within different countries. Do these differences reflect a selection of migrants with previous indication of mental illness or a predisposition to such illness? Are the migrants ill when they move and do they come for treatment, either as a result of their mental state, or to seek a more congenial environment for their problems? Do migrants live in areas of the city in which they are differentially exposed to conditions of life that might induce mental breakdown? Are the differential rates of reported mental disorders merely a reflection of other factors, such as social class position, ethnic group membership, age and sex placement: all groups in which migrants are often heavily represented? Or do the stresses and strains of urban living, the cultural conflicts encountered, and the difficulties in adjusting to these new conditions, induce mental breakdowns? Much research still has to be done on the health effects of migration. Migration implies a change of environment, and therefore necessary adaptation to a new environment. As long as that new environment is not sufficiently equipped physically and socially to make the chances for a good adaptation acceptable, it might be advisable to exercise great care in using migration as an instrument for population redistribution, especially in newly developed countries. Exchanging one environmental problem for another means at least in the short run no solution at all.

NOTES

1. Published as 'The Chaotic Society: Product of the Social Morphological Revolution', in *American Sociological Review*, 34, 1, February 1969, pp. 1-19.
2. *Ibidem*, p. 3.
3. *Ibidem*, p. 4.

4. *Results of the Symposium on the Impact of Urbanisation on Man's Environment, 13-20 June 1970,* published by the Institute of Physical Planning and Demography of the University of Amsterdam in cooperation with NIROV, 1972, p. 6.
5. Hauser, 'Chaotic Society', p. 4.
6. Cf. also Kingsley Davis, 'The Origin and Growth of Urbanisation in the World', in Charles B. Nam (ed.), *Population and Society*, Boston, 1968, pp. 411-412; and Gerald Breese, *Urbanisation in Newly Developing Countries*, Englewood Cliffs N.J., 1966, p. 137.
7. Kingsley Davis, 'Origin and Growth', pp. 414-415.
8. Kingsley Davis, 'The Urbanisation of the Human Population', in *Scientific American*, 213, September 1965, pp. 40-53.
9. *Ibidem*, p. 44.
10. *Ibidem*, p. 47.
11. For the underdeveloped countries, for example, this might be a very questionable assumption, especially in the intermediate zones between rural and urban where such a definitional question is most important. On the other hand, it seems to me that this functional criterion is not unidimensional from a sociological point of view, especially in the highly developed countries: earning one's living purely in agriculture these days means a highly rationalised conduct of business, necessitating a rather high degree of 'mental urbanisation', so that even in such a functional definition it is only the residential aspect that clearly discriminates between farm and urban population.
12. A. L. Epstein, 'Urbanisation and Social Change in Africa', in Gerald Breese (ed.), *The City in Newly Developing Countries,* p. 248.
13. T. G. McGee, 'The Urbanisation Process: Western Theory and Third World Reality'; introductory chapter to his book *The Urbanisation Process in the Third World*, London, 1971.
14. McGee explicitly refers in this discussion to the publications of A. O. Hirschman, *The Strategy of Economic Development*, New Haven, Conn., 1958, and of John Friedmann, 'The Strategy of Deliberate Urbanisation' in: *Journal of the Institute of American Planners,* XXIV, 6, November, 1968, pp. 364-373.
15. McGee, 'The Urbanisation Process', p. 13.
16. Bert F. Hoselitz, *Sociological Aspects of Economic Growth*, New York/London, 1965; 4th impr., p. 161.
17. *Ibidem*, p. 162. Discussions on this subject during the Leiden course placed much emphasis on the difference between *generative* and *parasitic* cities, within the framework of the more general problem of the carrying capacity of a city. Bert F. Hoselitz, in *Sociological Aspects of Economic Growth*, New York/London, 1960, pp. 187-188, suggests that a city should be designated as generative 'if its impact on economic growth is favourable, i.e. if its formation and continued existence and growth is one of the factors accountable for the economic development of the region or country in which it is located.' Hoselitz considers a city to be parasitic if it exerts an opposite impact.

    It is difficult to say anything concrete on the issue of carrying capacities at the highest possible level of abstraction because relational systems between urban centre and hinterland show too much variety. Moreover, there is no general agreement on which criteria can be regarded as necessary and sufficient for adequate quantification of the carrying capacity of an urban system. As the density dimension inherent to the urban phenomenon significantly distinguishes the city from a rural system, at least a psychological or psycho-sociological dimension should be included in measuring the carrying capacity of urban systems, in addition to criteria of a more physical nature. The carrying capacity of a rural system may be largely determined in itself (for example, the number of population who can obtain their subsistence from that rural area at the given natural soil conditions and at the given agrarian technology). In determining the carrying capacity of an urban system, however, that system cannot be regarded as standing on its own: its hinterland has to be taken into account. Cities have the ability of (or can only exist by) overreaching the carrying capacity of their own territory because they have the power to extend and exploit their rural hinterlands. It is in this regard that the difference between generative and parasitic cities seems to be most relevant to our theme. In line with Johan Galtung's 'Structural Theory of Imperialism' (*Journal of Peace Research*, Vol. 8, 1971, pp. 81-117), the beachhead city in a developing country can be regarded as aiming at a parasitic function within that framework of underdevelopment only in order to enable American and European urban systems to execute their (real or presumed) generative functions to the benefit of US and European economy. In other words, urban systems in Europe and the United States have proved capable of extending their hinterlands to such a degree that nowadays they even include most of the so-called Third World.

18. Epstein, 'Urbanisation and Social Change', p. 254. Samir Amin, in his paper 'Under-populated Africa' to the Population Conference of Accra, 1971, p. 12, regards this phenomenon of circulation as an expectable consequence of what he calls the 'marginalisation of the masses', as it is caused by lack of employment opportunities in the peripheral regions as well as in the cities of those countries.
19. *The Impact of Urbanisation*, p. 9.
20. Kingsley Davis, 'Urbanisation of the Human Population'.
21. *Ibidem*, p. 50.
22. *Ibidem*, p. 44.
23. *Ibidem*.
24. The provisional results of the 1970 Census were published for each Union Republic in its official newspaper. The figures for the All-Union level are quoted from *Sovietskaia Latvia*, April 17, 1971, pp. 1-2.
25. V. Perevedentsev, 'Migratsiia naseleniia i ispol'zovanie trudovykh resursov', (Population Migration and Use of Labour Resources) in *Voprosy ekonomiki*, 1970, No. 9.
26. B. S. Khorev, *Gorodskie poseleniia SSSR* (problemy rosta i ikh izoutchenie) (Urban Population of the USSR); Moscow, 1968.
27. All figures are computed from the *Municipal Demographic Documentation* published regularly by the Netherlands Central Bureau of Statistics, which gives the vital numbers and rates for each municipality for every year.

28. Hilde Wander, 'Policies and Implementation Methods in the Internal Redistribution of Population', *Papers IUSSP International Population Conference*, London, 1969, Vol. IV, p. 3024.
29. Louis Wirth, 'Urbanism as a way of life', in P. K. Hatt and A. J. Reiss Jr. (eds.), *Cities and Societies*, 1959.
30. John B. Calhoun, 'Population Density and Social Pathology', in *Scientific American*, 1962; cf. also Halliman H. Winsborough, 'The Social Consequences of High Population Density', in Thomas R. Ford and Gordon F. DeJong (eds.), *Social Demography*, Englewood Cliffs N.J., 1970, pp. 84-90.
31. H. ter Heide, 'Population Redistribution Policies in Western European Countries', *Papers IUSSP International Population Conference*, Vol. IV, p. 2996.
32. Cf. for an analysis of these structural effects of urbanisation on rural population in Canada, Leroy O. Stone, 'Urbanisation and Rural Population Age Structure: Some Generalisations', *Papers IUSSP International Population Conference*, Vol. IV, pp. 2923-2934.
33. *Second Report on Physical Planning in the Netherlands*, The Hague, 1966, p. 42 of original Dutch version.
34. Paul Drewe, 'Steps Toward Action-oriented Migration Research', paper presented to the meeting of the Regional Science Association, Dutch-speaking Section, March 24, 1970, Rotterdam, p. 6.
35. Wander, 'Policies and Implementation Methods', p. 3025.
36. T. I. Zaslavska, 'Objectives and Methods in Planning Rural-Urban Migration', paper submitted to the 7th World Congress of Sociology, Varna, 1970, quoted from the original published by the USSR Academy of Sciences, Siberian Department, Novosibirsk, 1970, p. 5.
37. Perevedentsev, 'Migratsiia naseleniia". Cf. also N.P. Kalinovskii, *Raionnye razlichiia real'noi zarabotnoi platy rabochikh i sluzhashchikh* (Regional Differences in Real Wages and Salaries), Moscow, 1966 and V.I. Perevedentsev, *Migratsiia naseleniia i trudovye problemy Sibiri* (Population Migration and Labour Problems in Siberia), Novosibirsk, 1966.
38. Perevedentsev, 'Migratsiia naseleniia i ispol'zovanie trudovykh resursov'.
39. *Ibidem.*
40. *Migration Against the Plan?'* Radio Free Europe Research Bulletin 0716, September 1, 1970.
41. Everett S. Lee, 'A Theory of Migration' in *Demography*, III, 1, 1966, pp. 47-57; also in J. A. Jackson (ed.), *Migration*, Cambridge University Press, 1969, pp. 282-297; Calvin Goldschneider, 'An Outline of the Migration System', *Papers IUSSP International Population Conference*, Vol. IV, pp. 2746-2754.
42. Karl W. Deutsch, 'Social Mobilisation and Political Development', in *The American Political Science Review*, LV. 3, 1961, pp. 493-514.
43. John F. C. Turner, 'Uncontrolled Urban Settlement: Problems and Policies', in Gerald Breese (ed.), *The City in Newley Developing Countries*, p. 508.
44. George C. Myers, 'Health Effects of Urbanisation and Migration', *Papers IUSSP International Population Conference*, Vol. IV, p. 2950 (a summary). Quotations here are from the original.

8. Urbanisation and the spatial concentration of decision making

J. G. M. HILHORST
AND
J. G. LAMBOOY

This paper examines the cumulative nature of the concentration of people and decision-making in time and space. The extreme complexity of modern industrial society is traced back to the relatively simple situation of a homogeneous and closed plain with emerging specialisations. Although some of the processes discussed correspond to those treated by van Benthem van den Bergh, this paper has a clear identity of its own through the due allowance made for distance and spatial diversity. The contributions by Burger, Du Boff, Kuijsten, van Raay and Weissmann are also of relevance to the line of argument developed. Reference may also be made to Lugo's chapter on energy availability as a potential limiting factor to the development and ultimate maintenance of highly complex agglomerations.

1. INTRODUCTION

This paper is concerned with a number of processes that contribute to the formation of cities and large agglomerations. These processes are economic, political and sociological in nature; they are bounded by the level of technological development of the society in which they occur and influenced by that of other societies. As such they form a complex whole that can perhaps only be approached but never fully grasped in terms of a model, even if this would remain at a fairly high level of abstraction. One of the basic assumptions of the paper is that man is socio-political in nature and that he shows this by striving to maintain or improve his relative social position.

In our opinion, the study of urbanisation is of great relevance to that of the relation of man to his environment. Cities are the cumulative expression of man's use of the earth and of his cultural development. Modern society is an urban society, and modernisation is frequently another word for urbanisation. Cities have become centres and the main production centres, at least if measured in monetary variables.

Increasing attention has to be given to whether or not the process of continuing urbanisation can be pursued, if we take environmental problems into regard. Have the cities outgrown our capabilities for managing? Are the social costs too high? To what extent can deconcentration and decentralisation be planned, for instance, leading to spread effects towards the peripheral parts of the country or of the world? To what extent can we govern these processes?

Clarification of these problems needs a thorough analysis of the basic forces of the urbanisation process as well as of those parts of the decision process which are related to it.

Tables, 1, 2 and 3 show the cumulative process of concentration into urban units.

Table 1. Percentage of world population in cities of more than 20,000 and more than 100,000 inhabitants

Year	*> 20,000*	*> 100,000*
1800	2.4	1.7
1850	4.3	2.3
1900	9.2	5.5
1950	20.9	13.1
1970		23.2

Source: UN Statistics.

Table 2. Growth in percentage of cities (>100,000) from 1800-1970

Period	*World*	*Asia*	*Europe and USA*
1800-1850	76	24	184
1850-1900	222	59	337
1900-1950	254	444	160
1950-1970	106	156	58

Source: UN Statistics.

Table 3. Growth of the five main agglomerations in OECD countries 1950-1970 (× 1000)

	Population	
Agglomeration	*1950*	*1970*
New York	12,300	16,100
Tokyo	6,300	12,200
London	10,400	11,500
Los Angeles	4,000	9,500
Paris	6,000	8,700

Source: OECD statistics.

2. SPECIALISATION AND URBANISATION

2.1. *Activity spaces*

As in most development processes, urbanisation should be studied in a framework that allows explicit recognition of the importance of time and distance as factors influencing this process.

The factor time will be introduced here by taking into account the cumulative character of the urbanisation process, while distance will come mainly in terms of economic distance, that is, the 'opportunity cost' of bridging geographic distance.

Let us consider a possible urbanisation process over a long period. In a relatively homogeneous plain a number of people live who mainly devote their available time to farming. For reasons of security and of access to their fields, the farmers will live in small settlements rather than on their own. The people living in each settlement will form small communities whose members will occupy various relative social positions, partly determined by the main kind of economic activity in which they are engaged. Some people in the various settlements will gradually introduce improvements in their production methods and may produce a surplus over what they need for their own subsistence. Some or all of this surplus will be exchanged among people living in the same village, who will attempt to acquire especially those commodities that enhance their relative social position.

If the opportunities for exchange are rewarding, the people producing surpluses may specialise even further, and by their example may induce others to adopt the innovations of specialisation and exchange. Obviously, a person who specialises in a certain activity cannot go beyond a certain limit which is determined by the number of hours in a day and the time he considers necessary or is expected to use for leisure and rest. The incentive to further specialisation will be all the greater if it is likely to be rewarding in terms of social position.

This poses a series of problems. The first is inherent in the process of specialisation itself, namely, that in the village where he lives the demand for the results of a man's activities may not be sufficient. A second problem is that if a person fully specialises in a given activity, he exposes himself to the risk of dependence upon the decisions of others to exchange their products for his.

The first problem may be solved by the specialist if he succeeds in finding a market for his product in other villages. This will be the easier if he can count on relations (perhaps relatives) there, but he will probably have to compete with others, either from his own village or from elsewhere. This process of competition in space is one in which those who have to travel far in order to market their product are at a disadvantage, especially since travelling implies that less time can be devoted to producing the commodity that is to be traded. This disadvantage can be solved in two ways. The first is that further specialisation is pursued for a number of activities, for instance, by introducing the specialisation of trader-transporter. The second solution is that of moving the activity to a place that is more central with respect to the market, that is, the various villages in our plain. For some activities this may be the only solution. Both solutions can be combined.

This process does not imply that all specialists will leave the non-central villages.[1] Those specialists will remain who can fill their time by satisfying the demand exerted by the villagers as long as this provides them with the means with which to maintain or improve their relative social position. These activities thus need smaller 'activity spaces' than those of the central locations.

It is important now to draw some conclusions from what we have seen so far, namely, *that activities apparently have their own spaces.* Thus, we have seen that some activities – in the sense of specialisations at a given level of functional differentiation – can provide a person with a living on the basis of the market that exists in a small village. (A modern example of such an activity would be a grocer who could earn a decent living in a village of about 1,000 inhabitants.)

We have also seen that other activities have a larger space and need the populations of various villages for optimal economic functioning, given certain levels of income and production, transport and communications technology.

Finally, we can see that activities whose products cannot, or cannot easily, be transferred, that is, activities which we now classify as part of the tertiary sector, tend to find a location that is central with respect to the space in which they act.

2.2. *The concentration of decision-making*

The second problem inherent in full specialisation is related to an increase in the dependency upon buyers. One partial solution to this problem is found in the introduction of a generally accepted means of exchange: money. Another partial solution exists in specialising in those activities for which demand is high. A third alternative is in forming trusts – either in a form such as the guilds, or in the forms adopted by the present-day international concerns. Whereas the first solution aims at getting in return for one's products a commodity that can easily be used in exchange with many others, the other two solutions aim at obtaining a firmer grip on the market. Both latter alternatives carry the seeds for dynamic development; the first posits the seeking of new specialisations not only in terms of product differentiation but also in terms of fulfilling as yet unsatisfied wants, while the second permits – although not necessarily – the concentration of research in new production methods and the development of power in political decision-making.

We shall now concern ourselves mainly with the central village in order to see how it develops both internally and in relation to other villages. The specialists in the centre whose activity spaces include the non-central villages have a series of common interests, even if they are direct competitors. They will therefore tend to cooperate with or at least support any efforts to establish law and order in the plain – at least inasfar as these efforts cover their activity spaces. Although other groups[2] will be also interested in formalising and enforcing rules of behaviour, the various kinds of specialists may themselves initiate this process by supporting certain groups in exchange for protection, etc.

Another force that works towards creating an important function in the central village is that producers in non-central villages who cannot change their location without abandoning their activity, will prefer to exchange their produce in the central village where buyers from there and elsewhere concentrate. Thus, the central village will acquire a market that should be seen not only in terms of exchange of goods but also in terms of exchange of information.

The latter function of the market is often entirely disregarded in central place theory, which normally works on the hypothesis that information on markets, technical knowhow, etc. is evenly distributed. However, this function is not only important from the point of view of how a common value system may come about in the activity space of the central village, but also for understanding why it is that information is *not* evenly distributed. Whereas the people from non-central villages will bring information from their environment and will only have time to speak with a few persons from other villages, the craftsmen and others in the market in the central village will obtain information from all other villages.

The fact that the central village is the centre of a communication field is of great importance for its further development, as we shall see later in more detail. However, inasfar as the effectiveness of decision-making is determined by the information available concerning a given situation, the decision-makers in the central village are clearly in the advantage, and it becomes possible for them to exert a form of extractive domination.[3] So far, we have not explicitly introduced the specialisations of trader-transporter, transporter and trader, and we have mainly spoken of activities that produce *material* commodities. The various specialists, such as farmers, artisans, cattle-raisers etc., have been assumed to transport and market their own products.

However, if demand for farm produce becomes high, there will be an advantage in concentrating on working the farm and in using the services of someone who collects it for transport to, and sale in, the market. This kind of specialist normally uses more advanced transport technology than is (economically) available to the farmer, and can be observed at work in many of today's poor countries. In some cases, he experiences competition from people who specialise in bringing producers and their produce to and from a market, but generally there is a certain separation in markets for these services: the transporter-trader or middle man is concerned with bulk such as the season's crop of maize or cacao, whereas the transporter is concerned with shuttling people who engage in petty trading of eggs, chickens, vegetables and so on.

The middle man will normally prefer the central village as his location, since there he will be at the centre of the communications field that is of importance to him. There is also the market in which he sells and which, in a homogeneous plain, is almost equidistant from the non-central villages, that is, most centrally situated with respect to total demand. The same will apply to people who specialise in rendering transport facilities.

This concentration of productive and service activities in the central village makes it an attractive location for new and related activities such as money lending, warehousing, repairing of transport, and catering, if the commercial activities there reach a level that is sufficient to warrant such an emergence of further differentiation.

The cumulative process described above will occur in a number of central villages in our plain, at least, if it is large enough to sustain their populations. Assuming this to be the case, we may expect that a number of people in the various central villages will attempt new specialisations. In doing so, some will discover that the size of the market in their central village and in the non-central villages related to them is insufficient. At what might be called a higher system's level, there will now develop a process of competition that, along the same line of argument presented above, will lead to a concentration of certain types of specialisation in the central village that is most central to the other central villages. This centre of centres we shall call a town.

Again, if the plain is large enough and given certain levels of technology and income, there will be an opportunity for more than one town to emerge. The various specialists in these towns will eventually start competing with each other and one of the towns will conquer a position of pre-eminence and emerge as the city.

Obviously, the larger the system becomes, the stronger the needs for establishing an administrative and legal order. Parallel with the development previously described, there will be a need for increasing specialisation in administrative and legal functions. Thus, certain professions in these fields will develop.

We shall see a rather equilibrated situation in which economic activities are distributed over the various levels of central places in accordance with the levels of income prevailing in the system, the number of inhabitants and workers, and the cost of transport incurred by those who make use of the various functions of these central places. Administrative activities will tend to follow a similar pattern, in which the cost of communication or transmission of information from top to bottom and the cost of generating information from the bottom upwards will be important criteria; these criteria will acquire different scopes depending upon the competences assigned to the various levels of administration. If these are fairly limited at the lower levels in the hierarchy, the central villages and towns will not represent important concentrations of decision-making power. Although they are centres of communication fields, most important information will only be available in the central city of the system, and people can exert influence only by participating in information exchanges. In cases of a high degree of centralisation in formal (and therefore of informal) decision-making, communication between centres of equal order will be rather unimportant, that is to say, there will be little interaction between such centres. There will instead be a strong tendency for concentration of private (as opposed to but interrelated with public) decision-making in the central city. This will reinforce the cumulative effects discussed before.

2.3. *Additional complications*

So far we have concentrated on giving a heuristic model of historical development that probably will not be encountered in any period for any specific area. Partly, of course, this is due to the fact that we have assumed a perfectly closed system. Obviously this is not the case. External relations can be of extreme importance. These can be economic or cultural relations. The result is that regions are open, not closed systems, although the degree of openness varies between regions.

Related to openness are colonisation processes. However, all these influences have in common that they reinforce the tendencies of centralisation and concentration inherent in the process of specialisation. In certain cases, such as colonisation, the city that until the arrival of the colonisers used to be the summit of the hierarchy may lose this position to one that is better situated to link the system to another one, perhaps on the seaboard from where the system's resources are exported. Thus, Freetown took the place of what the city of Bo was in an area that is now part of Sierra Leone, and Lagos acquired a position that used to be taken by cities such as Kano and Ibadan.

Similarly, but for other reasons and at another level, Lourdes would still be a miserable village had Bernadette not had her revelations there and had a healing well not started to flow there, while nobody might know of Mecca had Mohammed not been there.

Of the various external influences, the two most important are perhaps trade and war. Both are forms of communication between central place hierarchies that permit the transmission of new products and new technology, while they may also lead to a rearrangement of relative social positions. We shall limit ourselves to trade.

Inter-system trade is accompanied not only by the introduction of new commodities but almost always also by the presence of 'strangers', that is to say, traders from other systems. In fact, the trader-transporter may be the first 'stranger' to arrive and his arrival on the scene in our plain may essentially influence the process previously described. It may especially affect it in that the trader-transporter will enhance certain activities whose products are in high demand outside the plain while he may at the same time effectively compete with other activities because of the products he brings for exchange.

A second aspect of inter-system trade is that it follows certain routes chosen for efficiency reasons particularly for this activity. Thus, the effects in terms of transfer of technology, competition gains and losses, as well as in socio-political change, are bound to occur more easily and quickly along these routes than elsewhere.

A third aspect is that the inter-system trader will tend to choose as main stops on his way those places where the market is greatest, that is, the main cities of hierarchies of settlements. (In fact he may be forced to do so by the rulers of such towns, in exchange for safe conduct.) The importance to be attached to this is that it makes such a main city perhaps the most important link with the rest of the world, so that its inhabitants have access to more information than those in other places. The set of reasons why such cities are also attractive to invaders or why religious centres such as Medieval Rome and Moscow are poles of attraction to economic activities, are normally indicated in the economist's jargon by the term 'agglomeration economies'.

3. URBANISATION AND INDUSTRIALISATION

3.1. *Agglomeration economies*

Agglomeration economies may be defined as economies that occur in those places where large concentrations of activities have taken place. They may be divided into two classes: external economies and scale economies.

In this context we shall understand by 'external economies' the cost savings that originate from factors outside the activity itself, but bound to the environment of the activity's point location. Examples of such economies are the municipal fire brigade, the presence in town of specialised brokers, a reservoir of skilled manpower, lower freight rates, etc. 'Scale economies' represent the cost savings that occur because of the scale of operations of an activity. The simplest example of such economies is perhaps that the cost of the capital invested in a factory per unit of output will go down if the factory starts to work in two shifts instead of one. Agglomeration may induce such economies by the large market which they constitute.

It will be clear that agglomeration economies form extremely strong forces in the process of cumulative growth of urban centres.

Whether agglomeration economies acquire a certain significance for the central city of a given hierarchy largely depends upon the city's size in absolute terms and in terms relative to the size of the second and third order towns. As we are looking for factors contributing to urbanisation it becomes important to see what other factor(s) there may be at work that can bring a city or town to that size.[4] The number of non-agricultural population who historically cluster in cities and towns in a closed system obviously depends on the capacity of the system's farmers to produce sufficient food for the city people and for themselves. For any given open settlement system, however, this is not necessary, since the system may import foodstuffs that the farmers do not produce. Thus, the size of the non-agricultural population depends upon at least two factors: the capacity to produce food and the system's capacity to import foodstuffs. The latter capacity is in turn determined by the system's ability to export. Exported products may of course be agricultural, but they may also be of mineral or industrial nature, or even services such as transport or trade.

If the external demand for minerals is high this may give rise to some urban development, but this is generally not of great significance as long as processing activities do not become associated with the mining activity. Similarly, although some towns have developed because they were the home ports of sea-going vessels, their growth should be seen more as a result of other activities connected with sea transport (trade, banking, shipbuilding).

The growth of industry, together with or after that of trade, may therefore perhaps better be singled out as factors which provide the stimuli that result in agglomeration economies.

3.2. *Scale enlargement and industrial complexes*

The industrialisation process has been one of the most important transformative forces in our society. It has tremendously influenced our relations with nature and is one of the main causes of urbanisation. Until about 1800, the labour class worked in small establishments such as farms and craft workshops. The Industrial Revolution made it possible to create large production units with hundreds or even thousands of workers. This was regarded as a better use of production factors, especially of capital, in order to reach relatively low average costs. An essential feature of industrialisation has proved to be the urge to increase the size of the production units. Huge production complexes arose all over the industrialised countries. Iron and steelworks, textile industries, shipbuilding yards, metalworking industries, and so on, developed as signs of man's power to produce more and more on less land surface.

In agriculture land was a principal production factor. The landowning class was often also the ruling class, occupying the most important positions in the army and the court, or vice versa.

Urbanisation had already attacked the position of the landowners. The craftsmen, guildsmen, traders, administrators and the clergy formed a new class: the 'bourgeois' or the 'citizens', whose influence was based on information, political structures, and control of production factors.[5] The bourgeois formed the base of the new industrialised society. Urbanisation and industrialisation became correlated. The crafts in the existing cities provided the base for the technological knowledge needed in the industrialisation process. Many cities which are now seen as dominant urban centres were important even before the Industrial Revolution. In those centres new industries developed gradually and cumulatively out of the existing crafts and commercial groups.

However, a new type of cities, the size of which was largely determined by the needs of large-scale production, emerged. The German Ruhr-cities (Essen, Darmstadt, Düsseldorf, etc.), the English Manchester and Newcastle, and the American Pittsburgh are examples of this type of mine-and-basic-industry-oriented 'Black Areas'. They are typical of the urban centres which did not fit into the old system described in Section Two.

The increasing size of production units created an enormous demand for labour in the near proximity of the firms, with subsequent urbanisation. At the same time the productivity of agriculture increased, also made possible by industrialisation or mechanisation of that production process. A push effect on labour from agriculture and a pull effect of the new basic industries in the new cities explosively enhanced the urbanisation process. The 'Black Areas', in particular, increased their size tremendously.

However, industrial development did not only occur in areas with new and large industrial complexes. Many old cities such as Paris, London, Amsterdam and Birmingham, with diversified economic structures, kept pace with the Black Area cities. Many other old cities degraded. Only those cities where the new needs for scale enlargement could be satisfied, or those of important financial or political significance, acquired or maintained good positions in the new urban hierarchy.

At the present time we see that cities that had attained pre-eminence before the Industrial Revolution now maintain a dominant position, whereas the former mono-industrial boom-cities in the Black Areas have often become 'problem cities'. The really important cities are still those that were socio-political, financial and trading centres before the Industrial Revolution.

As we have said, industrialisation brought with it a need for big production units, at least if measured in numbers of workers and production volume. If these units are measured with another 'measuring rod', namely, *land surface*, we can conclude that the scale is decreasing as compared to agriculture. Formerly, the production of food for the cities occurred mainly in the surrounding area. Increased urbanisation, caused by the need for workers for the growing manufacturing industries, made it necessary to create food producing areas in other parts of the country or the world. The urban populations and the production of industrial goods in the western countries did not give rise to increasing demands for land for agriculture in their own rural areas; this need came to be satisfied in the first instance in 'colonies' for food production, such as Canada, Australia, Siberia, Argentine. It is necessary to stress this fact because ecologists often believe that an ecological unity exists between the cities and the direct surrounding areas. This is not true with regard to food production. That relation is world-wide.

As we have indicated, there was later a sharp increase in the productivity of land (and labour) that can partly be explained in terms of industrial inputs such as chemical fertilizers and pesticides and partly in terms of change of main crops, in which industrial crops feature as an important element. The prairies of the US were taken from the Indians in order to secure the demand for food in Great Britain and in what later became the Northeastern Seaboard urban Megalopolis (Boston-New York-Baltimore), and later for the main centres such as Chicago and the Pacific urban agglomerations.

Industrial development and the rise of income cumulatively caused the need for food and resource areas external to the metropolitan regions. The Netherlands, for example, has to import more than 50 percent of its food, expressed in caloric value, and nearly 100 percent of its mineral resources (excluding natural gas). The USA is becoming increasingly dependent on external resource areas for oil and metals. Obviously, this has political consequences.

The industrialised part of the world can be compared to the former city, the hinterland being the food and raw materials producing rest-of-the-world or the 'periphery'. Hence, the 'world-centre' has succeeded in its striving for dominance because industrialisation has made it possible to enlarge the scale of its food and raw materials providing area, whereas its productivity per unit of land surface has increased tremendously.

3.3. *The rise of the service sector*

We have already emphasised the significance of the old diversified socio-political, administrative and financial centres. Before the Industrial Revolution these functions did not take a high percentage of the labour force, estimations of the male working population engaged in this sector remaining below 10 percent. The development of the economy, in the sense of rising incomes and productivity, made it possible to satisfy demand in 'luxury' and expensive goods such as education, medical care, repair, and in those retail shops which specialised in luxury goods. At the same time and strongly related to this development, the activities in the tertiary sector mentioned previously such as banking and administration, increased in order to satisfy the needs of the growing manufacturing industry. Moreover, new types of tertiary activities such as research, insurance, new education types and certain transport services, stimulated the development of industry. The tertiary sector is intimately involved with general economic development, and is a condition for and a result of this development.

Obviously, the growth of the tertiary sector should be reflected in the structure of the labour force. In the developed countries more than 50 percent of the labour force is engaged in this sector, reaching even 70 percent or more in the main metropolitan areas.

This development is not only reflected in the structure of the labour force but also in the spatial structure. Again, there is a strong tendency among activities with the highest floor-productivity (i.e. the highest value-added per unit of land surface) to become 'centralised', that is to say, to seek each other's proximity. More and more, manufacturing industry migrates to the periphery of the city regions or even to rural areas, thus becoming a main competitor to agricultural land use. Manufacturing industry has reached a low worker-output ratio but an increasing land-surface-output ratio. Thus, in competing for land in the built-up areas industry is in a relatively weak position, and it is diminishing in importance as an urban activity. Urban activities have to be 'economic' in their use of an important and scarce factor in urban areas: land surface. Since various parts of the tertiary sector have better possibilities to satisfy this need to economise, it is understandable that the rising demand for tertiary commodities (services) has caused a spatial competition between the secondary and tertiary sectors which is most clearly expressed in the explosive growth of the offices sector in the bigger agglomerations.

The former industrialisation process had socio-political consequences: the process of the increasing tertiary sector has similar results. The rise in productivity of manufacturing industry had its effects on the spatial 'location shift' of agricultural production, particularly that of food. What is the result of the increasing emphasis on the production of tertiary goods on the location of industry? Will industry be 'displaced' towards countries or regions where land and labour are plentiful? And are the developed countries going to specialise in the production of services, whereas the developing countries have to specialise in that of agricultural and manufactured goods? What will be the socio-political consequences of this process?

To answer these questions we have to return to the analysis of activity-spaces. The production of food and raw materials is surface and resource-oriented. In principle, these products are not so distance-sensitive and can be commercialised over the whole world if shipped and transported by methods which result in scale economies, such as mammoth tankers. Other products, and particularly services, are highly distance-sensitive. Services in general have to be 'consumed' at their place of production. Now, if indeed there is a growing demand for services, a spatial concentration of these activities in the bigger urban systems or metropolitan areas will be the consequence.[6] But within the urban systems we see a deconcentration at a micro-geographic level: population (the richer part of it) is suburbanising, as well as industry, and also that part of the tertiary sector such as retailing, which has a strong localisation linkage with the population in residential areas. The scale of deconcentration of the space-consuming manufacturing industry, however, is not comparable to that of food production. The latter has been deconcentrated towards other regions, the spread of living and of manufacturing industries is *within* the metropolitan areas or *between* metropolitan areas: in development axes, where scale economies can be reached in production and transportation. Between the main centres again, an enlargement of scale in transport occurs in the main 'feeder roads'. Manufacturing industry localises in those places where land, labour and connections exist with main feeder roads and hence with raw materials and the urban decision-making centres.

3.4. *Remote control and urbanisation*

In the preceding sections we have examined the process of economic and spatial specialisation, the rise of agglomeration economies, and enlargement of scales. We have stressed that even in the early stages of the process the size of the developing system created the necessity to organise it by a more efficient administration and a legal order. In these stages of the development process a relatively simple hierarchical ordering of settlements would suffice for a spatial order in which information and control could be secured. The spatial position of the main city was strengthened by the construction of a communications structure in the form of a cobweb. Economic, political and military dominance went hand in hand. The road structure of France and the position of Paris is quite instructive in this respect.

Industrialisation, with its enlargement of scale and the creation of big new agglomerations based on the 'black area' industries, caused the disruption of many former spatial equilibria. Central-place hierarchies were changed, new selection processes occurred, structures were blurred, but one position was not essentially attacked: that of the main politico-economic centres such as Paris, London and New York. On the contrary, these centres often strengthened their position: decision-making was once more centralised. A new spatial hierarchy was under construction with primary cities of world significance, based on the control of capital, information and military power. The peripheral world regions were brought under control of these centres. Within the metropolitan areas a similar process occurred. The position of the central city remained important because of the increased technical possibilities for communicating with remote places by telephone and telex.

This process of controlling increasingly larger and more complexly related communication fields had been enhanced by technological possibilities for storing information with computers and data banks. These have enabled increasingly more complex formal decision-making structures of which not only multinational firms but also defence organisations such as the Warsaw Pact and NATO are clear examples. These formal structures, however, do not entirely satisfy the needs of decision-making summits of these and similar kinds of organisation. As before, they require the possibility to short-circuit communication processes and therefore there is a persistent tendency among principal decision-makers to strive for spatial proximity in order to be as quickly informed as possible, particularly by face-to-face contacts.

The process of increasing domination by a small number of world centres is thus based on increased centralisation in the decision-making process. At the same time, as we have described above, the executing units, particularly the manufacturing of goods, have been diffused outwards. The production process has been 'split' into two parts: the decision-making and the executing parts. The first (the offices) are centralised and often spatially concentrated, whereas the second are dispersed.

Huge office buildings are physical expressions of the need for spatial proximity of and to the decision-makers and also of the domination of cumulatively wider areas. The activity spaces of the main industrial, banking and political establishments of the world meet each other, or partly cover the same areas. The world is partitioned into large sectors or 'influence-spheres'. As we have already emphasised, the need to establish an administrative and legal order becomes stronger as the system becomes larger. In former ages colonies and 'dominions' were possible; new, 'remote' control has replaced them.

As in preceding stages of the process, professions will develop. Increasing specialisation in the new remote control functions occurs: 'quaternary functions', which form the top of the decision-making pyramid. These are professions linked to decision-making, management, research and information storing. A new system of administration and legal order on a world scale has not yet developed. No formalised integration of the new activity spaces has come into being. Political control of these processes has to be a main goal, in order that a better world may be possible.

4. CONCLUSIONS

Urbanisation is an extremely complex phenomenon that has to be clarified before we can construct a successful strategy for environmental control. Modern society and urbanisation belong together. Obviously, this process has reached a stage in which negative external effects such as pollution can be overwhelming. Do we have the position, the possibilities and the political structure that can assure a new and better future for our cities? The answer depends on the sociopolitical and technical abilities of our urban society.

Whereas sources of pollution used to be concentrated in central areas, the demands for higher incomes in peripheral areas, the competition for land in the main cities and the improved facilities for transport and communication have helped to spread pollution over larger areas. The risk is that, with the simultaneous concentration of decision-makers, this phenomenon will not be experienced as a danger to the quality of man's environment and that no adequate policies to counter its negative effects will be adopted.

NOTES

1. Obviously, there is a limit to the influence of lower production cost which is determined by the cost of transport of a given good to non-central villages. Outside that limit, the specialists from the central village will not be able to compete. This critical distance for the good is called the 'range of a good'. The minimal market size for the survival of the activity is the 'threshold area' or 'minimum activity space'.
2. We shall return to this later when discussing other city-forming factors.
3. Obviously, this result can be disrupted when exchange with other regions develops. For example, location in proximity to the border with another system can result in a transport advantage, as we shall see in section 2.3.
4. By size we not only understand number of inhabitants but also their income, both important as determinants of demand.
5. In a number of countries, of course, accumulation of capital was enhanced by formal or informal processes of colonisation.
6. Wider use of modern means of communication and transport may perhaps curb this trend to some extent. For reasons mentioned above, there will remain a need for the spatial concentration of decision-makers.

9. The challenge and the direction of change: some observations

E. WEISSMANN

This contribution contains a concise discussion of some realities of man's relationship to his environment and of the general steps that need to be taken to balance these two components. The author asks hard questions about priorities. To stop growth where it hurts and to redistribute it where it matters is advanced as one of man's challenges of today. Subsequent papers by Du Boff, Burger, Lugo and Syatauw and that by Benthem van den Bergh, elaborate some of the statements on current societal problems and offer additional substance to the desirable direction of change.

DEVELOPMENT AND THE ENVIRONMENT

Man with all the physical and intellectual capacities he enjoys has existed for hundreds of thousands of years. In fashioning his first shelters, man set in motion a dynamic and potentially highly productive process of adapting the natural habitat to specific needs and to his liking. But with the appearance of larger human settlements in the more fertile river basins of Asia, Africa and Europe a mere ten thousand years ago, the society of man started on the difficult road of development. Struggling first to survive and then to advance, in this relatively short time man has degraded the environment, more recently at a terrifying pace. With the emergence of new and more intricate technologies, simple man-made shelter gradually grew into hamlets and villages, the more complex trading towns and walled cities, centres of industry and commerce, metropolitan agglomerations and, finally, to urbanization's ultimate product, the megalopolis. Here the traditional rural and the most advanced urban ways and forms often co-exist in clash and chaos; and in sharp conflict between the man-made and the natural environment. As a result, most nations, and more particularly the more affluent ones, now face seemingly irreversible trends of depression of the human quality of life.

Two broad interpretations of the interaction of man and environment are possible. The more obvious is: a slow, gradual biological and social evolution of man and then, suddenly, man beginning to destroy the natural habitat that sustains him. Alternatively, the present conditions can be seen as an entirely new stage of environmental and human development: man supplementing nature and forming to a large measure an environment, urban in character, presumably more convenient as human habitat, and more efficient as agent of further development. Total accommodation and dependence on the natural environment is gradually shifting to partial and increasing control of the environment. By deliberately applying science and the technologies we now possess, and hopefully working with, rather than opposing and blindly destroying nature, we are now capable of improving our environment.

URBANIZATION AND THE ENVIRONMENT

Urbanization is the milieu in which conflict, interaction and change manifest themselves most forcefully in the social, the physical, the economic and the political sense. But the city itself is also the vehicle by which the benefits of society's growth and productivity ultimately reach larger numbers of people. Unfortunately, the once viable relationship between Nature and the environment built by man of pre-industrial society is now radically disturbed by an urban environment haphazardly built. Transport and worldwide communications networks have now linked together man's cities around the world, transformed the character of human relations and the structure of societies; and have created in every corner of the globe an acute environmental and urban crisis. Inordinately vast resources and capital are now required to restore the balance.

For this, however, a shift is also required from the dominant economic and technical criteria for development to social and human values as criteria. Since most planners still restrict themselves to the former criteria, a radical redirection of priorities in the allocation of resources is essential. Economic 'efficiency' is a relatively simple concept, readily amenable to the use of mathematical methods and the computer but it is far less reliable as a guide to the human use of a nation's productivity and its long term needs. Some planners and some nations are beginning to conceive and test new approaches and new planning tools and techniques by blending economic and social criteria or adjusting productivity and human progress to one another; or rather, projecting productivity as an instrument of social and human development.

The essential relationship and interaction to be understood is thus between the controlled man-made environment and the natural environment, which man must respect in order to survive and develop. Under conditions of traditional cultivation, when the two environments were generally in balance, there tended to be more unity between the constructed and the natural environment, between endowment by nature and endowment by man. Nature's ecological cycle and man's agricultural cycle complemented one another in a reciprocally-beneficial relationship. Shelter too was a suitably controlled extension of man's natural habitat. But harmony turned into conflict as man applied new and more complex technologies more generally in different kinds of development pursuit; and technical and economic criteria began to monopolize priority in the allocation of resources at the expense of environmental quality and human and social benefit.

Recently, the Club of Rome has given the world carefully computerized projections of impending doom, projections readily produced by duly applying all the routines and procedures of natural science and engineering technology but omitting some of the essential and social factors. At the United Nations Conference on the environment in Stockholm, the officials of the establishment and many activist groups forcefully brought to the world the realization of the critical state of human affairs and the extreme urgency of common action, national and international, individual and communal. A number of clear conclusions and propositions emerge from these events.

1. Under the impact of scientific and technological progress the trends concerning population, sources of livelihood and ways of living are rapidly changing our society from a predominantly rural-agricultural to an infinitely more complex urban industrial-agricultural society.
2. These dynamic factors influence each other in terms of their own growth and in the rate and direction of change, which in turn are crucial for both spontaneous and planned development.
3. Changes are taking place at exponential rates which require a high degree of operational flexibility in concept and planning, and a shift of emphasis from detailed sectoral and national to comprehensive planning at all levels.
4. In many countries the regional approach has become an important mechanism for the implementation of national and sectoral development objectives and policies and for the protection of the environment.
5. In the process of development new entities are emerging as a result of economic, social, physical and political integration that are cities in the socio-economic sense and regions in the geographic and the political-administrative sense (city-regions).

6. The term region (a state, a province, a metropolitan or a city-region) implies concern with given physical conditions and resources, a given group of people and a given institutional structure as part of a nation.
7. There is an urgent need for meaningful participation of citizens with the planners and administrators in the complex process of conceiving, projecting and implementing development activities intended for the citizen's benefit.
8. In human affairs, such as planning for socio-economic development, or urban and metropolitan growth, or planning for industrial or rural development, flexibility in concept and in method and procedure is essential due to the ever-changing nature of human society.
9. The concept of reciprocal, mutually productive relationships between economic growth and human development and the quality of environment, though present in theory, is as yet far from being generally adopted, much less practiced.
10. For the sake of man's survival in decency and freedom a shift is now needed in criteria for development from economic and technical efficiency as the nearly exclusive yardstick to social progress and the quality of life and environment as additional criteria.
11. This, in turn, may humanize development, a concept that is gathering increasing recognition among development planners, administrators and theorists and the man in the street, as a means of 'resolving' the 'crisis' in development planning.
12. For the first time in history it now appears feasible: as the society of man we already possess the science, the technology and the required resources with which to influence to a large extent the direction of further development, the quality of the environment, and the nature of our society.

THE CITY-REGION CONCEPT

In this context the concept of city-region suggests itself as an approach to the task of restoring or enhancing development in harmony with nature's ecology and beauty, spreading material growth and enriching human progress and culture. At times the aim may be the loosening of urban agglomerates for higher efficiency, or simply for enlarging the human quality of life. At other times the city-region may offer a suitable framework for the requisite concentration for development. It can take any shape and structure that geography, technology and human ingenuity and institutions can conceive and produce. What I suggest implicitly is not a prescription for 'the city of the future', but rather the formulation of ground rules now for a dynamic process of balanced socio-economic and environmental development by planning city-regions as part of national or international development.

The city-region is a composite system of an infinite variety of economic, social, physical and political phenomena reacting upon one another. Any plan or projection for the 'mega-system' must therefore embody at least the following four major systems:

1. *A social system* – designed to further the development of 'urban man' now becoming ever more highly productive, disposing of vastly more time and resources for leisure, learning and culture; more thoroughly informed and therefore also better prepared to participate more directly and meaningfully in decision-making concerning his welfare.
2. *An economic system* – designed to further the development and application of technologies for growing productivity of man and machine and an equitable distribution of the material wellbeing thus made possible; enjoying ample opportunities for creative participation in the society's economic, human and cultural development.
3. *An environmental system* – designed to further urban growth and environmental development within the larger ecological region; a physical environment where both economic and social capacities are multiplied and the human qualities of life enlarged; where man intervenes as a creative builder; not a despoiler of nature.
4. *A political administrative system* – designed to further the setting of development objectives and policies with true citizen participation; and determining through due political processes the means and methods of projected development in a meaningful dialogue between the planner and administrator, and the citizen.

To facilitate the dialogue and promote productive interaction within each of these four systems and among them, a highly sensitive planning and monitoring system is needed, capable of responding instantly to the potentials and consequences of fast-rising productivity and to the human need for continued growth and development in dignity and freedom. If so conceived and practised, planning could move from conjecture to a truly dynamic instrument of growth and development in harmony of man and nature.

THE ENVIRONMENTAL AND URBAN CRISIS

But how are we as a society at present tackling this admittedly complex and tough job?

In the affluent part of the world the environmental crisis takes the form of unwanted concentrations of activities, structures, things and people in urban complexes such as the Eastern Seaboard Megalopolis in the United States of America, or the great urban industrial complexes and corridors of Japan and Europe. And in the developing continents there is a relentless and chaotic agglomeration of people and poverty in amorphous metropolitan areas where explosive expansion is less due to the 'pull' of economic growth and improved human conditions than it is to the massive flight of rural people from misery, disease and hunger. The crisis is a manifestation of rapid progress in technology which promises abundance, but challenges at the same time our society's ability to accept change and to use its immense new productivity to better human conditions.

The oft-stated purpose of economic growth is social improvement. But human progress is not at all an automatic consequence of economic growth. To obtain it, a society must allocate to human development a suitable share of the wealth it produces and must plan for an appropriate distribution of the social benefits it can offer. However, we are so much preoccupied with the pursuit of growth alone that we continue locating new economic activities primarily on the basis of the investors' short-term benefit instead of long-term regional and national benefits; and concentrating on the requirements of the world market in preference to a nation's own needs, so much so that the urban problems and environmental degradation in the so-called Third World often are a direct result of the demands for primary goods by the affluent part of the world.

When, in the process, external investment and aid are offered, the already considerable limitations imposed by obsolete concepts of economic balance and efficiency are compounded by political and ideological issues. In truth, by this means the dependent relationship between the big and the rich powers and their former colonies continues or even re-establishes itself. This then restricts even further the prospect of using the society's accrued and potential resources for the establishment of a viable world society and a viable world economy. But these are the two basic factors for the pre-industrial nations to use their own natural wealth and human capabilities for their own benefit, and the two basic conditions of their breaking-out of the vicious circle of underdevelopment. Very humbly I submit that the blind pursuit of economic growth, the blatant misuse of technology for individual and corporate benefit, and the resistance of affluent societies to reassessing the values and criteria concerning their own growth are not only widening the gap between the rich countries and the poor and degrading the environment on earth in the process, but also are frustrating the legitimate desire of the Third World to develop.

THE QUESTION OF RESOURCES

My final point concerns resources. For the sake of technical efficiency and obsolete economic concepts we still accept all kinds of restrictions on human dignity as the price of growth. These restrictions might have imposed themselves in an era of scarcity when social development had to be limited to what supported the society's economic goals. But now, as the world is reaching the threshold of affluence, the dilemma facing the rich nations is how to define the way and quality of life they desire as societies, as well as to define the contribution they are ready to offer toward making the world economy and the world society viable. Or they must continue to arm and to 'police' the world in the vain hope of protecting their dominant position and thus arresting social and political change.

In fact, negotiating the needed shift in attitudes and values concerning national development and international aid, away from exclusively economic criteria and foreign policy reasons to social and human development as goals may well become the major challenge our society will face in the remaining years of this century. Or the industrial society as known in the west may perish.

The world's annual outlay for the 'defense establishment' amounts to over 200 billion dollars. Five nations alone spend more than 80 percent of these public resources on highly obsolescent but exorbitantly costly offensive armaments. These are tested as to their capacity for destroying human life and the environment that sustains it in unequal contests by wars brought to distant countries. Recent history demonstrates that even the richest countries cannot have both 'guns and butter'. Nevertheless, preciously scarce resources are being poured into new weapons systems at the time when the 'overkill' factor has already reached a level at which the nuclear arsenal of one of the superpowers alone can destroy all large cities in the world, not once but many times. In this climate of an arms race among the large and rich nations, other countries, including the developing countries, are compelled to devote substantial portions of their wealth to the military at the expense of economic and social development.

In another area, the trend towards more leisure, learning and culture is already significantly reflected in the highly developed countries' consumer habits. In the United States, for instance, some 150 billion dollars are spent annually in the pursuit of leisure, mostly of a spectator-non-participant type. Also, a large international oil company has recently spent 100 million dollars on finding a new name. With resources so considerable already being spent for economically 'non-productive' pursuits, public resources in the case of armaments, and private in the case of leisure and public relations, it is really not a question of scarcity but of misallocation. It seems cruel that in these circumstances so many people in the world, including some in the most affluent countries, should have to be hungry, illiterate or ridden by curable diseases for reasons of 'economy'. There are, of course, limits to the ability of rich nations to divert resources to alternative uses; and limits to the capacity of the developing countries to absorb effectively such resources as loans, grants, or reparations for misuse and exploitation. But how are we ever to discover where these limits lie unless we move from speculation in conference to a real test?

Could it be that in their own interest nations will pool their resources and knowhow to reverse trends and redistribute growth where it matters, stop it where it harms? If it can be done, we may witness the end of the 'pre-history of man' and see the first steps leading to genuine human development in our time.

10. Man, organization, and the environment

JAMES F. MORRISON

Human organisation is a crucial factor in increasing man's capacity to exploit (or over-exploit) his environment and in making it possible to solve the long-term problem of the proper balance between what the environment can provide by way of air, water, energy, raw materials, and waste-disposal capacity, and man's demands for these environmental services. Rational and effective collective decision-making and problem-solving depend, however, not only on the development of appropriate organisational structures, but also on the achievement of changes in popular values and world views. Inevitably there are important obstacles to realising either of these essential requirements and these are further elaborated in the papers by Burger, Bendavid, Du Boff and Tellegen.

It is clear that in recent years there has been a growing world-wide awareness of man's intimate interrelationship with and ultimate dependence on his natural environment for survival and the enhancement of the quality of human life. Rather than viewing this growing awareness as something completely new, however, it is more accurate and perhaps more useful to interpret it as a reawakening of this dependency relationship at a new and higher level of understanding. Throughout most of human history, and even today in most of the less developed parts of the world, people have lived in a precarious and uncertain relationship with their natural environment and have shared traditional belief systems and institutions that have emphasized in some way man's total dependency on his natural (and/or supernatural) environment. It has been only quite recently – and even now in only a part of the world – that the scientific and industrial revolutions have brought about not only great advances in man's ability to modify and control his environment, but also a rapidly spreading popular faith in man's ability to conquer nature and in the inevitability of human progress and unlimited economic growth. The fact that the scientific, industrial, and more recently, the agricultural revolutions have made it possible for increasing numbers of people to live in highly populated urban areas within the context of a largely man-made environment has undoubtedly been in some large measure responsible for the erosion of the traditional belief systems and institutions more oriented toward nature and god(s) and their replacement by faith in technology. The more 'mature' belief systems and institutions now in the process of emerging, while rejecting the 'technology and economic growth can solve everything' optimism of the industrial revolution, nevertheless promise to retain an important place for science, technology, and industry in the new synthesis with renewed respect for the natural environment.

Ironically it has been largely the successes rather than the failures of our scientific, technological, and industrial achievements that are now forcing us into a more mature awareness of our dependency on our natural environment. Man's attempts to use and modify the gifts of nature to his own advantage have always had an effect on the natural environment – often a significant one – but it has only been in the last few decades that the level of our scientific discovery, machine technology, and organizational skills have made it possible on a world-wide basis for our population level and consequent demands on the environment for energy, water, air and other raw materials, open space, and waste disposal to grow beyond the capacity of our environment to provide for our needs (at least at current levels of knowledge, technology, and organization). The supplies of energy, raw materials, and open space are clearly more and more out of balance with the current and projected rapidly increasing demands of our growing and ever more consuming population. In addition, the environmental crisis threatens to make worse the already existing economic disparities and tensions both within countries and between them. Consequently we find growing awareness and concern about man's relationship with the natural environment, but no real solutions have yet been found.

It is clear that in the long run the supply of energy, raw materials, open space, and natural waste disposal capacity – and the demand for them – cannot remain permanently out of balance, though in the short run the imbalance can be maintained by lowering the quality of life. In the long run, however, some sort of restoration of the balance is inevitable, either by increasing supplies and/or by reducing the level of demand.

Using the first strategy, *supplies can be increased* in a number of ways:

1. Discover new supplies of existing resources (not a real option for land or air),
2. Stretch existing resources by greater recycling of resources once mined (not an option for energy though some waste heat could be captured and other forms of now discarded waste could be transformed into energy),
3. Develop new knowledge and technological applications that make possible

a. more efficient exploitation of known resource deposits (i.e. better mining, transportation, and refining methods)
b. more efficient use of energy resources
c. more efficient utilization of refined resources (i.e. better transportation and manufacturing methods; better product design to reduce manufacturing, operation, and maintenance costs and to increase the useful life and versatility of the product)
d. more efficient recycling
e. development of substitute resources for scarce ones (though this solution often requires increased energy use),

4. Move population and/or industry nearer to supplies to make resource exploitation cheaper,
5. Make more use of human energy (e.g. require people to sort their own garbage to make recycling more feasible),
6. Reduce unnecessary duplication and waste in the economy to free resources for other uses,
7. Develop new organizational and management methods that make possible the above developments,
8. Develop new applications of labor, management, capital, and energy to make possible the above developments,
9. Pass new laws and regulations that make possible the above developments,
10. Utilize government intervention (e.g. taxes, subsidies, transportation rate regulations) to change the relative profitability of using poorer or less accessible resource deposits, recycled materials, or new types of resources in place of scarcer ones – or let nature and the market take their course to achieve the same results more slowly as the price of the scarce resources increases,
11. Change public attitudes to favor the use of previously unused methods or resources or of government regulation,
12. Eliminate certain uses of some resources (e.g. land for parks, golf courses, extensive private yards; e.g. silver for coins) to free them for other uses – in other words, reallocate the usage of resources,
13. Redistribute concentrations of existing supplies held by a few individuals or countries in order to make them available to others.

It is important to keep in mind, of course, that not all of these methods can be used in every case and that the use of one of these methods to increase the supply of one resource may hasten the depletion of another (e.g. more energy may be required for refining or transporting a substitute resource. Moreover, many supplies, especially of stored energy, are ultimately limited and increasing supplies of that resource can solve the problem only temporarily).

As an alternative or complementary strategy, *demand can be decreased* in a number of ways:

1. Reduce the population level, thereby decreasing the level of consumption indirectly,
2. Reduce consumption levels directly by
   a. removing the scarce item from the market and/or
   b. substituting another product for the scarcer one
   c. rationing
   d. increasing prices (but this puts the burden on the poor)
   e. decreasing wages or redistributing them to favor consumption of more abundant resources
   f. lowering consumer desires and/or changing them to prefer more abundant resources
   g. increasing the efficiency with which consumption takes place (e.g. increasing product life and versatility, increasing the number of people who use a given product, increasing population density and the efficiency of urban design to minimize the amount of energy, raw materials, and transportation needed in the urban infrastructure and everyday operation of the city, reducing the frequency of changes in product style changes)
   h. designing more labor-intensive industry and encouraging less energy and capital-intensive industry, recreation, and life-styles
   i. increasing taxes and spending the money in ways that make a minimum demand on scarce resources – or spending it to develop new resources in accord with the first strategy.

Reducing demand, however, is clearly not an easy option, as some reduction in the quality of life or at least alteration in popular life style is required – at least in the short-run. Moreover, it runs the risk of increasing inequalities and raising tension levels as previous expectations are upset.

The central questions here are two: (1) To what extent and how soon can new discoveries in science and technology and new developments in the socio-economic and political sphere increase our raw material and energy supply? In other words, can supply keep up with growing demand? If not, as many argue, (2) will the balance between supply and demand be restored through the age-old impersonal mechanisms of nature and the market, forcing man to change his ideas, his institutions, and his behavior only after successive and increasingly serious disasters have brought misery and death to hundreds of millions and drastically lowered the quality of the natural and man-made environment and the general quality of life for most of the remaining population and probably further multiplied already existing inequities and tensions – or is it possible that enough people and strategically-placed leaders in society will recognize the danger in time and somehow manage to bring about a conscious reorganization of national and international society so that these otherwise inevitable disasters and serious deteriorations in the quality of human life can be avoided or at least minimized?

It is the major thesis of this paper that it is in the area of human belief systems (or social thought) and organization, not in the area of technological discovery, that the key to the problem of restoring the environmental balance with minimum loss of life and suffering is to be found. Technology will no doubt play an important role, but without the proper context of social thought and organization, technological innovations are more likely to continue to create more problems than they solve.

The important role of scientific discovery and the application of machine technology in the industrial revolution and the consequent increasing impact on the natural environment have been widely discussed. More neglected, however, has been the role of human belief systems and social organization (including political and economic organization) in these developments. Without changes in belief systems and advances in human organization and management that have enabled societies to become larger, more complex, and better able to mobilize resources for scientific discovery and technological innovation and investment in economic infrastructures and applied industrial technology, the continuing industrial revolution would have been impossible. Likewise, scientific knowledge and technology are usually awarded the leading roles in proposed solutions to our environmental problems. The importance of changing our social thought and institutions, while often acknowledged in passing, is all too often passed over quickly or ignored entirely.[1]

The levels of scientific knowledge and technological development themselves, of course, affect the development of belief systems and institutions by limiting the choices open to societies, opening up new possibilities for development and helping to create new behavior patterns and values; but at the same time, belief systems and institutions are important determinants of whether the level of scientific knowledge and technology is advanced and applied in practice. The social thought patterns and institutions of a society may or may not provide a framework that stimulates scientific investigation and applied technological development. More specifically, societies differ in the degrees to which they create an intellectual climate that stimulates and rewards such development and provide formal institutions and financial support for such efforts. Even when scientific knowledge and machine technology are readily available, it is a society's belief systems and institutions that play an important part – along with the level of economic development and capital availability – in determining their impact. In China, for example, many of the technological processes important in Europe's industrial development had long been known but not widely applied. Likewise, in the less developed parts of the world today available technology is not uniformly applied due to differences in belief systems and institutions as well as differences in economic development and potential sources of investment capital.

At this point it seems useful to say a little about human society and organization in general. To begin with it may be helpful to be a little more specific about the analytical components that need to be considered when we talk about human society, belief systems and institutions, and seek solutions to the environmental crisis. First of all, on one level of analysis, there is the collective belief system – or the world view, intellectual paradigm, or system of social thought – of a society. In brief, the belief system includes the collective memories of the society; the way it perceives and interprets the reality of the world and explains how it works; and the way it categorizes, organizes, and relates things. It also includes the society's shared values, goals, priorities, expectations, and norms. [See point five below for a discussion of non-shared beliefs.] A key part of the belief system is the relating to the appropriate institutions and rules of the game for making collective decisions, resolving conflict within the system, and protecting the society from outside threats – i.e. beliefs relating to the political system, its proper role in society, the degree to which obedience to government is required, etc. Another close related key area relates to the appropriate institutions and rules of the game for producing and distributing goods and services in the society – i.e. beliefs relating to the economic system.

Second, on another level of analysis – the behavioral or operational level – there are the various social institutions that structure the behavior of individuals (e.g. governments, economic enterprises, schools, churches, family). These institutions (or patterned social behavior), of course, correspond to and are made possible by the collective belief system on the first level of analysis discussed above.

Third, on the same level of analysis as the institutions, there are the actual substantive decisions that are made by the various social institutions – and the impact of these decisions on the natural, man-made, and social environments.

A fourth major component (also on the second level of analysis) is the distribution of capabilities (or power) in society – both between various social groups and between political institutions on the one hand and other organizations and individuals in the society on the other.

A fifth component (this one on the first level of analysis) is the distribution in society of the values, goals, expectations, and beliefs about how the system does in fact and should operate – a fact which can be used as a measure of the cleavages and degree of consensus in society, both over specific issues and over the appropriate institutions and rules of the game for collective decision-making and conflict resolution.[2]

There is also a third level of analysis that should be mentioned briefly: namely, the individual, who acts within the context of the collective belief system and institutions of society, and of the belief systems shared by the many organizations and groups that make up a society.

Although these analytical divisions are to some extent arbitrary, the point is that when we begin talking about what changes are necessary to restore the balance between man's demands on the environment and its capacity to provide what man needs to survive and preserve a high quality of life, all five of these major components of human belief systems and institutions need to be considered. It is important to ask how existing reality in each of these areas – the social belief system, operational social institutions and rules of the game, actual substantive policy decisions, the distribution of power, and the distribution of beliefs, values, and goals – hinders man's world-wide ability to restore the balance and what changes need to take place before this can happen. The questions can be asked with regard to the environmental problem at the local, regional, national, or international levels. In using this schema at different territorial levels of analysis or even when applying it to different countries or localities within a given country, it is important to remember that there will be great differences in the extent to which there is a well-developed collective belief system and central institutions. At the international level, and even at the national level in many countries, there is little consensus about many issues and often weak, ill-defined, and/or unpopular central institutions that can rule only through the widespread use of coercion.

Another way of looking at the problem of man, organization, and the environment is to take a structural-functional systems approach and list the basic functions that have to be performed successfully in any society or organization in order for it to survive over time. There have been many such lists developed by anthropologists, sociologists, and political scientists – most notably by sociologist Talcott Parsons – but the following composite list will suffice to illustrate the approach; with institutions commonly performing these functions noted in parentheses.

1. Procreation or continual recruitment of outsiders into the group (The family; the personnel department; proselytization or recruitment committees)
2. Communications and intelligence gathering and analysis – in relation to the natural, man-made, and social environment (Language, speech and writing; scouts and advance men; scientific research; libraries; propagandists; media)
3. Socialization and assimilation of new members into the group; imparting group goals, values, beliefs; providing meaningful roles (Schools, churches, welcoming committees, orientation meetings, the family)
4. Definition of group goals and purposes; providing meaning and direction for participation (Political and religious leadership; social clubs, political organizations, churches)
5. Production (or conquest) of sufficient goods and services to meet group goals and provide a continuing incentive to remain a member of the group (Economic and political institutions)
6. Collective decision-making, conflict-resolution, integration (Political and economic institutions; churches; social organizations)
7. Adaptation to existing and changing environmental conditions, and defense against and accommodation to outside groups (Scientific research, trial and error learning, and borrowing from other groups; planning departments; political and economic institutions; military institutions).[3]

It is important to note that in different societies these functions may be performed by different institutions. Each function may be performed simultaneously by a number of institutions, and a given institution may perform more than one function.

The purpose of presenting these functions here is not simply to make lists, but to emphasize in a different way that even 'simple' societies are in fact rather complex, dynamic units that both depend on the natural environment and at the same time use it to perform functions (and pursue goals) that may be quite separate from the environment. Much human effort is inevitably involved simply in maintaining the social system or pursuing collective goals, even though they may at times be harmful to the environment. This functional approach, however, also suggests that in the long run one of the fundamental requirements of social system survival is that an adjustment be made to the environment (including the natural, man-made, and external social environments). Finally, this approach illustrates the importance of social organization to human life and suggests that virtually all individual activity is ultimately dependent on the social context, including family, community, nation, specialized organization, or private club; even social deviates are dependent on the larger society in some ways and in other ways on their own sub-groups of deviates which are necessary to sustain their deviance over time. Society and human organization, in short, play a key role in mediating the individual's relationship with his physical environment and, at the same time, themselves constitute a major part of the total environment with which the individual has to deal. In any case, the point is that man must remain constantly alert to the adequacy of the performance of his social organization – in relation both to human relations and relations with the natural environment – if he is to enhance the chances of his survival.

It can be argued that human history is in a sense the history of the successes and failures of the groups or organizations which man has formed to improve his individual and collective chances for survival and attainment of his goals. Very little human behavior at any stage of historical development takes place outside the context of human social organization, directly or indirectly. It is through organizations that human beings manage to (1) resolve conflicts, harmonize their goals and develop new collective goals, (2) concentrate knowledge and information to increase decision-making rationality and effectiveness, (3) combine their individual talents through coordination and specialization of labor, (4) mobilize, concentrate, and direct greater quantities of human labor, raw materials, and energy resources and (5) apply them more efficiently and effectively to achieve their goals. Although the forms of social organization have changed as societies have become larger and more complex – with decreased relative importance for the family and religious institutions, for example – some form of human social organization has been a constant factor in human development. While the various functions noted above have to be performed by all societies or organizations to survive over time, some organizations and societies manage to perform them more effectively than others (because of differing degrees of social consensus, leadership abilities, population values and skills, etc.) and/or find themselves in natural environments more conducive to effective performance of these functions and attainment of their collective goals. (The substance of the collective goals of societies also differ, of course – in part due to adaptation to the environment, but also in part to extraneous factors or chance – and these different goals may be important not only in determining the course of societal development, if environmental conditions are favorable, but also in determining the chances of the society's survival. Some goals, for example, may make it more difficult for a society to adapt to changing environmental conditions than if its goals were different. A society with high consumption and immediate gratification goals may not have accumulated enough surplus to tide it over difficult times or may find it more difficult to reduce its consumption levels without creating severe social tension and friction.)

This brings us to a third way of viewing the role of organization in man's relationship with his natural environment: namely, concentrating on the problem-solving capabilities of societies. Although this third approach is closely related to the others, the first two provide a more general framework for looking at societies and their relationship to the environment, while this approach concentrates more specifically on the mechanisms and processes by which societies recognize, define, and solve their problems including those relating to the natural environment. To be more specific, collective problem-solving systems include our collective capabilities

1. to recognize problems before they begin to develop – a kind of early warning system involving the collection and analysis of information based on some understanding of how natural and human systems work;

2. to understand accurately the nature of the problem, its causes, and the obstacles standing in the way of dealing with it once the problem does arise;
3. to develop a set of solutions (goals/visions of alternative futures) relevant to the problem and a set of strategies for implementing them;
4. to achieve a clear choice by the members of the society between the alternative solutions and to mobilize adequate support for the solution to insure its effective implementation;[4]
5. to implement the solution quickly and effectively throughout the society (in all geographical areas and among all social groups);
6. to monitor objectively and accurately the impact of the solution implemented; and
7. to undertake quickly any modifications of the solution implemented if it proves to be less effective than expected.

It should be noted, however, that in most societies at most times, most 'collective' decisions are not the product of conscious, centralized, and/or rational decision-making by the public or their chosen representatives – or even by authoritarian rulers claiming to make decisions in the name of the people. On the contrary, most of the 'decisions' that affect the fate of a society while made collectively are not made consciously and are the result of largely uncontrolled – and perhaps largely uncontrollable forces – such as the pre-existing structure of social beliefs and institutions, the operation of the market, or the unforeseen consequences of many individual or collective decisions made in quite different contexts. For example, 'decisions' to increase or decrease the rate of population growth, to develop suburban sprawl, or to increase drastically the world demand for energy fall into this category.

Although it is highly debatable whether it will ever be possible – or even desirable – to achieve such social consensus, centralized authority, and knowledge of natural and human systems that truly collective world-wide (or even national) decision-making can be achieved, it is clear that we could increase significantly the degree to which we exercise conscious control over our socio-economic development. At present most people – and perhaps even most politicians and elected officials – are not really fully aware that their society is inevitably, if unconsciously, making collective policy decisions that control its destiny. These policy decisions may be made directly by the central government and its agencies, or more indirectly through the decisions of local governments, large and small economic enterprises and other private organizations, and individuals as they interact with one another through formal government channels, socially, or in the market place.

These policy decisions – involving the making of laws and the allocation of resources in society – help create the framework of incentives and sanctions within which decisions are made by government agencies, economic and other private organizations, and individuals, and are the key determinants of the future course of the society's development.

The policy decisions made by government may cover a wider or narrower range of societal activities, depending on the complexity of society, the level of economic development, the strength of the government in relation to the rest of society, and the degree to which there is consensus that the proper role of government extends to these areas of life and consensus over what policy should be in the area.

Policies also differ from society to society in the extent to which the policy is well-defined and consistent internally and with other policies. It is not unusual – especially in complex and dynamic societies – for policies to be ill-defined with considerable latitude for contrary action by different groups. (In fact, this is one of the major means of conflict resolution in society – to let different individuals or groups do different things, even at the long-run expense of society, in order to avoid open conflict by openly making a decision that is inevitably unpopular with significant groups in the society.)

Considering the importance of these abstract collective policy decisions, it is a little surprising that they have been so neglected by social scientists as well as by private citizens and policy makers. Individual policy decisions or even a few policy areas have been investigated fairly thoroughly by scholars, planners, and policy makers, but little has been done in the way of taking a comprehensive, yet fairly detailed overview of just what our national or international policies are and what impact they are likely to have over time. Part of the explanation for this failure no doubt lies in the extraordinary complexity of society, the number of bits of information that have to be analyzed and the contradictions involved in each policy area. Part of the answer is also to be found in the fact that many of our collectively-made policies are not made by government, so we take them for granted or assume they are beyond the sphere of conscious public control. Still another part of the explanation lies with our tendency, until recently anyway, to assume that everything is going well and that the decisions made by the market or individuals pursuing their own interest will most likely contribute to further inevitable progress. Whatever the reasons, it is clear that we seldom take the kind of overview of our society and its effective public policies and their consequences that is necessary if we are to begin to exercise more conscious control over our collective destinies.

It would perhaps be instructive for someone to go through each of the major policy areas and attempt to outline just what our collective policies are in the area and assess what their probable consequences are. Although the divisions are somewhat arbitrary, the following list probably covers the policy areas most relevant to man's relation to his natural environment and gives some idea of the scope of our collective policy choices:

1. Land use and reclamation
2. Energy use and development
3. Water use and supply (quantity and quality)
4. Raw material use and supply
5. Waste disposal – solids, liquids, gas, radiation – and pollution control
6. Science and technology
7. Population growth and location
8. Human resource development
   - Education and training
   - Rehabilitation
   - Health
   - Welfare
   - Recreation
9. Economic development and stability
   - Rate of economic growth and investment
   - Production mix and quantity
   - Location of economic growth
   - Fiscal and monetary policy
   - Wages
   - Employment
   - Goods and services delivery system
10. Public finance and income distribution
    - Taxation
    - Budget allocation
    - Income redistribution

Welfare services
11. Government operation and services
12. Government regulatory action
13. Urban design and development
14. Housing
15. Transportation
16. Communications and mass media
17. Culture and recreation
18. Public safety – police, fire, safety
19. Defense
20. Public participation in government and community life
21. Trade (foreign)

In assessing our public policies in these areas it is important to recognize that there will inevitably be certain contradictions or conflicts between policies in a given area and between areas. Given the complexity of society and the diversity of group interests, the fact that no policy affects everyone equally, and the fact that even individuals have conflicting short-run and long-run interests, this is not surprising. Nevertheless, good organization may minimize the conflict by suggesting new ways of harmonizing opposing interests.

It has been suggested earlier that it is desirable for us to increase our awareness of just what our collective policies are in various areas so that we are in a better position to evaluate their rationality and effectiveness and work for policies that are more likely to take us where we want to go. At the same time it is important to recognize that – because of conflicting group interests in society – as we begin to make our basic decisions more consciously and openly and more through centralized institutions, the greater the danger of sharper conflict and increased political tension. (Good policies should be designed to minimize the loss to any group and to maximize the benefits to as many as possible, but someone is bound to come out with more costs or fewer benefits than others, and even when those who are affected are compensated generously for their losses, many still cannot accept the change.) In the area of energy policy, for example, when decisions are made by the market or behind closed doors by an economic and political elite, there is more of an air of inevitability about the decision and it is harder to find anyone to blame or anyone to serve as a focus for public protest action. Therefore, even those who are hurt by the policy decision are more likely to accept it without open protest and adjust quietly to it.

Nevertheless, until basic policy decision-making becomes more conscious, rational, and public, there is little chance of making policy serve genuinely public needs rather than the narrower economic interests of those (usually minorities) who have vested interests in existing policies. At the same time, there is certainly no guarantee that more democratic and public participation alone will solve the problem either, as the requirements of environmental protection or resource conservation often mean the necessity for the public to make sacrifices they are unprepared to make.

The accompanying diagram illustrates some of the major relationships and flows in a rational policy-making system and indicates how specialized policy impact analysis and policy design agencies can have some potential impact on the formal decision-making process – if their services are welcomed by formal decision-makers and if ideological rigidity and/or public pressure for specific solutions is not too great.

While the above pages have concentrated on the importance of belief systems and organizations (or institutions) in man's relationship with the natural environment, and the need to improve the degree to which our problem-solving systems operate effectively, the last part of this presentation will focus on the problems of achieving that objective.

Another major thesis of this paper is that even if the importance of the role of belief systems and social organization in the environmental equation is properly acknowledged the problem is not so much that social scientists have not yet discovered what needs to be changed in order to rationalize our collective problem-solving capabilities, but rather that human belief systems, organization, and behavior on a mass scale are very resistant to change and not particularly responsive to even the most unanimous and unimpeachable conclusions that may be reached by scientists (natural or social). (Witness the lack of response to recent discoveries about the impact of cigarette smoking on health.)

In other words, the point of view presented here is that the basic problem we face today in dealing with our environmental problems (as well as with most of our other problems) is not so much the lack of scientific knowledge or technological knowhow – in either the natural sciences or the social sciences – but rather one of how to alter our local, national, and international systems of human thought, organization, and behavior – or, to put it differently, our collective human decision-making and problem-solving systems – so that we can restore the balance between what we demand of our environment and what it can provide.

Diagram showing the interrelationships of the various parts of the collective decision-making (or problem-solving) system of society

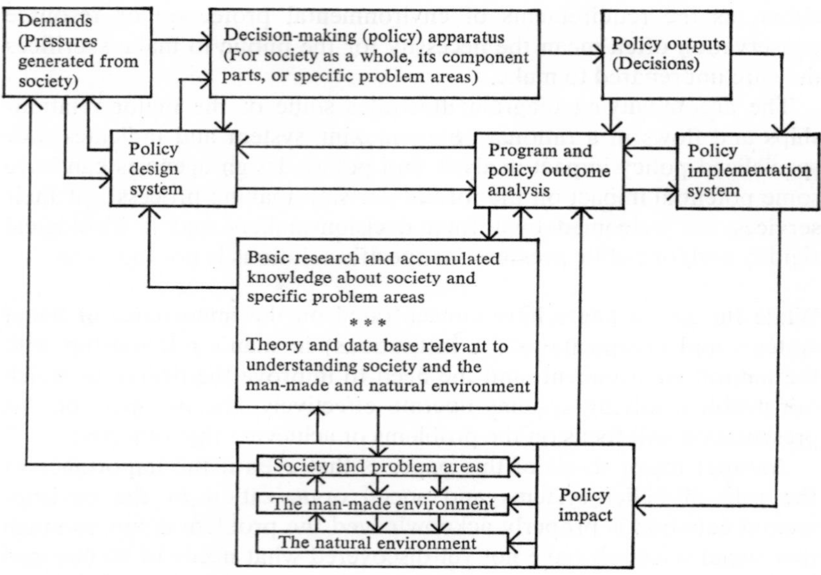

We know, for example, what governments can do theoretically to regulate the economy and individual behavior to bring them more in line with our natural environmental limitations. Governments, for example, can carry out campaigns to change public belief systems through their ability to control school textbooks and curricula, generate news for the media, print books and posters, hire writers and speakers, buy or receive free radio and TV time and advertising space in magazines and newspapers, influence or, in some countries, control the content of the media, etc. Governments may also create new regulatory agencies or strengthen old ones and establish new rules governing the behavior of producers and consumers. They may set minimum quality or safety standards; allocate raw materials or limit the use of certain raw materials; control the amount or circumstances of production or use of products or ban their production or use entirely; regulate interest, investment, wages, profits, money supply, credit rates or prices; control the disposal of waste, and in other ways affect production and consumption. Governments also have the power to impose license fees, effluent charges, taxes, tariffs, and quotas, or pay subsidies, give out grants, make loans, and provide tax write-offs and credits, thereby indirectly affecting prices, competition, and production. They may also enter the market directly through engaging in the growing, mining, production or importation of goods. They also affect the market through their purchase of goods and services – either for government or public use or reallocation within the society. Governments also affect the quantity and quality of the labor supply through population policy, health policy, education policy, welfare policy, transportation policy, and military conscription policy. They also affect the economy through collecting, analyzing and distributing information about the economy's behavior, about potential markets, and about production techniques. Governments also support the economy through directly or indirectly supporting basic research, the development of new technological applications, and financing the construction of a basic infrastructure of roads, ports, schools, hospitals, irrigation ditches, power plants, airports, navigation aids, etc. In addition, they provide direct and indirect support for the economy by enforcing contracts in the courts, collecting debts, regulating competition, protecting producers and consumers against theft and sabotage, providing police, fire, and other services, insuring depositors in banks and overseas investors, providing guarantees for loans, printing currency and minting coins, stabilizing markets, controlling inflation and depression, and on and on. In order to insure compliance with their orders governments also have an enormous array of sanctions. In addition to criminal prosecution (with fines or imprisonment – or harrassment) the government may allow civil penalties, undertake actions for damages, issue injunctions; give or withhold licenses, requested regulatory changes to contracts, grants, or loans; call for seizure and forfeiture of property; control raw material or energy supplies, and so forth.

But despite the tremendous potential power of governments to act to restore the balance, in practice even the most centralized and secure governments have done relatively little. There are no simple reasons as to why this is so, but we can easily identify a dozen obstacles to effective environmental action by government without resorting to conspiracy theories.

1. There is still no widespread sense of urgency that anything drastic needs to be done, or even an awareness that there is a problem in the eyes of many people. In other words, collectively we have not yet fully perceived that there is a problem serious enough to do anything about.
2. There is no consensus over the exact nature of the problem or how to deal with it – even on the part of those who are aware that there is a serious problem. The energies of the reformers are thus diluted and their potential allies confused. (Is the answer more technology and investment or lower consumption? Too many people or the wrong technology?)
3. The old paradigm or world view – that technology and economic growth can solve our problems, that progress is inevitable, that resources are unlimited and should be treated economically as if they were free, that consumption can continue to increase indefinitely, that private consumption is preferable to public consumption, that public planning and regulation of free enterprise are to be avoided wherever possible, and that the free competitive market is still intact and can solve our economic and welfare problems – has not yet really been seriously challenged and is still basically intact, even in the minds of those who recognize vaguely that there are serious problems.
4. Any real solution will be costly – not just to those with a big economic stake in the status quo, but also to the average citizen, who in many ways stands to suffer more than big business, as prices rise in response to the increased production costs that would follow the introduction of pollution controls, higher priced raw materials, more durable products, additional labor required in some aspects of production, recycling charges, etc. In addition, the dislocations in certain industries and geographical areas would be even worse. Certain powerful vested interests would certainly be hurt. Additional costs would fall on the wealthier in general because of the need to provide relief for those at the bottom end of the economic scale who would be hit hardest. Even many of those who already recognize the problem and strongly favor doing something about it might well balk if they knew the full price.
5. Although there would be long-run gains to be had from taking action now – at least in the sense that long-run costs would be reduced – a great many people, if not most, tend to prefer deferring the costs until later, even if they will be significantly

higher then – the classic short-run vs. long-run cost dilemma. This tends to be true because people feel a greater pressure from short-run costs (especially in countries such as the US where their economic appetites perpetually outpace their incomes), because there is always some uncertainty that the costs will be greater in the future, and because it is easy to deny unpleasant future reality. The problem is complicated by the fact that the older population – which tends to be poor and hardest hit by the short-run costs involved – would have to pay the costs now and would benefit little from the long-run gains. As identification with personal interests tends to be stronger than identification with species survival interests, there is a problem here with interest cleavage along age lines.

6. Many of the proposed solutions – e.g. accelerated efforts at population control, abandoning the private automobile, rationing, increased regulation of the economy – bring with them significant non-economic costs that a great many people find intolerable. In other words, the magnitude of the short-run costs to many people is greater than the long-run costs.
7. The magnitude of the problem is so overwhelming that even many of those who recognize the problem see no solution or no way of implementing it. Under these circumstances most people see the rational solution as being to enjoy the goodies now while they are still available and relatively cheap. Unless everyone can be forced to make the sacrifice at the same time, most people see no point in making a significant personal sacrifice that can have little impact on the total problem.
8. Because people at any decision-making level short of world-wide (where there are no real collective decision-making institutions and unified action is most difficult) are involved in competition with others for scarce resources and markets, no producer (or employee) can afford to be a part of any corrective action that leaves his competitor unaffected.
9. Our political leadership, and most individual citizens, are diverted from the environmental problem by more immediately pressing or at least more dramatic issues.
10. The impact of proposed solutions on any individual to some extent remains an unknown and poses a potential threat. Most individuals, even those who might stand to gain from the proposed reform, invariably see some risk involved and can foresee the

possibility that the personal costs to them – in being dislocated, for example – might well be greater than the costs of doing nothing. The possible unknown costs and risks of change, in other words, are often perceived as being much higher than the relatively known costs and risks of doing nothing.

11. Generally speaking, the larger, more loosely organized, more complex and more diverse a social unit is, the greater the difficulty in getting consensus as to a solution to a problem. The environmental problem is clearly one that involves such a large, loosely organized, complex and diverse social unit.
12. The less developed countries of the world are most certain to be unhappy about many kinds of reforms aimed at protecting the environment, as these would certainly increase their capital and production costs and lower their rate of economic growth. Proposals for radical population growth control are also likely to be perceived as an imperialistic threat to their independence. These objections can be overcome only with a massive influx of aid from the developed countries that will be politically increasingly difficult to support because of rising costs and expectations in the advanced nations.

So much, then, for a brief and incomplete list of obstacles standing in the way of finding and implementing a rational solution to the worldwide environmental crisis. Although it is tempting to conclude with a pessimistic prognosis about the prospects for a solution, perhaps it would be better to close with a few observations about the problem of change in the environmental area.

First, we should emphasize that as a rule change – for better or worse – takes place slowly rather than overnight. Things are not likely to get worse – or better – with the speed suggested by many prophets of gloom – or of technological utopia. There will be time for making some adjustments to the changes and introducing some corrective measures. Some severe shortages and economic crises are undoubtedly inevitable before these corrective measures have been introduced but will hasten the process. The restoration of the balance between human demands and environmental capacity will undoubtedly involve both a reduction in consumption levels and technological innovations aimed at increasing supply. The problem of increased disparities between rich and poor seems likely to continue and the politics of distribution to become more acute. The extent to which continued crises produce meaningful reform in large measure depends on the degree to which the environmental reformers succeed in communicating to the public at large and to its educated and politically involved leaders of society the nature and urgency of the crisis and in agreeing among themselves on preferred solutions. The hard scientists must play a particularly important role in this communication process and should be careful to walk a thin line between stating the problem forcefully and dramatically enough to arouse concern and not overstating it (as have some already) to the point where credibility is lost. It would also be helpful for the natural scientists to work closely with politicians, journalists, editors, film makers, and teachers so that what they produce is more easily and effectively communicated to the public. Change must take place simultaneously on all levels – the public world view, institutions and rules of the game, substantive policies, redistribution of capabilities and of values – and in all policy areas, though there may be greater haste made on one level or in one area than in others at given times. Some policy areas, such as energy, water, raw material, land use, urban design, economic growth and employment, population, welfare, science and technology, public finance and taxation are probably more crucial in this respect, however, than others such as recreation, culture, government operations. Another key determinant of the ability to solve the environmental crisis with a maximum of speed and a minimum of suffering will undoubtedly be the extent to which the reformers manage to form effective, well-supported action organizations that can work not only to educate the public about the problem and possible solutions, but also work with important executive and legislative policy makers, the courts, sympathetic business leaders, and grass roots political organizations to push through the necessary institutional reform and substantive policy changes at all levels of government. Important also will be the degree to which environmentally-conscious people join the mass media staffs and major economic enterprises and manage to work their way up into positions of policy-making influence in these operations.

Important public officials or well-known public personalities, such as the President (or Prime Minister), governors, heads of government departments, leading legislators and party leaders, or news commentators, can play an important role in calling public attention to the environmental crisis and proposing or mobilizing support for needed legislation or public action, but this is not likely to happen until after a significant amount of pressure from the scientific community and considerable grass roots public opinion has already emerged to demand such leadership efforts.

In short, solving the environmental crisis depends less on great heroes or carefully calculated strategies formulated and carried out by a few revolutionaries than it does on the quiet, dedicated work of people throughout the social system – work by people who are aware that there is an environmental crisis, who are willing to devote many hours and years to working for reform, and who are wise enough to recognize that the problem will not be solved easily or quickly, patient enough to continue their efforts year after year, humble enough not to get carried away with the unique righteousness and infallibility of their own pet scheme, and flexible enough to work with others and to adapt their ideas to the changing times and circumstances.

NOTES

1. The fault here, however, lies not only with the natural scientists and engineers who often at least acknowledge the need for more attention to social, economic or political considerations, but also with the fact that until recently so few social scientists have been interested in environmental questions. Even now the number of social scientists doing serious work in this area is still relatively small.
2. Note that the first and second categories refer to beliefs and institutions that are shared collectively by society, while the fourth and fifth categories refer to the more divisive features of society, i.e. to the beliefs and institutions that are shared by only part of society.
3. The first three functions correspond roughly to Parsons' 'pattern maintenance' function; four and five correspond to his 'goal attainment' function; six to his 'integration' function and, in part, to his 'goal attainment' function; and seven to his 'adaptation' function.
4. This may involve both the necessity for significant popular involvement in the earlier steps of the problem-solving efforts and a high degree of pre-existing social unity and consensus on values, goals, priorities.

11. Economic ideology and the environment

RICHARD B. DU BOFF

Limits to Growth *was a common topic of discussion among faculty and students of the Leiden Course. Du Boff reviews some criticisms of this bestseller and exposes major inconsistencies in the arguments of some leading economists. Positive steps with which to decrease some impacts of current growth policies are suggested. The reader is encouraged to compare these with the views of Smerdon and Gaither, Tellegen, Lugo, and Weissmann. Also of interest is the extent to which we can turn to previous human experience for guidance; this question is touched upon by Van Raay and Van Arkel.*

The degree of opposition – if not violence of language – on the part of economists to new social theorizing appears to be directly proportional to the threat that such theorizing poses to their own vested interests. Once this rule of behavior is recognized, it becomes easy to understand why so many Western economists react with incredulity, mocking skepticism, or cold hostility to the rising concern over economic growth and ecological crisis. Any suggestion that economic growth – the cornerstone of the Keynesian welfare state – might breed serious contradictions or even sow the seeds of its own demise challenges the ideology, concepts and tools of the mainstream of the economics profession of capitalist nations and their Soviet communist imitators.

The attitude of economists toward questions of socioeconomic institutions and environmental disruption began taking shape in the late 1960s, but it crystallized in early 1972 with the publication of the Report of the Club of Rome's 'Project on the Predicament of Mankind', *The Limits to Growth* (hereafter, *Limits*).[1] 'It's just utter nonsense', commented one leading American economist, who asked a *New York Times* interviewer not to identify him. Another US economist, Nobel Prize winner Simon Kuznets, called *Limits* 'a simplistic kind of conclusion – you have problems and you solve them by stopping all sources of change.' In the view of Yale University's Henry Wallich, 'I get some solace from the fact that these scares have happened many times before – this is Malthus again.'[2] Everett Hagen of MIT found himself 'saddened that the treatment of an important subject should be so inadequate . . . The assumptions of their model are . . . peculiarly unrealistic ones, [and] hyper-Malthusian.'[3]

But these remarks proved to be comparatively mild. The wellknown British development economist Wilfred Beckerman dismissed *Limits* as 'a brazen, impudent piece of nonsense that nobody could possibly take . . . seriously'. For him, there is 'no reason to suppose that economic growth cannot continue for another 2,500 years'.[4] A London *Economist* editorialist and an American academic agreed: *Limits* reaches a 'high-water mark of old-fashioned nonsense', causing 'a flurry of alarming articles from the pens of those who don't know better and those who should know better'.[5] 'An empty and misleading work', claimed a trio of US economists reviewing *Limits* for *The New York Times*. 'Its imposing apparatus of computer technology and systems jargon conceals a kind of intellectual Rube Goldberg device.' 'Less than pseudoscience and little more than polemical fiction', *Limits* is 'not a rediscovery of the laws of nature but of the oldest maxim of computer science: Garbage In, Garbage Out'.[6]

To be reminded of the fact, however axiomatic, that the natural and environmental resources of our planet are limited, and that in less than two decades the Earth has been ravaged and poisoned far worse than over the entire preceding course of human history, seems to be subversive for these economists. But others are beginning to realize that it is environmentally impossible for the whole world's population to gobble up resources and to pollute the air, land, and water at the rate done today in North America and Western Europe. Is this disproportion to be permanent – one-quarter of the Earth's population consuming the vast bulk of its goods and simultaneously undoing the work of millions of years of organic evolution for all mankind? And how have *we* been chosen to enjoy so huge a portion of the world's resources of which our very use (apart from any exploitation and injustice in obtaining them) continues to bar access to them by the rest of humanity?

The obvious answers to questions like these undermine the moral legitimacy of our social system – and the economic growth ideology it presently rests upon. This is why environmental warnings like *Limits* have been greeted with a ferocity that goes well beyond correcting technical errors. Conventional economists in particular feel menaced by statements that not only will economic growth run up against unanswerable ecological barriers but that there is a widening array of problems that growth may *aggravate*, let alone fail to solve.

Perhaps economic growth as the answer to social problems always was inherent in the dialectics of market capitalism. Still, in my opinion, a qualitative change did take place as a result of the desparate and prolonged economic crisis of the 1930s. Never before in the long history of capitalism has so much stress been put on maximized national output – on generalized economic growth as the necessary precondition for social and political reforms. Naturally, this economic growth ideology has been absorbed by the bulwarks of industrial and technological power in capitalist nations – the major manufacturing companies and banks – and it is reflected in an insatiable hunger of corporate management for dynamic growth of sales and earnings. On a scale unmatched in the past 300 years, the representative capitalist business firm now plans and projects for the future, and it does so in a growth-maximizing framework. Profits are primarily for researching and marketing new products and for plowing back into further expansion, not for dividend payouts. The key management function in modern, large-scale business enterprise is tied to constant improvement of profits, cash flow, and overall sales, just as the viability of the capitalist political economy itself depends upon unceasing economic growth for delivering the goods to masses of citizens who are persuaded that the way to the good life is through accumulation of consumer durables.

Present-day growth ideology grew out of the experience of the Depression of the 1930s. The ruling circles of Western capitalist societies perceived that any repetition of the economic stagnation of that sorry decade would rekindle dangerous social tensions and anti-capitalist politics. Realization of the necessity for the state to play a new, expanding role in maintaining respectable levels of income, purchasing power, and employment coincided with the birth of Keynesian macroeconomics in 1936.[7] Aggregate economic analysis of inherent tendencies of free market economies toward periodic slowdowns and slumps, with depressed profit levels and rising unemployment, was seized upon as a rationale for government policies that would promote a high and sustained rate of economic growth, measured in terms of undifferentiated gross national product (GNP).

While the composition of GNP has retained significance for some purposes (usually having to do with perfunctory acknowledgment that, 'as we all know, the quality of life is the ultimate standard of human welfare'), enormously greater emphasis is now placed on increasing the GNP *regardless of its structure*. Any increase of final output tends to be desirable: it adds to GNP, reduces unemployment, and buttresses private business sales and profits. By the same token, redistribution of wealth and income remains an admirable ethical sentiment, to be sure, but its importance is strictly secondary; after all, if only the 'GNP pie' (or 'le gateau national', or 'de nationale koek'

– to illustrate how ideas are diffused internationally when they are useful to top policy and decisionmakers) is kept expanding year after year, everybody becomes better off as his personal slice grows in size, even if his share of the total 'pie' does not change or decreases somewhat.

Thus was the Keynesian Revolution of the late 1930s transformed into a system-reproducing mechanism. The most conservative implications of the new economics were selected out by Western power structures and their economists. Keynes himself might have speculated about the need to 'socialize investment' in private enterprise economies in order to attain full employment, and several of his contemporaries might have employed his analytical tools for essays in public planning of investment, production, and job creation. But there proved to be very little 'effective demand' for that kind of Keynesianism. Instead, the radical implications of Keynes' economics for the role of the state, income distribution, and economic planning were by-passed in favor of a basically conservative doctrine: government would sponsor economic stability by assuring high levels of purchasing power in the economy, which in turn would undergird markets for private investment, production, and marketing activities.

From this setting emerged the fullblown ideology of economic growth, neocapitalist style. Aggregate and unrestrained economic expansion came to be offered as a solution to broad social problems – unemployment, poverty, inequality of income and property holdings, shortages of public goods, and deadening, alienating forms of work and consumption. Social goals could now be cast in terms of aggregate production targets, or a GNP growth rate which by definition *any* increase in output helps fulfil. With growth as the foremost priority for political leaders and their economic advisers, it would be a simple matter to de-emphasize the competing claims of subsectors or micro-centers of the society – they would all eventually obtain what they needed from the society's expanding economic surplus, its 'growth dividend'. The serviceability of such aggregate economic growth, with its trickle-down benefits for everybody at some (unspecified) time in the future, for ruling classes and political elites in capitalist nations should be self-evident. It preserves social tranquillity while imposing few strains on the existing structure of production, property ownership, economic rewards, or the political interest groups and social classes that support and depend upon them.

The environment debate offers us an illustration of economic growth ideology in action. The way the economics profession in general has responded to *Limits* provides a case study of how growth practitioners tear problems out of their historical and social contexts, isolating them from the forces that produce and shape them, and with which they continuously interact. Problems are not treated as integral parts of ongoing social processes but rather as separable, individual issues. Thus, the bulk of conventional, responsible criticism of *Limits*, and similar ecological hypotheses, turns out to be at best partial and at worst pedantic and contradictory.

Most of the economists' objections to *Limits* fall under five general themes.

(1) *Limits* assumes geometric (or, as mathematicians call it, exponential) growth rates of population, industrial production, and food output, that sooner or later must encounter resource constraints – shortages of natural resources (land, minerals, metals, fossil fuels) and deterioration of environmental resources as pollution begins to wreak havoc on water and air. Through systems analysis the complex interrelationships among population, food supply, industrial production, natural resources, and pollution are also traced through, to determine how they feedback on one another and under what circumstances we may expect economic-ecological harmony and stability or a convulsive collapse of either population (from starvation or disease), industry (from resource scarcities), or agricultural output (from pollution or demographic pressure) so that the world system grinds to a halt.

Economists reply that the multiple relationships or feedback loops in *Limits* are underspecified and that several of them are incorrect. Birth rates, for instance, are not a function of only the other factors in the *Limits* model (the level of industrialization and the food supply) but also of death rates. The connection between industrial production and pollution is less stringent than *Limits* takes it to be; even with existing technologies much of today's pollution could be avoided with little loss of output. Nor will growth of production simply use up material resources until supplies dwindle to zero. The day of exhaustion will be put off by economizing: as a resource becomes scarcer its price will rise, furnishing an incentive to use cheaper materials in its place. Furthermore, the dismal forecasts in *Limits* might be altered if logarithmic functions were introduced instead of exponential functions. Finally, demands for capital goods and raw materials may be overstated, since the *Limits* projections of manufacturing production are built upon unrefined, physical GNP. Consequently, the model discounts possibilities for expanding the output of intangible services, and it disregards the fact that at least in Western countries some 75 percent of the increases in output per manhour are attributable to productivity advances, and only one-fourth to actual increases in capital equipment (including land).

(2) Projecting present growth rates exponentially into the future is a hazardous business. Many of the underlying data that prevail at present can, and probably will, shift over time, and the longer the time span the greater the possible change. English economist W. Stanley Jevons in the 1860s predicted that British coal reserves would run out in the twentieth century, and in 1889 Sir William Crooks foresaw mass starvation within six decades because of exhaustion of Chilean nitrates; both men arrived at such conclusions by extrapolating contemporary use rates against then known supplies. Lately, British editor Norman Macrae has suggested that projection of the trends of the 1880s might have shown the cities of the 1970s buried under horse manure. Then too, we are told, no one can really be certain that economic growth will go on interminably.

(3) *Limits* rules out social adjustments – man's capacity for adapting himself to new conditions. It would be unrealistic to expect people to sit idly by as disaster creeps up on, and then overtakes, them. Man, who has been wonderfully innovative for centuries, will not suddenly become inert. The social transformations of which he is capable can render any long-term model useless. Society and politics are not easily fed into a computer. (This argument is now applied to population growth. Industrialization has led to voluntary fertility limitation in the West, and we are advised to anticipate a similar result as psychosocial and ecological parameters begin to affect all of the world's people.)

(4) 'There is no technical reason why technical advance should not continue indefinitely', writes Hagen,[8] in pointing to the most commonly heard criticism of *Limits*. The epochal importance of technological progress is virtually denied in the *Limits* analysis of economic growth. Technology, economists insist, can be expected to help us control pollution, step up food output many times, and create *new* resources

(as well as save on inputs of existing resources), just as it has in the past.[9] The public appears to be unaware how cheaply pollution can be abated by means of techniques now known (for the United States, it would require 'only' the annual increase in its GNP over the next few years, according to some estimates). There seems to be even less appreciation of the fact that new resources are invented thanks to economic and technological growth. Natural gas was not a resource 100 years ago, and petroleum was hardly used. Men have quite literally created hydroelectricity, aluminum, plastics, and synthetics, and soon the 'breeder' reactor and controlled nuclear fusion of hydrogen may permanently solve our energy needs. As for the food problem, consider the historical progression in agricultural productivity, from the two to the three-field system, to crop rotation and cultivation of legumes and selective livestock breeding, to fertilizers, hybrids, and now the miracle wheat and rice strains of the green revolution. And if man ever discovers the secret of photosynthesis he might be able to produce all his food on a few square kilometers of good land.

(5) *Limits*, a number of economists have protested, ignores the problem of poverty in both the industrialized and the underdeveloped countries. Economic growth, more than anything else, will be required for the elimination of poverty, undernourishment, and lack of life's bare necessities. Even for the world's wealthiest nation, 'growth is the only way in which America will ever reduce poverty', say Passell and Ross.[10] Without sustained economic growth there can be no social surplus for dealing, not only with poverty, but with pollution, urban agglomeration maladies, and other dilemmas arising from scarcity, or insufficient access to society's resources.

What strikes the historical and ecological-minded social scientist is not that these five themes are wrong – some may be, others are not – but that they either focus, one at a time, on variables with which economists can feel comfortable (prices, resource supplies, productivity ratios, pollution as an external diseconomy, properly specified mathematical functions) or criticize *Limits* on grounds that tend to undermine the basis of their own economic methodology. To attack *Limits*, economists must now affirm how quickly and unpredictably data can change over time, a warning that would, if faithfully obeyed, shake the foundations of their own neoclassical, partial equilibrium analysis. Likewise, they are now forced to place considerable stress upon the prevalence of complex and subtle interrelationships among economic and noneconomic variables in 'the real world', an unusual posture for most economists and one which will surely cause long-time observers of the economics profession to rub their eyes in disbelief. To hear some reputable conservative economists express grave concern over poverty should also come as no small surprise: the zero-growth stationary state idea is 'an upper income baby', one such economist asserts. 'They've got enough money, and now they want a world fit for them to travel in and look at the poor.' A more liberal-oriented economist echoes that objection to *Limits*: 'Can you expect billions of Asians and Africans to live forever at roughly their standard of living while we go on forever at ours?'[11] – these comments, from men who heretofore have not exactly distinguished themselves for their outspoken concern over the plight of the Third World or the sickeningly lopsided distributions of income in their own nations and internationally.

To repeat, what is at issue here is not the honesty or the sincerity of mainstream economists but their inconsistent social analysis and their selective invoking of economic dynamics and noneconomic influences on human behavior. This is why their salvoes against *Limits* must be interpreted as largely ideological. The same can be said of their strictures against using exponential growth rates for estimating the future. They themselves are primarily responsible for discovering and popularizing 'compound interest' economic growth, and prescribing it as the surest path toward national development and human satisfaction. It is with remarkable ill-grace that growth-preaching economists should disparage the growth projections in a work like *Limits*, whose professed aim is to inform the public at large about the perils of unchecked, exponential increase in environmentally disruptive forces, especially economic growth.

To sharpen our understanding of how economic growth ideology can triumph over genuine *social* science, we might look more closely at some specific criticisms of *Limits*. Growing shortages of any natural resource, economists maintain, will be accompanied by a rise in its price for users, who will be stimulated to search for a cheaper substitute. The market economy therefore carries its own automatic solution to raw material scarcities, a solution which several economists claim (erroneously) that *Limits* overlooks.[12] But would private business firms view this profit-threatening increase in the price of a critical resource input with equanimity merely because economists tell them that it is a signal to seek a less costly alternative? Firms utilizing such materials as essential inputs count on their continued availability at some specific range of prices. The struggle of capitalist industry to ward off resource cost increases is fraught with explosive political implications, both in domestic energy policies inside Western Europe and North America and in the foreign policies of these rich nations toward Third World countries on whose minerals, metals, and oil they are becoming more and more dependent. Yet even if we are satisfied with the answer that 'this is a noneconomic issue', the social rationality of the market price system is not rescued. For in natural resources we are not dealing only with matters of short-term relative scarcity but with possible exhaustion of this planet's irreplaceable endowments. The economists' vaunted price system is anything but a reliable social measure of resource abundance. The discovery and exploitation of a rich pocket of ore may drive prices down, but it hardly means that there is more of the resource than there used to be. On the contrary, it means that the total accesssible supply of that resource is being depleted at an accelerated rate.

What, next, of the faith of economists (and so many others) in technological ingenuity to save us from resource depletion, pollution, and food shortages? Do not *Limits* and other such exercises in futurology assume that technologies and resources grow at linear rates while everything else grows exponentially? (*Limits*, at least, does not.)[13] Leaving aside the possibility that high technology production is actually rendering us more dependent on a handful of diminishing resources (a possibility that the US Department of Commerce considers realistic),[14] and forgetting for the moment that these vital resources – aluminum, cobalt, chromium, tungsten, nickel, among others – come mainly from Third World regions, we would still face another unpleasant fact: every technological change has social side-effects, some of them unforeseeable. By now it is a stock judgment to point out that the green revolution in many poorer countries has created at least as many problems as it has solved; it has dangerously escalated social and economic inequality, for example.[15] *Limits* itself draws attention to the effects of urbanization, the twin-brother of industrialization.[16] The ills of modern-day urbanization show that there are some problems not susceptible of purely technological solutions – criminality, drug abuse and alcoholism, congestion, uglification, loss of space and privacy, as well as imbalanced food diets, disappearance of open land, the breakdown of the natural controls and regulatory mechanisms built into the Earth's ecological cycles, and the social disintegration and morosity which seem to be ineluctable consequences of uncontrolled economic growth. Reliance on nuclear power technology to meet skyrocketing energy demands in Western countries is also giving rise to some truly nightmarish dilemmas, namely, how to dispose of and store radioactive wastes. Scientists estimate that nuclear wastes will have to be kept under surveillance for thousands of years; the materials are so hot that they remain in a constant self-boil for an indefinitely long time. The complications connected with disposal via burial are now so great as to have set off hunts for alternatives like shooting the wastes off into outer space or sinking them beneath the Antarctic ice sheet – exotic suggestions that again promise at least as many problems as solutions. (The irrelevance of such tremendously high cost technologies to 75 percent of mankind is another factor that might be noted here.)

Once technology is viewed in this light, it becomes irrelevant to charge the authors of *Limits* and other ecologists with technological Malthusianism. While Thomas Malthus may have assumed technology more or less stagnant, ecologically and socially concerned people see modern technology as intrinsically dynamic – and all the more menacing as a result. Exponential technology in private hands bids fair to aggravate our crises faster than it helps reduce them to manageable proportions. Mushrooming consumer 'product development', thousand-fold increases in pollution sources within a decade or two, pesticides that permeate biological food chains to the extent that they would continue to be transmitted from one generation of animals to the next even if their use were halted immediately, not to mention a drastic multiplication of the power of the state itself in information control and surveillance of private citizens – all of this we owe to technology. Do we need yet another round of technological progress to resolve them, and then perhaps another . . .?

Finally, of course, advocacy of faster economic growth for enabling us to deal with pollution, resource and food deficits, and poverty is the ultimate resort of conventional economists – the linchpin of their ideology. An expanding 'growth dividend' is the very first requirement for coping with social problems; it is of greater importance, and it is far more readily available, than institutional changes in society, including the distribution of income and power. (This is theme No. 5, described above.)

Responding in 1972 to a typical statement of this growth doctrine by Passell and Ross, *The New York Times*' Anthony Lewis wrote:

> ... the economists' claim that economic growth is the way to a more egalitarian society is in fact a transparent fraud ... Anyone who thinks the American pattern of economic growth is a path to social justice could not have lifted his eyes from a textbook for years. The result is no different if one looks at the distribution of wealth among nations. The disparities between the richest and the poorest are getting worse, year by year. Growth is a cop-out, a way of avoiding the real social and moral issue of equality. Facing the ecological truth about our planet should help us to face those issues at the same time.[17]

One of these issues, as Lewis notes, is the staggering disparities in income between the affluent industrialized nations and the rest of humanity (not to mention the gaps between rich and poor inside the developed nations). If *Limits* is correct in holding that sustained economic growth cannot go on indefinitely, then clearly the only way the lot of the poorer nations' people can be improved is through a global redistribution of wealth, income, and consumption. Several orthodox economists, who had never until quite recently been known to consider income distribution as a hot social issue, now criticize *Limits* for desiring to stop growth and thereby freeze the poor in their poverty and misery. (Here too the charge is incorrect: *Limits* does face this issue, at least as squarely as many economists.)[18] Environmentalists should have no hesitation in arguing the issue of income inequality. Once again, the mainstream economists themselves have lauded economic growth as a *substitute* for income redistribution. As American economist and former Kennedy administration adviser Walter Heller has put it, 'When the cost of fulfilling a people's aspirations can be met out of a growing horn of plenty – instead of robbing Peter to pay Paul – ideological roadblocks melt away, and consensus replaces conflict.'[19]

The proposition is as fallacious socially as it is untenable ecologically. For all the impressive quantitative economic growth in the West since 1950 income differences remain grotesque, with the top five percent of income receivers in most capitalist nations getting as much income as the lowest 35 percent combined, and the upper fifth getting six or seven times as much as the poorest fifth. If growth has given higher money incomes to many of those at the bottom of this economic ladder, it has done so at a terrible social cost – by reinforcing unequal personal enrichment as the motive force in the economy. Consciousness of this kind of self-perpetuating economic inequality cannot be permanently suppressed, for reasons cited by the great English economic historian R. H. Tawney over 50 years ago:

Hence the idea, which is popular with rich men, that industrial disputes would disappear if only the output of wealth were doubled, and every one were twice as well off, not only is refuted by all practical experience, but is in its very nature founded upon an illusion. For the question is not one of amounts but of proportions; and men will fight to be paid £30 a week, instead of £20, as readily as they will fight to be paid £5 instead of £4, as long as there is no reason why they should be paid £20 instead of £30, and as long as other men who do not work are paid anything at all.[20]

But not only does modern economic growth generate human dissatisfaction and frustration as fast as it satisfies the demands of household consumers. The belief that such growth will furnish us with the means for dealing with problems like environmental destruction falls into two fatal traps.

One of these traps is the treadmill effect of a growing, free-market produced GNP, which creates disproduct or disamenities as an integral part of *the very same process* by which it turns out more 'goods' (whatever the degree of imbalance between 'goods' and 'bads' during any one period). An increasing number of social scientists share the view that undifferentiated growth produces diseconomies or disamenities faster than amenities.[21] I have already referred to some of these costs of economic growth – *negative* GNP like the frightening deterioration of urban life, rising noise levels and nervous tensions, esthetic degradation, reduction of living space and nearby countryside, a mounting incidence of industrialization-related diseases (cardiovascular ailments, strokes, ulcers) – as well as environmental pollution. A further paradox is that statistically measured economic growth not only is accompanied by disamenities, it is augmented by them. GNP totals register both the value of cigarette sales and the costs of treating associated cases of lung cancer and heart disease. The rising expenditures on pollution control are also added into the GNP and thus increase it. Our celebrated economic growth, then, may result in no real addition to our social wealth if we subtract from GNP, as we should, all of these (growing) costs of producing it. And it could well leave us even worse off if we make another necessary deduction from it: an annual deduction analogous to the capital consumption allowances by which private business firms estimate the portion of their plant and equipment used up and worn out in the course of the year. This new deduction would take into account depletion of natural and environmental resources – the irreproducible original capital of our planet.

The other trap is that economic growth appears to strengthen those institutions that are the causes of our social contradictions in the first place. Such growth, and its capital accumulation exigencies, create power positions that henceforth direct and guide the income-generation process *and* the economic surplus that flows from it. Ruling classes and political elites, who possess action-initiating power in the spheres of investment, pricing, technological innovation, and the division of labor used in the production process and in private and public bureaucracies, cannot be expected at some later stage to relinquish control over the resulting 'growth dividend'. Those who held decisive power at the beginning of the income-generation process can be expected to utilize any eventual surplus to further their own goals, not those of liberal economists and other sincere reformers. And the more robust the growth, the larger the growth dividend likely to be appropriated by ruling classes to consolidate their own privileges. If these goals and privileges *are* the main causes of our social ills (including environmental decay), and if economic growth does fortify them, then it is obvious that more growth is not the way to the better society.

The foregoing does not mean that no environmental improvement measures at all can be hoped for within the institutional context of contemporary corporate capitalism. It merely implies that the burgeoning economic surplus will be diverted toward environmental, and other broadly social, ends only insofar as those ends happen to coincide with the priorities of the ruling elites. Additionally, to the extent that public spending may be necessary in order to clean up the environment and prevent further despoliation of it, our options appear to be *narrowing* as economic growth speeds up. Crushing evidence on this point is offered by a statistical study of economic growth in Western Europe during 1960-1970, by European Economic Community economist Michel Albert. Nations which had the highest rates of economic growth (in GNP) were the ones that turned in the worst performances in the public sector (output of collective goods such as medical and health facilities, low-cost housing, mass transport, and so forth). Outstanding in this perverse achievement were France and Italy. Why? Simply because vigorous economic expansion in present-day capitalist societies, featured by a bilateral monopoly in key labor markets and chronic wage and profit, cost-and-price spirals, is generally accompanied by stronger inflation. To combat rising prices, governments follow the path of least resistance: they cut back on public outlays that are not 'instruments of reinforcement for industrial power' (with France again the leading example). Result: an increasing tendency for faster economic growth to retard public investments that benefit the mass of citizens, especially lower income families. 'It must be admitted', concludes Albert, 'that the rise in the rate of real growth, far from favoring improvement in the area of collective equipment, can, under certain circumstances, act as an obstacle and even lead to its relative regression, not only in the short term but over the intermediate term.' Conversely, because the Western European experience particularly since 1965 shows that the more slowly growing nations maintained better growth rates in public spending, 'it might be easier for the countries of the [European Economic] Community to achieve rapid development of their collective equipment with a moderate growth . . .'[22]

Albert did not include the United States in his survey, but there the situation was essentially the same. The post-1966 inflation triggered by Vietnam war expenditures led straight to the liquidation of many Kennedy-Johnson 'great society' social programs, and the 'growth dividend' stemming from accelerated economic expansion from 1962 to 1969 was returned to middle and upper income classes through a series of tax cuts, rather than spent on public goods.[23]

Spaceship Earth is indeed a closed system, though we may not know exactly where or when its boundaries lie. In the words of British scientist Robert Allen, 'If you're going to jump out of an airplane, it's better to have a parachute than an altimeter'.[24] *Limits*' own virtue is in predicting ultimate outcomes, and it is imperative to demonstrate these truths in striking fashion, because human behavior will have to be adjusted to them. We have as well a moral obligation toward unborn generations not to rely upon discoveries and technical innovations before they have been made to push back the limits to growth. We might hope for a future extension of these limits, but it would be reckless and irresponsible to take such extensions for granted. Technological reductionism and faith in the growth dividend represent gambling with the wellbeing of future generations, nothing less.

Yet if orthodox economists were dedicated *social* scientists, they would find ample room for criticizing *Limits* and other partial analyses of the environmental crisis. Readers of *Limits*, for instance, will find no mention of war and the arms trade, imperialism and neocolonialism. The global nature of the model prevents an examination of the *structural* problems of this Earth and above all its division into two parts, one rich and the other poor. Naïve growthmanship, on the other hand, supposes that the poor three-quarters of the world can become as rich as the wealthy quarter by following the same avenues of economic growth and by copying (or integrating themselves with) multinational corporations, homogenized urbanization patterns, a manipulative technology, and a 'rational' state bureaucracy that carries out social and political 'modernization'. But these are the very institutions that have so brutally divided the world's people, worsened international income inequalities over the past 25 years, and tightened the dependency of poorer, peripheral areas on the industrial centers. The metropolitan nations and regions of the world treat all the rest as virtual colonies that supply cheap raw materials, foodstuffs, and labor power and as 'developing' markets for their own 'high mass consumption' goods. No doubt, this international division of tasks makes for sizeable increases in global output, but it depends upon vast imbalances in political influence and military might, and it reinforces the hierarchical structure of the international economy and a mode of production that is careening toward ecological calamity.

This is why environmental and political logic are intertwined and inseparable – and why both are the negation of corporate capitalist logic. Capitalism, more than ever before, is based upon dynamic growth of sales and profits, powered by complex technologies that allow expansion-minded corporations to break out of (what for them are) the narrow confines of the natural ecological cycles (land, air, water). Their feverish drive for ever-expanding markets is accompanied by an increasing propensity to pollute unlikely to be checked simply by levying selective effluent taxes on the worst polluters. The impact of imposing environmental costs on private businesses, either by taxing them and/or forcing them to invest more in pollution control equipment, will likely be to increase prices to final consumers, decrease sales and profits, or retard growth itself (probably some combination of all of these, depending upon the demand and productivity characteristics of the particular industry). Moreover, even if pollution per unit of output should be, say, cut by half, a doubling of GNP thanks to uninterrupted growth would leave us right back where we started, only this time with a more seriously depleted resource stock and a worse disposal problem to which pollution control equipment too would have contributed.[25] One way or another, any diversion of profits and capital investment from the pursuit of growth is a violation of the competitive rules of the game of big business, and it will undoubtedly be resisted as such.

So politics and environment are at one. Modern capitalism, and possibly Soviet communism too, fuse them. To regard them otherwise is to divest them of their critical social content and to lapse into piecemeal solutions that border upon elitism or right-wing reaction. Behind exclusively 'anti-population explosion', conservationist 'return to nature', and 'quality of life' ideologies lurk repressive political measures that are sure to be proposed as the only workable and practical solutions to imminent demographic and environmental disasters. Add to this the 'corporate responsibility' movement in the United States and former European Economic Commission President Sicco Mansholt's campaign to build up a stronger Common Market political arm and planning agency to meet the ecological challenge, and one has two poor candidates as forces for the radical transformation of society in North America and Western Europe. All of these diverse ideologies and movements tend to seduce people away from more fundamental social crises. They take a problem of political-economic structure and priorities and convert it into a plea for technocratic reform and individual morality.

Man's exploitation of the environment is a function of a massive, quantum jump in economic and financial concentration, technological virtuosity, political centralization, and communications media saturation in relation to the private citizen. In other words, man's exploitation of the environment is a function of man's exploitation of man and woman. Ecological issues and answers are interwoven with those of social change and human liberation.

The first step, then, is not to elevate defense of the environment over all other elements in this social whole. Environment must not be preferred to the root issues of poverty and inequality, personal alienation and despair, imperialism, war and the arms race, racism and sexism. All are structurally linked. They can be unravelled only through political organizing, and formulation of unified social and economic programs aimed at laying down foundations for a new society. Only then will we be able to move away, *in an egalitarian manner*, from our present system of highly unequal conspicuous consumption of goods and of prodigiously wasteful, capital-intensive production. To achieve an ecologically sane, economically rational society will require *growth*: growth in human services, not a further proliferation of privatized gadgets. It will likewise call for a sweeping redistribution of income, rural and community redevelopment, experimentation in intermediate technologies, and some decentralization of decisionmaking power in economic production and governmental administration.[26] Popular education and agitation will be needed to move toward genuine democracy, where people regard themselves as potential contributors to the social good – as citizens rather than as consumers.

How to take the first small steps in this direction is the political question looming up before us all.

NOTES

1. D. H. Meadows et al, *The Limits to Growth*, New York, Universe Books, 1972.
2. *The New York Times*, 27 February 1972.
3. E. E. Hagen, 'Limits to Growth Reconsidered', *International Development Review*, June 1972, pp. 10, 12.
4. W. Beckerman, 'Economists, Scientists and Environmental Catastrophe', *Oxford Economic Papers*, November 1972, pp. 327, 333.
5. S. F. Singer, 'Population and Pollution: do we dare to grow?' *The Nation*, 27 November 1972, p. 528.
6. P. Passell, M. Roberts and L. Ross in *The New York Times Book Review*, 2 April 1972.
7. The seminal publication was J. M. Keynes, *The General Theory of Employment, Interest and Money*, London, Macmillan, 1936.
8. Hagen, 'Limits to Growth Reconsidered', p. 13.
9. *Ibidem*, pp. 12-14; Singer, 'Population and Pollution', pp. 527-531; and for similar Soviet optimism, N. Timofeyev-Ressovsky, 'The Biosphere is 10 Times Richer than we think', *UNESCO Courier*, January 1973.
10. P. Passell and L. Ross, 'Don't Knock the Trillion-Dollar Economy', *The New York Times Magazine*, 5 March 1972. This theme is elaborated in the Passell-Ross book, *The Retreat from Riches: Affluence and its Enemies*, New York, Viking, 1973.
11. These two wellknown American economists are quoted in *The New York Times*, 27 February 1972.
12. See *Limits*, pp. 54-67 for a discussion of this point.
13. *Ibidem*, pp. 54, 64, 86 and chapter IV.
14. See 'The US Searches for a More Realistic Trade Policy', *Business Week*, 3 July 1971, esp. pp. 65-67, and Peter G. Peterson (Special Advisor to President Nixon on international economic policy), *The United States in a Changing World Economy*, Washington, US Government Printing Office, 1971, Vol. I, pp. 10-11 and Vol. II, pp. 15-16.
15. See H. M. Cleaver Jr., 'The Contradictions of the Green Revolution', *Monthly Review*, June 1972, summarized in *American Economic Review*, May 1972, pp. 177-186.
16. *Limits*, pp. 145-150. In Paris the average speed of a public transport bus was 14 kilometers per hour in 1952, and 8 in 1970, or the same speed in 1970

as a horse-drawn omnibus in 1900: a perfect illustration of one benefit of a technological innovation (the internal combustion engine) being cancelled out by another, uncontrolled use of it (in the private automobile). On main thoroughfares of some other French cities – Marseille, Lyon, Strasbourg – bus speeds have fallen as low as 5 kilometers per hour. See Claude Julien, *Le suicide des démocraties*, Paris, Grasset, 1972, p. 75. In the United States the automobile explosion has virtually annihilated surface public transportation as an effective and dependable means of getting people from one destination to another. According to a Gallup survey, *The New York Times*, 30 May 1971, 81 percent of American workers travel to and from work by automobile. In West Germany, the second most car-using country of seven surveyed, only 45 percent of workers commute by car.

17. *The New York Times*, 6 March 1972. Lewis was commenting on the Passell-Ross article, 'Don't Knock the Trillion-Dollar Economy'.
18. *Limits*, pp. 178-182, 191-195.
19. W. W. Heller, *New Dimensions of Political Economy*, Cambridge, Mass., Harvard University Press, 1967, p. 12. See R. B. Du Boff and E. S. Herman, 'The New Economics: Handmaiden of Inspired Truth', *Review of Radical Political Economics*, August 1972 for an analysis of the ideology of 'Keynesian' economists in the United States.
20. R. H. Tawney, *The Acquisitive Society*, New York, Harcourt, Brace and Howe, 1920, pp. 42-43.
21. See E. J. Mishan, *Technology and Growth: the price we pay*, New York, Praeger, 1970 and *The Costs of Economic Growth*, London, Staples, 1967.
22. Commission des Communautés Européennes, *La croissance du coût des infrastructures et des équipments collectifs et le problème que pose leur financement pour un développement harmonieux de la Communauté*, par M. Albert (Conférence Industrie et société dans la Communauté Européenne, Venice 1972), esp. pp. 14-19 [my translation RBD]. In West Germany, 'When he took office in 1969, Mr. Brandt pledged himself to reform. But . . . reform, in such pressing fields as education, costs money, and the need to dampen inflation dictates that federal, state, and local governments spend less. Broadly speaking, this contradiction has been overcome by putting off reforms.' J. A. Morris Jr. in *International Herald Tribune*, 20 March 1973.
23. See Du Boff and Herman, 'The New Economics', pp. 56-62.
24. Quoted by Edward Goldsmith in *Le nouvel observateur*, 19 June 1972, p.v.
25. See Barry Commoner, *The Closing Circle. Nature, Man, and Technology*, New York, Knopf, 1971, chapters 9, 10 and 12; R. England and B. Bluestone, 'Ecology and Class Conflict', *Review of Radical Political Economics*, Fall-Winter 1971, esp. pp. 39-51; and Jason Epstein, 'Can We Afford Sliced Eggplant?', *The New York Review of Books*, 5 April 1973.
26. See J. Hardesty et al, 'Political Economy and Environmental Destruction', *Review of Radical Political Economics*, Fall-Winter 1971, reprinted in W. A. Johnson and J. Hardesty (eds.), *Economic Growth versus the Environment*, Belmont, Cal., Wadsworth, 1971; also 'A Blueprint for Survival', *The Ecologist*, January 1972.

12. Developed and underdeveloped: a radical view of constructive relationships

AVROM BENDAVID

The deep and serious questioning of fundamental tenets of the industrialised 'developed' world – of which Du Boff's contribution to this anthology is an excellent example – leads quite naturally to a re-examination of the principles of development being exported to the 'underdeveloped' (or 'developing' or 'less developed') world. This chapter continues the re-examination by picking up the thread where other recent writers have left off. It is found that previous attempts to define development have failed to recognise that this term necessarily encompasses culturally defined values exclusively, especially at the operational level, and this failure in turn may account for much of the dismal performance of development assistance in the past. The implications for development assistance in the future are vast. These are examined, and a new basis for constructive relationships is proposed.

There is, particularly in the Western world, a growing wave of self-examination reaching deep into the structure of values that for so long have been taken for granted. Basic premises of life in the industrialized countries are being questioned, and some are coming under serious attack. Among them is the desirability of continued economic expansion, with its inevitably attendant environmental deterioration; heightened complexity and anxiety in the conduct of personal affairs; growing welfare disparities; increasing concentration of power in the hands of managers of economic empires; and increasing specialization upon which economic growth feeds but which leads to an alienation from the natural and social environment, and perhaps ultimately from the self.

In the past few years the development assistance establishment has been undergoing an intensive soul-searching as well, partly influenced by the introspective fashion of the times, but clearly stimulated by a well-founded disappointment with the fruits of its labors over the past two decades or so. Here, too, the most fundamental assumptions are being questioned: Is development to be thought of only in terms of economic growth? What about 'nation-building'? The alleviation of human misery? The distribution of global power? Do the 'developed' countries really have the development knowhow to provide technical assistance uniquely suited to the problems of the 'underdeveloped' countries? Are they really interested in bringing about a world of truly independent developed countries? And more. The discussion has reached the point where the entire question of development assistance is up for reconsideration.

Increasingly, there is recognition of the fact that the societies that have emerged in the affluent countries, and their associated values and life-styles, are merely that – i.e. what has emerged, for better or for worse – and are not necessarily superior to or desirable over possible alternatives.[1] This has vast implications for a reconsideration of constructive relationships between the developed and the under-developed.

THE NATURE OF UNDERDEVELOPMENT[2]

When the missionaries set out to save the souls of peoples with different religious traditions, their objectives could be conceptualized with relative ease. Simply a matter of bringing people from a less desirable state, nonbelief, to a more desirable state, belief manifested in observance of the prescribed code of living and religious rites. To achieve this would require an education to certain attitudes and skills, and provision of the requisite minimal physical facilities.

Development assistance to the Third World, encouraged by the successes of reconstruction aid after World War II, was undertaken with a similar kind of approach. The approach has proven to be much too simplistic, is probably responsible for much of the failure, and is the source of so much of the confusion over the matter to this day. George Axinn has stated it succinctly: 'The assumption was that development, undefined but identified through indicators, mostly economic, proceeds along a uni-dimensional scale; and that all of the world's nation/states – if not the multiple sub-cultures within them – could be rank ordered by some formula from the "most developed" to the "least developed".'[3] To this should be added that the very choice of the world 'developed' makes clear that value judgements are involved, and that the former is the desired situation, to be sought by 'less developed' peoples. Today, our understanding of the matter has been broadened so that we include not only – and perhaps not even primarily – economic indicators. But the basic conception of development as a process through which a society moves from a given (underdeveloped) socioeconomic condition to another, more desirable (developed) socioeconomic condition as a consequence of the provision of education to the appropriate attitudes and skills, of technical assistance, and of basic infrastructure, remains essentially intact.

The problem begins with the attempt to define the developed socio-economic condition; that is, the state to or toward which development and development assistance seek to advance the relatively underdeveloped. For it is by virtue of certain societies being there already that they are thought to have the knowhow to instruct others. Moreover, implicit in the definition is the key to understanding the nature of underdevelopment.

We begin with a flat assertion. There will never – can never – come a time when every person on Earth will have a command over material resources equal to that of the average American or even West European today. It should be clear that this does not mean merely that the underdeveloped countries cannot expect to reach per capita GNPs in the $3,000-$5,000 range. It means as well that they cannot possibly seek ultimately to reproduce either the 'socio' *or* the 'economy' part of socioeconomies already in that range.

Owing to this, as well as to the fact that human misery does not seem to have declined much even in underdeveloped countries 'on the move' by the usual criteria, many have argued for a redefinition of the objectives of development. They suggest that rather than pursue a 'Western model', the poor countries should look elsewhere for their definition of what it is to be developed. Most authors, however, have fallen into the trap of seeking a universal meaningful definition of development, and this has resulted in their doing the looking – and the finding – on behalf of the countries they have prejudged as underdeveloped.

Dudley Seers, in his ground-breaking and now famous address to the 1969 SID World Conference,[4] for example, first argues that neither the experience of the developed countries nor governments of the underdeveloped countries can provide the values which define development meaningfully. He finds that, 'Surely the values we need are staring us in the face . . . if we go back to the question . . . what are the necessary conditions for a universally acceptable aim, the realization of the potential of human personality?' The implicitly universal answer which Dudley Seers provides is income, 'Enough to feed a man, [and] also to cover basic needs of clothing, footwear, and shelter.' Furthermore, 'Another basic necessity, in the sense of something without which the personality cannot develop is a job.' Moreover, 'Equality should [also] be considered an objective in its own right.' And finally, 'The fulfilment of human potential requires . . . adequate educational levels, freedom of speech, [political liberty], citizenship of a nation that is truly independent, both economically and politically, in the sense that the views of other governments do not largely predetermine his own government's decisions.'

While we may wish to grant the universality of the aim of 'fulfilment of human potential', can the interpretation of this aim, and therefore the requirements for it, be other than subject to variation depending on culture? It is indeed puzzling that Dr. Seers first insists that development involves value judgements, then dismisses the values implicit in the development of the West as well as those proclaimed by Third World Governments, and lastly asserts on behalf of the underdeveloped peoples what the correct set of values should be, rather than concluding that the matter should be left for them to decide. Before exploring this critical issue, it may be instructive to observe how a representative of a poor country 'looks elsewhere'.

Mahbub ul Haq, of Pakistan, delivered a much-quoted address to the International Development Conference in the spring of 1972.[5] In it he declared that, 'To conceive of the objectives of development in terms of Western living standards or to focus on the widening gap between the rich and poor nations is not meaningful at all . . .' Haq suggests that 'the developing countries have no choice but to turn inwards . . . and to adopt a different style of life more consistent with their own poverty . . .' Development goals should be 'elimination of malnutrition, disease, illiteracy, squalor, unemployment, and inequality'. Underdeveloped countries should not merely be concerned with 'how much is produced, but what is produced and how it is distributed'. It is clear that 'this requires a redefinition of economic and social objectives . . . of truly staggering proportions.'

By whom? Why does anyone outside the nation in question have to define social and economic objectives? Why is it that the reformers themselves – both from the rich and from the poor countries – always find that previous definitions of development were lacking, and proceed to offer new definitions that supposedly differ only in magnitude in their applicability among the myriad cultures of the Third World? On the strength of what superior insight can it be claimed that this time development *really is* being defined correctly? Why do development's most eloquent spokesmen continue to agonize over and probe this issue when their own statements have shown – perhaps without their realizing it – that it is in fact a non-issue for international purposes?

The plain fact is that it is not a definition of development or its objectives *per se* that is being sought. What is being sought is a *workable* definition of development in order to salvage from the failures of the past – failures owing largely to then current definitions of development objectives – a continuing justification for development assistance and the presence of the development establishment. Development assistance based on these new definitions is destined only to bring about further disappointment. For the definitions will be workable only in development assistance terms, conforming to the development assistance establishment's frame of reference, and not reflecting the values and realities traditional and relevant to, and definable only by, the individual societies in question.

Is equality – economic or social – the same for the Indian as for the Swede? Is human dignity the same for the Syrian as for the American? Is employment the same for the Englishman as for the Thai? Yet the givers of development assistance in any form cannot provide it without being in agreement with its intended use. And this means that development objectives and the techniques for achieving them (implicitly, the nature of underdevelopment as well) must conform to a framework of logic deriving from their – the giver countries – perception of the world and attitude-value systems. They know no other reality.

The question can and has been raised whether those who provide development assistance have succeeded in eliminating unemployment and poverty, in promoting equality and fulfilment of human potential, in controlling what is produced and how it is distributed sufficiently at home to be instructing others in these tasks. But quite apart from that, their accomplishments at home have been exclusively and inextricably bound up with their history of economic growth. So that, for example, the development establishment[6] cannot conceive of accomplishing even the most limited development objectives outside a framework of modernization and expansion of the commercial economy.

To cite but one case, most writers on the subject, including the two quoted above, see employment as one of the keys to equality, particularly economic equality, human dignity, and to the elimination of poverty (however that is defined). This means more jobs. Inevitably, then, the underdeveloped countries must look to economic growth, particularly industrial growth. Other interpretations of equality, human dignity, even poverty, and certainly other means of achieving them – if necessary under local interpretations – simply do not exist in reality as they perceive it. And while the development establishment is intellectually flexible to a surprising degree, and becoming more so, more jobs still means an entire complex of priorities, human resources, concepts, attitudes, infrastructure, institutions, and so on, modelled on patterns perhaps slightly modified, but essentially originating in the experience of the developed countries.

Thus, even when the givers of development assistance try to turn away from a definition of development in their own image, even when they try to be responsive to more limited, meaningful, and relevant development objectives such as those called for by Seers and Haq, they cannot really succeed. At best, the effect of the redefinition will be to replace a preconceived 'destination' of change with a slightly less presumptuous preconceived 'direction' of change. In the end, the development assistance givers will directly or indirectly promote and impose a concept of 'developed' defined in their own image.

And what is the status of this image? There is serious doubt that those who people the poor countries, given any real choice, are interested in emulating the rich socioeconomies. There is even a good deal of agonizing in some recipient governments over the conflict between what they have been given to understand as necessary progress, and the maintenance of traditional life and values. More significantly, a great debate now rages *within* the industrialized countries concerning whether they are really developed in any but a narrowly and culturally defined economic sense, if that. Their basic value systems, even the striving for improved technology and greater economic efficiency, are now being questioned. Many in the 'advanced' countries have begun to turn to more 'primitive' societies for guidance to improve the quality of life, and even for superior types of technology. The debate will not be joined here. Suffice it to say that the fact that so much uncertainty prevails even at home must disqualify any overall definitions of developed, development, or underdevelopment based on the experience of the so-called developed countries.

Now it cannot be denied that there is human misery of the most basic kind in the world, and it would be inhuman not to provide help, when requested, to alleviate it. But if chronic problems of basic human misery, as any society views it in its *own terms*, can be alleviated without significantly altering the pattern of life, there remains no basis for labelling that society 'underdeveloped' even if it produces but $20 per person per year in its commercial economy. Development assistance, however, almost by definition seeks to get at basic human misery, if at all, not directly but by bringing about fundamental social change. Social change may be necessary, may be sought, and may come about in a society, but in any case it must be viewed by the outside world only as change, with neutral value, not as 'development' or 'progress', which are synonymous with some supposedly universal standard of 'improvement'. Development assistance is, in fact, most accurately described as 'foreign social change assistance'.[7] The givers of this assistance promote a transition from an existing societal form to one more like their own by tampering with the social, cultural, political, and even spatial fabric of the recipient society in the belief that this constitutes absolute improvement.

What is the nature of underdevelopment? There really is no such thing except as a society, by truly looking inwards, may wish to define it for itself. 'Development assistance', whether requested or not, constitutes nothing less than interference in the social evolution and historical self-determination of others.

THE NATURE OF CONSTRUCTIVE RELATIONSHIPS

If the foregoing holds, if the common distinction between developed and underdeveloped is but a figment of the imagination of the industrialized countries promoted with missionary zeal, and if development assistance is seen as more correctly labelled 'foreign social change assistance' with all that this implies, then any moral or practical justification for a continuance of official foreign assistance programs and the enormous establishment set up to promote and execute them would seem to evaporate.

The specter of representatives of the governments of a rich and a poor country collaborating to alter the social fabric of the latter is shocking indeed. Yet it is a quite regular occurrence, despite the fact that it represents a level of interference in the culture and traditions of the poor nation that would never be tolerated in the rich. It is made possible by the fact that both governments feel that the rich country can provide something that the poor country needs. They are convinced of this, despite the lack of substantial evidence, because the members of both governments have, effectively, been to the same school.[8] They do not come together as equals, but as developed and underdeveloped. The basis for a truly constructive relationship is missing.

The basis for such a relationship – one based on equality and mutual respect – can be expected to evolve only if and as international programs related to development are phased out. This means that all official undertakings founded upon a developed-underdeveloped, advanced-traditional, or any other implicitly superior-inferior relationship would have to be brought to a close.

Having gone this far, development assistance may, in net, have created more misery than it has eliminated. In many cases, the very dynamics of change which it has promoted have fostered conditions of human misery nonexistent previously; and this would seem to confer upon the development assistance establishment the responsibility to attempt to mitigate the situation it has created, and certainly not to exacerbate it, as it withdraws. Moreover, development assistance has become so intertwined with the economies of many countries, that to pack up suddenly and leave would create nothing less than a calamity for millions of people, and probably result in the downfall of not a few governments.[9] For these reasons, the withdrawal and dismantling would have to be accomplished carefully, perhaps over a period of several years. But it is a necessary first step, and ultimately it must be total.

For there really is no justification for governments or international bodies to be in the foreign social change assistance business. We have all – donors and recipients alike – become so used to the institutions and practices of this business as a fact of life, that the suggestion to discontinue it may at first seem more incomprehensible than is justified. After all, there are many businesses in which governments do not engage even if requested. And once it is generally accepted that governments do not provide foreign social change assistance, it is unlikely that others will request it. Governments are not, for example, in the foreign architectural improvement business; and the governments of poor countries do not, as a rule, ask the governments of rich ones for assistance in improving the general physical and functional qualities of their structures.

The concept and practice of development assistance must be written off as perhaps a well-intentioned error born of post-war confidence and exuberance. There must arise a general recognition of the fact that no society, no foreign expert, no multinational organization can provide the guidance for achieving a society that is in any general sense superior to or 'more developed' than any that already exists.

It must be stressed that a clear distinction should be made between disaster relief and development assistance. The former is temporary emergency aid aimed at directly alleviating acute human misery resulting from natural catastrophe, war, and the like. It is given in a selfless and humble spirit, and is not designed to 'develop' the recipient. Caution must be taken, however, not to generalize from the humanitarian motives of disaster relief operations a rationalization for development assistance through the process of coming to view selected characteristics of the so-called underdeveloped countries as chronic disasters.

Poverty, inequality, unemployment, human dignity, and other culturally defined terms must be interpreted as appropriate by any society (as may the means for dealing with them), and may figure in a program of self-development (which may or may not include economic expansion) it may wish to undertake. If so, it must be left to design and undertake this program in its own way, and within the limitations of its own resources. In its worst and perhaps most common form, development assistance not only instructs nations in 'overcoming' these problems, thereby tampering with their creative social processes, but promotes solutions beyond the capabilities of their own resources, thereby ensuring an erosion of their sovereignty.

Development assistance is a rather recent phenomenon. But nations have been learning from each other throughout recorded history. For the most part, and with the exception of cases of military conquest, societies have influenced each other through trade and other forms of personal contact. Over time, some have had major influences on others. Architectural styles, systems of government, technology, crops, even culinary arts have been exchanged. Introduced through personal contact, however, they usually passed through an extended filtering process before being generally accepted. In the course of this filtering process either the society gradually adjusted to the new idea or the new idea itself underwent modification to meet the requirements of the society. And of course, many new ideas introduced this way never won acceptance. In any case, as a result of the filtering process, serious disruption generally was prevented.

Times have changed, and rapid communications are nearly universal. Still, there is a vast difference between the introduction of new ideas in the course of normal relations between equal societies, and the virtual imposition overnight of entire complexes of institutions, technologies, attitudes – indeed, ways of life – that results from the operations of the development assistance establishment as it is known today. Accordingly, the disruption has been staggering, and one is hard put to justify the high price that has been paid by those affected.

We propose a movement toward constructive international relationships, based on equality, self-respect, and mutual respect among societies, regardless of relative per capita GNPs or differences in cultures and values. This means that development assistance is replaced by a non-system in which ideas are exchanged as people and goods flow back and forth among nations. George Axinn has proposed the notion of 'iterative reciprocity' which 'suggests continuous growth and benefit to each participant',[10] a concept that may be relevant in this context. With official development assistance programs terminated, individuals and private organizations may still be called on to contribute their skills to the solution of specific problems in countries lacking those skills,[11] but they must go not as experts in development, as representatives of any government, or as part of any official development program.

If this new posture can be assumed; if the rich countries can shake off the conviction that they have the gospel and the compulsion to spread it; if the Third World societies can see themselves for what they are – burdened with some urgent human problems to be solved, but not 'underdeveloped' or worse yet 'developing'; perhaps truly constructive relationships can be established that will contribute to the development of both the rich and the poor, each in accordance with the priorities of their own unique social systems.

NOTES

1. Indeed, it is widely agreed that these societies will have to undergo traumatic alterations before the end of the century merely to survive. This on grounds of resource depletion and environmental contamination alone.
2. We wish to stress at the outset of our argument that our remarks are addressed to an audience assumed to be sincerely interested in what it understands as the development of underdeveloped countries – and anxious to take steps to promote it without regard to the effect on the power or economic bases of the developed countries. Any other assumption would make this essay and all others like it superfluous exercises in a vacuum of unreality. This they may be, but discussion of the matter will be left for other forums.
3. George H. Axinn, 'Linkage Versus Intervention – An Alternative Strategy for International Assistance in Rural Development', paper presented to the Annual Meeting of the Rural Sociological Society, Baton Rouge, Louisiana, August 1972, p. 2.
4. The quotations in this paragraph are all from Dudley Seers, 'The Meaning of Development', paper given at the 11th World Conference of the Society

for International Development, New Delhi, 1969, under the original title 'Challenges to Development Theories and Strategies'. Reprinted by the Agricultural Development Council, Inc., New York, 1970.

5. The quotations in this paragraph are all from the excerpt of the address which appeared in the May 1972 *Newsletter* of the Society for International Development, p. 4. The precise citation given there was: Mahbub ul Haq, Senior Advisor, Economic Department, World Bank, in an address (expressing his own personal views) to the International Development Conference, Washington, D.C., April 20, 1972. For purposes of clarity, the order of the quotations has been changed, but their intent is presented intact.
6. Despite the fact that the 'development establishment' is international, its members – whether development assistance scholars, givers, or receivers – are schooled in the ways of the industrial countries to the point where it makes little difference what their actual cultural origins are insofar as their basic 'mental set' with regard to development is concerned.
7. 'Social change', in this context, must be understood in a broad sense. It includes, for example, measures that facilitate the maintenance of power in the hands of groups that might otherwise not succeed in maintaining it, or the preservation of an unpopular nation-state form, as well as the more readily apparent forms of social change.
8. There exists another possibility, of course. Namely, that collaboration of the type described is undertaken because it serves certain personal interests. But to consider this in the present context would take the discussion further afield than is desirable.
9. This alone provides an excellent indication of the nature and failure of this kind of assistance.
10. Axinn, 'Linkage versus Intervention', p. 16.
11. In an earlier draft of this essay the following passage appeared: 'The condition which justifies a form of official assistance by those capable of providing it is that in which large numbers of people are chronically plagued with malnutrition and poor health to the point where pondering development objectives in any other sense is to them an irrelevant exercise.' It has since become clear that even bilateral or multilateral health and birth-control programs addressed to the limited objective of enabling a society to determine its own course and with its own means by helping it to free itself of the ravages of chronic human physical misery of the most basic kind invites a measure of interference and experimentation that may well ultimately prove more damaging than helpful. However, this is a prime example of an area in which individuals or organizations have much to contribute, when requested, as may international agencies that do not relate such assistance to the notion of development.

SELECTED REFERENCES

Axinn, George H., 'Linkage Versus Intervention – An Alternative Strategy for International Assistance in Rural Development', paper presented to Rural Sociological Society, Baton Rouge, 1972.

Haq, Mahbub ul, address to International Development Conference, Washington, D.C., 1972. Excerpt in Society for International Development *Newsletter*, May 1972, p. 4.

Hochschild, Steven F., 'Technical Assistance and International Development: A Need for Fundamental Change', *International Development Review* supplement 'Focus Technical Assistance', 1972/4, December 1972, pp. 15-20.

Jacoby, Erich H., 'The Dilemma of the World Bank', *Rapport*, the Review of the Swedish International Development Authority, III, 7, November 1972 and *Development and Change*, IV, 3, 1972-1973.

Meadows, Donella H. *et al.*, *The Limits to Growth*, New York, Universe Books, 1972.

Myrdal, Gunnar (abridged by Seth S. King), *Asian Drama*, New York, Vintage Books, 1972.

Seers, Dudley, 'The Meaning of Development', New York, Agricultural Development Council Inc., 1970 (reprint of address given at the World Conference of the Society for International Development, New Delhi, 1969, under the title 'Challenges to Development Theories and Strategies').

Weintraub, A., E. Schwartz, and J. R. Aronson, *The Economic Growth Controversy*, White Plains, International Arts and Sciences Press, Inc., 1973.

13. Ecological viability: political options and obstacles

W. BURGER

'The simple life is a minority taste.'

John E. Sussams, *The Ecologist*, July 1972.

Burger's contribution picks up the thread of Du Boff's concluding remark on the political dimension. The prospects for improvement seem slim if societies do not succeed in incorporating the environmental realities of a resource-limited earth into the political arena. The author points out the dangers of dogmatism and ideological prejudice and reviews numerous fallacies pertaining to the environmental crisis and its solution. Finally, the author emphasises public opinion formation as the mechanism for enabling the political process to meet the ecological challenge. The correspondence with views expressed by Tellegen may be noted.

I. INTRODUCTION

'If we plan remedial action with our eyes on political rather than ecological reality, then, very reasonably, very practically and very surely we will muddle our way to extinction', thus reads paragraph 162 of the 'Blueprint for Survival'.[1] But the opposite strategy may also produce unattractive results. If we attempt to plan remedial action while ignoring political reality, very surely we can only do so with the help of some absolute central power which may, very reasonably, transform our society into an ecological paradise with, very practically, a fair chance that it will have the social and cultural characteristics of a forced labour camp. No-one would like to opt for either of these two strategies. But what alternatives do we have?

L. J. MacFarlane, in a comment on the 'Blueprint' writes, 'the failure to give any thought to the vital political implications and aspects of the "Blueprint" seriously mars . . . the chance of its being accepted or applied.'[2] To call this limitation a failure is not, in my opinion, quite justified. To develop ideas about future, more responsible, societies is as necessary as to explore the political possibilities for the realization of any such better society within, or departing from, a particular socio-political and cultural reality. On the other hand, over the last few years much has been written about how bad the present situation is and how much better it could be in the future, but very little about the political road that might lead to such a better future. It is high time to lessen this disproportion in order that many valuable ideas on the environmental issue may not be doomed to political sterility.

I shall attempt in this paper to explore some political aspects of the ecological problem and also its possible solution, taking the socio-political and cultural framework obtaining in the highly industrialized world as my frame of reference. The paper first charts the most common lines of thought on the ecological situation, distinguishing some implicit and explicit ideological elements. An estimate is then made of the political significance of these elements in terms of their potential to ward off or perhaps to hasten the physical collapse or socio-political bankruptcy of the industrialized world. The last section deals briefly with vital aspects of public opinion formation that may enable the political processes to meet the ecological challenge.

II. POLITICAL JUDGEMENT AND IDEOLOGICAL PREJUDICE ABOUT ENVIRONMENT PROBLEMS

II.1 *A paradox: a long-term and yet urgent problem*

In *The Closing Circle* Commoner refers to what he sees an 'an air of unreality about the environmental crisis',[3] a perception which most people will experience regularly and which I consider of the greatest political significance. The air of unreality may alternate with a sense of urgency when we read about the disasters impending unless we act quickly. Objectively, the problem calls for immediate if not radical action, for determined efforts to introduce changes that will aim for, and in the long run will produce basic reforms.

That nevertheless the problem often has an air of unreality can be traced to the fact that we do not perceive the destruction of the environment as an immediate threat to our present wellbeing. Very few of us are so seriously affected in our daily lives that our usual, more direct problems in the spheres of personal relationships, work, career or family-life are pushed into the background.

Commoner places his main emphasis on the 'apparently hopeless inertia of the economic and political systems'.[4] We must indeed take very seriously the psychological tendency of people who are confronted by bigger problems than they feel able to handle, to show an escapist reaction and to leave the solutions to those whose job they feel it is to solve great problems.

The lack of reality about the ecological crisis thus seems to result from the disparity between its objective magnitude and the lack of felt urgency on the one hand, and on the other the discrepancy between what we objectively think should be done and what we feel is practically feasible. In accordance with a wellknown socio-psychological 'law', this ambiguity creates widely divergent opinions about policies to be followed, in which ideological prejudice and wishful thinking form major components. This being an important factor in political reality, it seems worthwhile to briefly inventorise the most common views regarding man and environment in the present phase of history.

II.2 *Two types of opponents to reform*

1. A decreasing but still influential strain of thought actually denies the need for any particular attention to the ecological issue. Its apologetic arsenal is basically that of liberal capitalism and classical economics. Although its adherents acknowledge the existence of some environmental problems, they consider that these should be handled as any other problem that accompanies social and economic progress. Temporary shortages of raw materials have so far been overcome by intensified exploration efforts and the introduction of substitutes. Science, technology and the market mechanism give modern society an enormous adaptive capacity which can be relied upon to keep pollution within socially acceptable limits. As long as we keep the basic structure of our developed societies intact, especially its main driving force of sufficient opportunity for free enterprise and healthy competition with government regulation to check temporary imbalances, nothing need be worried about. A no-growth policy is viewed as particularly dangerous since only growing economic surpluses can enable industrialised nations to make the necessary expenditures for pollution control and other 'social' expenses that may be deemed necessary.[5]

Many of these growth-optimists and defenders of the structural status-quo stigmatise the story of impending ecological catastrophe as being invented by the enemies of capitalism who want to undermine the belief that capitalism is a basically good system by which to organise production. To add to the confusion, however, there are also renowned social-democrats who ascribe the no-growth ideology to the middle and upper class origins of its protagonists, who have everything they want and now tell others that further growth is no longer possible, thus 'kicking the ladder down behind them'.[6]

2. Some opponents of liberal capitalism, especially orthodox Marxists, also show a belief in the blessings of industrialisation, technological progress and material growth, that has lost little of the strength it had

in the 19th century. Quite logically perhaps, these people see the recent growth of official attention to environmental control as part of a conspiracy, in this case of monopoly-capital or the exploiting classes. As a consequence of its choatic development the capitalist system now faces great problems; while avoiding a discussion of the real causes, capitalism seeks to postpone its own collapse by trying to ease the tensions created by its inner contradictions through slowing down economic expansion and technological progress. In vain, of course. The no-growth ideology should be strongly opposed, not only because it is immoral in view of the poverty prevailing in large parts of the world, but because it is a false solution to a problem which need not exist at all. Only after revolutionary transformation of our production relations will it be possible to successfully tackle the environment problem; until then we should not allow it to divert our attention.

Granting that we should not have any illusion that the environment issue will be taken advantage of by political interest groups if they see a chance to do so and whatever the merits of their views in other respects, the opponents to reform evidently bet heavily on future uncertainties. Can we really be sure that ecological disasters will be prevented either by timely discovery of new technological or economic devices, or by a timely collapse of capitalism? It seems rather a gamble to do little other than wait for history to follow its 'natural' or 'necessary' course and not show any inclination to allow, even temporarily, certain political changes of strategy or other purposive moves, if only for gaining time or as a safety measure.

II.3 *Four types of reformers*

Contrary to the optimistic opponents of reform, the 'reformers' though not necessarily pessimistic, have less confidence in the general validity of a particular political doctrine.

1. An important category of reformers believes and expects that the ecological crisis which threatens all human beings irrespective of nationality, race, class or religion, will at last bring the longed-for harmony to our societies and to the world as a whole. The impending disaster will convert sworn enemies into allies, make rival groups join in making the sacrifices necessary to avert the catastrophe.

If this view were merely naïve, to be unmasked as soon as reality claims its rights, it might be discarded as politically unimportant and therefore irrelevant to our analysis. But political danger lies in the fact that the expectation of a public consensus often is a mere expression of the demand that consensus should actually come about. If, for instance, underprivileged groups and countries refuse to line up for national or international programmes to prevent ecological disaster under terms stipulated by the ruling powers, moral indignation about their irresponsibility may then all too easily prepare the ground for holy wars. New socio-economic regimes aiming at no growth, for instance, may be forcibly imposed on us with the argument that we should no longer waste our time and energy on political issues which have become inappropriate in this critical phase of human history. Contemporary holders of political and economic powers will take upon themselves the 'historical, though not always pleasant' role of saving mankind (or Europe, the United States or East Asia) from ecological holocaust.

It is unnecessary to argue, on the basis of recent historical experience, that if such views become widely shared fascism will lurk around the corner. Paradoxically, because this strain of thought does not recognise any political problem it is politically very dangerous.[8]

2. In a similar rather a-political ideological frame is couched a more sympathetic, but I fear in its pure form rather ineffective line of thought often found among liberal reformers who also have an over-optimistic belief in the power of reason. But conscious of the danger of ready-made solutions imposed by power elites, they argue for societal reform mainly along educational lines: help the masses of the population to realise what we, as a collectivity, are doing, and each individual will regulate his private and public behaviour in an ecologically more responsible manner. The problem is thrown into the consumer's lap. Aren't we all consumers? If we change our demands, the producers will have to follow in order to meet them. If we limit our demands, economic growth and technological innovation will automatically slow down.

This argument reveals the inability of many well-meaning middle class citizens to see the rationale of large sections of the population who refuse to make sacrifices for the public benefit: not owing to 'labour class materialism' as is so often alleged, but because they feel they have been consistently denied a fair share of the national wealth for as long as they can remember. Consumers who wish major changes to be made in the range of goods offered to them will indeed face considerable short-term sacrifices. The production system will deliver new types of goods only after great delay and probably against higher prices. Furthermore, a buyers' strike intended to force down levels of material consumption will not rally much support among people who already consume little beyond their basic necessities – in most societies the majority of the population.

This does not mean that activities to increase consumers' awareness about harmful consumption habits will not have results. But structural reforms are unlikely except perhaps indirectly, once it is realised how limited is the consumers' control of the socio-economic process.

The two types of reformers discussed so far, whom we might call 'corporatist-centralist' and 'liberal-educational' respectively, both have their leftist counterparts.

3. Leftist centralist reformers are as convinced as those Marxists who would prefer to await a dialectical turn in the social history of the West, that an ecologically more favourable socio-economic system will never be established within the framework of industrial capitalism. But the strength of their conviction, combined with their sense of urgency regarding the environment problem, makes them ascribe similar views to large and rapidly growing numbers of people. These reformers predict that public debate about the ecological crisis will soon cause a major shift to the left among the majority of politicians in the Western capitalist welfare states, thus making these nations ripe for basic reform. The people who matter politically will gradually become convinced that nationalisation of the key industrial, financial and insurance sectors, curtailment of national and international economic competition, and a systematic policy for decreasing income differences, can no longer be avoided. This 'socialist revolution' will clear the way for an international policy on ecology that is centrally guided per country or world-region. Social unrest will be kept at a minimum as the price for the reforms in terms of reduced material wealth and consumption will primarily be paid by the higher and middle income strata.[9]

According to this model, political struggle that leads to important structural reforms is preconditional to an effective environment policy. However, its adherents often create the impression that this 'revolution' is at first confined to the political and cultural elites, who will then persuade the public at large to accept the new societal structures. It might be feared that in such a reform elitist and technocratic tendencies will be hard to control, so that conditions will be unfavourable for the long-term development of a more radical cultural and ideological reform movement that has its roots in the population as a whole. If this is a prerequisite to a democratic society of mature citizens, a 'revolution from above' may well defeat our ultimate social ideals: it may buy us a physically viable future but at the price of further postponing a really humanised society.[10]

4. Leftist reformers who consider this price too high and who fear that even a post-revolutionary society, if it is elitist and centralist may tend to develop corporatist or even fascist tendencies, form a fourth group which might be designated as 'radical ecological activist'. Social and political action at the base of society occupies a central place in the strategy of these reformers. They try to prevent anti-social or ecologically harmful decisions being taken by local authorities, government departments or political parties by organising those population groups who are most seriously threatened. They also lobby for the acceptance of alternative plans and projects that are developed with the help of experts, technicians and scientists who join their ranks.

Perhaps it is reasonable to say that the activists are less naïve in their thinking on societal change than the three other reform groups. They have no illusions about the rationality or goodwill of political and economic power-holders or official experts and authorities, whether in a capitalist or a socialist society, unless these are constantly and forcefully reminded of the immediate needs of particular groups of people, communities, neighbourhoods and regions.

At the same time the activists expect that continuous confrontation and the resulting conflict will produce increasing awareness about how society operates, not only among the population at large but also among people in leading and executive positions, and far more quickly than through educational action of the liberal enlightenment type.

They acknowledge the importance of education but place strong emphasis on its philosophy and ideology which, in their view, should in the first place form people who know when, why, and how to be effectively disobedient. Such a philosophy should ultimately guarantee the effective exposure and counteraction of manipulative practices by persons in power positions who may pervert positive results obtained in the regular political process.

Diagram 1 summarises this classification of main trends of thought on the politics of environmental control and the necessity for societal reform.

Diagram 1.

	'The problem will take care of itself'	'The problem is urgent and requires basic reforms'	
		Advocates of centralist reforms	Advocates of reform at the base of society
'rightists'	growth-optimists	the corporatist reformers	liberal educational mobilisers
'leftists'	revolutionary optimists	state-socialist reformers	radical ecological activists

III. THE BATTLE IS ON

III.1 *Political consensus decreases*

A wide array of opinions on the environment issue does not necessarily produce a low degree of political consensus. If particular views should dominate among a large majority of people and their leaders, other opinions would be doomed to political insignificance. But the opposite is the case. Until recently few people of whatever political conviction ever questioned the positive value of rapidly developing industrial mass production to provide consumer goods and durables in ever greater varieties and quantities. The majority were willing to accept that governments and industrialists, helped by expert technicians and economists, should direct and accelerate that development. Now, however, there is a tendency in all ideological corners of our industrialised societies to take a critical view not only of the production system as such but also of the values underlying our societies. The increasing awareness of wrongdoing, requiring a basic review of much that has been taken for granted in the past, naturally assails the various established economic, social and political institutions – government departments, planning agencies, labour unions, political parties of all kinds. These are often forced onto the defensive and then show greater readiness to seriously consider the need for increasing control of free enterprise, higher taxation and greater expenditure on government measures and programmes for pollution control, research into new forms of energy, greater care in planning and expanding industrial regions, etc.

Perhaps rightly, many would interpret these tendencies as a general shift to the left of overall political opinion. In my view, however, it is not realistic to expect that large working majorities of leftist political groupings will soon be willing to radically attack the ecological problem.

For the time being this shift merely seems to sharpen conflict and to increase antagonism.[11] This is not so much due to diverging views regarding the many technical and economic questions that need to be solved, however important these may be. It is more because of the realisation that, however the ecological problem is to be tackled, considerable sacrifices will have to be made. In spite of growing perception of future disaster, most people think that there is still time in which to settle differences of opinion about who is to make these sacrifices in the first place. And this is, I think, the main reason why we should prepare for a prolonged political battle over a very long-standing political concern: how to share the burden of our collective survival.[12] This crucial point will be elaborated more fully in the following section.

III.2 *The bill will be high: Who is to pay?*

An interesting estimate has recently been made of the enormous resources squandered in the United States for purposes of very doubtful or even negative social benefit under the present system of production and consumption.[13] However useful and necessary such estimates may be, in my opinion they are more pertinent to the question of which type of society (not necessarily less prosperous) we may conceive for the future, than that they provide much insight into the short and medium-term costs of establishing such a society. Indeed, the impression may be created that the costs of following the path to an ecologically more responsible society are negative. If we would stop being so wasteful we could increase our material prosperity and at the same time safeguard our ecological future. Although of course it is correct that we should try to finance environment control by reducing expenditure on things that are least useful or possibly even harmful, I tend to hold the view that, at least for the phase in which our societies are restructured on new production and consumption patterns, we should prepare ourselves for a drastic lowering of our material living standards. I cannot imagine such a restructuring without the following short and medium-term consequences:

- a politically-imposed decreasing profitability of that (large) part of existing 'conventional' capital which, in its utilisation, is wasteful of natural resources and detrimental to the environment;
- high investments to be made in new industrial equipment to enable ecologically more acceptable production processes;
- major expenditure for scientific research to develop alternative technologies;
- retraining and re-education of large sections of our labour force;
- unemployment problems through the contraction of certain economic sectors and branches of industry before sufficient new employment opportunities in others can be created.[14]

Countries embarking on such policies will need to face two serious secondary economic consequences:

- a dramatic shrinking of government budgets owing to decreasing tax income or, if this is not feasible, a sharp increase of taxation rates;
- a thorough revision of external economic relations by subsidising or terminating the export of non-competitive commodities and setting-up import barriers to some goods while liberalising imports of others. For example, natural products may be imported to substitute those synthetics whose production can no longer be tolerated at home; natural products grown at home may be made competitive to imported synthetics.

Economic retaliation will only aggravate the problems of ecology-minded countries or world regions which are forced to steer a course of greater autarchy in a world which, as a whole, is not yet ready to make short-term sacrifices in order to prevent longer-term ecological calamities.

The political consequences of costly ecological reforms must be tremendous. Is it unrealistic or pessimistic to predict that, at the outset, the privileged socio-economic strata in those countries that are determined to attack the ecological crisis will at best only support a policy which spreads the economic burden over the different population groups proportionate to their present levels of income?

But this would imply that people in the lower income stratum would have to suffer indefinite prolongation of their present condition of relative or even absolute poverty. Absolute increases of material wealth can no longer mitigate the felt injustices or large income differences.

H. C. Wallich has written: 'growth is a substitute for equality of income. So long as there is growth there is hope, and that makes large income differentials tolerable.'[15] In other words, the rapid pace of economic growth in the industrialising and industrialised countries bought them their relative social and political peace; but as we have since realised, this was done at the expense of nature's future capacity to sustain the human race. Now, for the sake of our future survival, to return to nature what we owe her at the expense of our under-privileged groups not only appears ethically unjustifiable but politically not very promising.

The alternative – during the phase of transformation – can only be to maintain the present material living standards of the low income stratum, or to allow even slight improvement, while sharply diminishing the affluence of the higher income groups. There may be immediate improvements in the quality of life for large sections of the population, but no-one can fail to see the political obstacles to such policies. As Peter Bunyard has phrased it: 'One cannot help but ask, how in a capitalistic materialistically oriented society like ours would the establishment sell . . . the idea of qualitative growth to its electorate.'[16]

III.3 The dim prospect of political halfheartedness: the crisis is exported

Given the state of affairs described above, there is a great probability that political struggle over the environment issue may be avoided as soon as it produces the first political defeats of sincere reformers. A political confrontation is necessary on such normative issues as western consumerism, mobilisation of labour and capital resources through the rat race called free enterprise and competition, and purposively maintained social and economic inequalities. If this does not earn the necessary support of the electorate, it must be feared that political leaders, whether leftist or rightist, will be tempted to transfer the aggravating ecological problem to the international political arena. Each country or each politico-economic bloc will desperately try to secure for itself a continued supply of natural resources and cheap raw materials from the Third World.[17] Major investments in the most severely polluting industrial sectors will be made in countries where widespread poverty and unemployment form a sufficient safeguard that the environment issue will not create much of a political problem.[18] The higher the investments, the stronger will be the pressures in the rich countries to maintain their control over the poor countries and keep them loyal to the interests of the investors. Little imagination is needed to foresee another round of imperialist military confrontations, not only between industrialised countries or their blocs but also with 'insubordinate' Third World countries. Such a course of events can only produce an absolute political, economic and moral impasse – even though the 'victory' of the rich industrialised nations over the rest of the world were not complete. For the world as a whole the ecological consequences will be disastrous whether or not large-scale wars are the result. The anticipation of such wars would cause an accelerating arms race which by itself would be totally incompatible with economic and industrial reform policies and would frustrate any attempt to diminish the squandering of raw materials and energy.[19]

The political attitude which acknowledges that measures must be taken to avert an ecological crisis but simultaneously stresses that they should not be allowed to basically change our socio-political and economic systems, differs only a shade from the shortsighted opinion that the ecological problem will take care of itself, if not in theory then at least in practice. Too much concern that the precarious balance of our economic or socio-political situation does not allow for radical policies can only result in such a slow change of the status quo that, in the long run, serious disruption along the lines just sketched will be unavoidable.

III.4 *The choice: radical democratisation or totalitarianism*

If the struggle for our ecological future is not transferred to the international political arena, it would signify that the industrialised rich nations recognise that they should primarily solve the problem among and within themselves.

From all sides appeals will be made for social and political solidarity in view of the emergency situation. Much moral weight will be added to this appeal by the fact that, under the assumed circumstances, the rich countries of the world do not want to make the poor countries pay the bill for the former's misbehaviour in the past.

But even after prolonged ideological debate will the leading elites and middle classes be convinced that solidarity should primarily mean solidarity with the underprivileged? Will they put their political weight behind a policy which over 10 or 15 years for instance, will drastically reduce income differences and other social injustices as a necessary precondition to popular response to a call for solidarity in undertaking ecological reform?[20]

The struggle over this issue will probably be long and exhausting: a highly critical period of social unrest, frequent political strikes, repeated electoral and parliamentary stalemates. The risk is that eventually these will not alternate with fruitful compromises and political breakthroughs in a direction that is socially and ecologically desirable but will cause a hardening of stands of the two major opposing parties and a complete political deadlock.

Conservatives who hysterically cry 'wolf' at the first signs of polarisation among the public, fearing that the forthcoming conflict might change the political status-quo, should be strongly opposed. In the name of peace and harmony they will probably try to maintain their own social, economic or political privileges. On the other hand, leftist dogmatists who reject compromise even when conflict has sufficiently matured that their fruits may be reaped, may invite the rule of violence to take hold of the political scene.

The longer a political deadlock lasts, the louder will be the calls for strong leadership, if not for one strong leader, turning the chances in favour of a reactionary takeover of power, very much as we have seen in critical phases of the history of Portugal, Spain, Italy and Germany between the two world wars, France during the Algerian crisis and, more recently, in many developing Third World countries which are unable to solve the problem of poverty.

Thus, not a victory of enlightened progressive thought in leading political and economic circles, as predicted by many of the more optimistic progressive reformers, but a victory of authoritarianism if not of brute violence, accompanied by the usual mystifying phraseology for popular consumption.[21]

III.5 *The method determines the outcome: fight for political consciousness*

What are the chances for a favourable outcome of the political struggle over the environmental issue? I have tried to show that the political and social conditions in our industrialised consumption societies tend to change many solutions to ecological problems that are advocated by different ideological circles into non-solutions, or to set in motion social processes that lead to what might be called 'political regression':

the formation of some central power which justifies the political means it utilises by the goal of saving our societies from ecological disaster. The reason for the strength of this propensity may have to be sought in the weakness of our democracies – not as reactionaries often use this term but in the sense that, in spite of mass education and other democratic institutions, we have not succeeded in creating a high level of awareness among the people about the structure, operation, virtues and defects of our societies. Western culture, like others, has been as successful in 'brainwashing' as in enlightening people. Moreover, the mass character of most of our institutions, whether in the sphere of social services, material production or culture, has seriously alienated people from their existential basis, their 'human condition'. Therefore, if we wish our societies to take the tremendous political hurdle of radically reforming our production system while avoiding totalitarianism, we have to ensure that people realise their cultural and political situation so that, as political force, they become sufficiently immune to those powerful weapons of the politicians: mystification and demagogy.

But we cannot wait for this cultural process to get under way before starting work on tangible measures with which to avert the more immediate ecological calamities. With few exceptions, the ecological measures that are now being planned or are already being undertaken in our industrialised countries under the pressure of established political forces can only be welcomed. But in view of the laggardness and conservatism of most bureaucracies, the numerous circumventions of laws and regulations, and the relative impotence of established political institutions in these and other respects, the political strategy which I term 'radical ecological activism' should have an important if not decisive role to play in averting major ecological disasters during the coming decennia. In several countries it has already produced substantial results, giving proof of great potential to heighten awareness among those directly involved in the actions and among the public at large about ecological problems and about ways in which official authorities and established politics tend to deal with them.

III.6 *Struggle for disorder, struggle for order*

From the previous section an important and for some of us perhaps consoling conclusion can be drawn: we must never rely on radical activism as the only strategy with which to safeguard our ecological, political and cultural future, just as it would be unwise to leave the urgent task of changing our political, cultural and economic aims and efforts to the established, regular political powers.

Radical activism alone would lead to chaos, unopposed ruling power would soon degenerate into absolute bureaucratic dirigisme, which would be hell. If radical activism does not want chaos and central planning and coordination does not wish to dehumanise society into a computerised robot, they need each other even though they are undoubtedly sworn enemies in daily political practice.

In other words, the best of all possibilities during the phase of transformation of our western societies is a process in which periods of sharp conflict alternate with periods of mutual accommodation in the relationships between different groups of the population, sectors of the economy or sections of the administration. Some of these will incline more to the side of the Establishment, others to the opposition. But their alliances should preferably shift rather than freeze, producing new power configurations which over a longer period of time, with or without political revolution, will allow for a process of social, cultural and economic development very different to that which the world has seen over the past few centuries.

Such a turbulent process, as I see it, is the sole guarantee that ecological goals will not be used to sanctify political means, i.e. that the physical survival of our societies will be bought at such a cultural and moral price that the whole effort may no longer be worthwhile.

IV. HOW TO WIDEN POLITICAL 'TUNNEL-VIEWS'. A CONCLUDING NOTE

It will appeal to reason that if public debate on the environment issue and its social and cultural ramifications is to achieve its goal of widening and ultimately destroying the 'tunnel views' of the entrenched political, economic and bureaucratic interests, it cannot afford to become dogmatic.

Although full elaboration of this theme would require another essay, it seems relevant to briefly summarise it here. Public debate will be tremendously important if we are to survive the political crisis that is hopefully ahead of us: hope based on the insight that a period of crisis is unavoidable if the environment issue is to be taken seriously in our over-developed western world.

The problem will be to cultivate a particular critical attitude towards our cultural values, science and technology, economic power concentrations (monopoly capital, conglomerates, multinational corporations), bureaucracies, and other nuclei of societal organisation; namely, a critical attitude which feeds on radicalism but rejects dogmatism and fanaticism. In the short run, we cannot simply discard our institutional and cultural heritage, however much we realise that it has created the bad situation in which we find ourselves. We have no choice but to keep it in operation for some time while we work towards its change and ultimate replacement by something better. This requires that at least in one respect we allow little room for compromise: we, as citizens of rich industrialised countries, must bring our political, economic and cultural power concentrations under control and break their monopolies. Although this in itself is a structural change, it means that the outward shape of our institutional framework need not change very much for some time to come.

For example: as long as we need large economic and bureaucratic organisations to provide us with our prime necessities, it is better to curtail their power, to prevent them from blocking necessary change, and even to involve them in long-term transformation of the structure of which they form part. Given the great complexity of our densely populated industrial societies, utter chaos and great human suffering seem inevitable with, again, great probability that reactionary forces will fill the power vacuum if we allow premature and precipitate destruction of our political, administrative and economic institutions. To get our own structures under control in order to reform them through a carefully managed revolutionary process, political debate must not only be intensified at all levels and in all corners of our societies, but a new conceptual arsenal must be developed by which ideological deadlocks may be prevented from blocking the political process. This is what I mean by 'avoiding dogmatism'. Although I would contend that compared to other political strategies the activist approach perhaps less easily falls victim to dogmatism – inter alia because it generally concentrates on concrete, limited, though 'exemplary' issues, thus sowing the foment of disobedience – tendencies of leftist dogmatism can nevertheless be observed, especially when activist movements become too strongly dominated by an established political or ideological force.

A new conceptual arsenal can, in my opinion, only be created during a debate on issues of public concern. However, it should be based on a methodical refusal to accept terms, concepts and slogans at their face value, whether these are used by our opponents or by our comrades-in-arms. General statements on policy issues should be made down-to-earth, qualified as to place, time and circumstance, in order to make them operational or to expose them as unworkable; again: in particular socio-historical conditions and time perspectives.

Most topical controversies in the discussion on man and environment suffer seriously from lack of specificity and of space-time qualifications of the stands taken, and therefore tend to get bogged down in inconclusiveness. Examples are: the discussion of growth versus no-growth, of the importance or unimportance of population control, of economic autarchy of countries or world regions versus international division of labour, of 'simple life' versus affluence as the prospect of people in ecological utopia, of industrial versus 'arcadic' economy, of pollution tax versus enforced pollution standards for production processes, etc., etc.

Slogans can fulfil a useful function in initiating the discussion of issues connected with the problem of man and environment, but the debate itself should aim at de-sloganising issues once they have reached the centre of public attention. In good Socratic tradition, we may thus help to prevent that mystification and false consciousness will once again predominate over real understanding. If in other respects we cannot be too optimistic about political consensus on how the ecological crisis should be handled, our politicians could perhaps reach agreement, at least on one general policy guideline: that in order to meet the political challenge ahead of us they should seek to ensure the highest possible political and social awareness of all people.[22]

How should this be done? By guaranteeing maximum openness in the process of economic, political and bureaucratic decision-making at all institutional levels of society; by developing sources of information about matters of great socio-economic relevance and facilitating public access to them by a liberal attitude towards extra-parliamentary political action; by demonopolising the mass media and liberating them from the grip of governmental and commercial interests; and finally and perhaps most important, by allowing scope for critical political education in schools – if only by reforming the teaching of history, geography, economics and civics – and by radically democratising schooling, in structural and pedagogical terms.

Many countries in recent years have shown promising achievements along some of these lines. However, anti-democratic forces with their wellknown phrases (that confusing the people would threaten our democratic institutions, that social and political stability is needed for development and that leadership and authority should not be further weakened) have managed to prevent or delay many new developments towards greater democratisation and political awareness.

NOTES

1. 'Blueprint for Survival', *The Ecologist,* January 1972.
2. L. J. McFarlane, comment on the 'Blueprint', *The Ecologist*, January 1973, p. 39.
3. B. Commoner, *The Closing Circle*, New York, 1971, p. 293.
4. *Ibidem*, p. 294.
5. Edward Heath, speaking at Nottingham University on 27 March 1973, declared: 'Economic growth gives us more resources to use for improving the quality of our environment . . . The new resources and the new technology now at our disposal, as the result of past growth, mean that we can now do more to make Britain a better country to live in. But if we are to continue to reap the rewards of growth and prosperity we must be prepared to . . . take the risks that will be needed to maintain it.' (quoted from *News Service*, Conservative Central Office, 27 March 1973).
6. *The Ecologist*, February 1973, p. 61, quoting a Labour Member of Parliament. Professor W. Beckerman, teacher of economics at the University of Southampton, declares that: 'I suspect that most of the people who are currently anti-growth are motivated by middle class judgements, and that if this were more apparent they would not receive such uncritical support.' Ibidem.
7. Professor W. F. Wertheim in 'Eclipse of the Elite' (valedictory lecture at Amsterdam University, March 1973) came very close to this line of thought when stating: 'Slowing down economic growth, slowing down population growth, a moratorium on technological development – these are the medicines since recently advocated by quacks not interested in fundamental change, in real cure'. [My translation, W. B.]
8. The conclusions to which centralist thinking can lead are demonstrated inter alia by Kenneth Boulding's ideas for keeping populations stable. Boulding proposes a system of licences for childbirth to be issued to each married couple. These licences may be bought and sold. Sanction against couples who have a child without a licence: a choice between a fine, a jail sentence or sterilisation. Boulding's proposal is sympathetically discussed by H. E. Daly in 'How to Stabilise the Economy', *The Ecologist*, March 1973.
9. A typical exponent of this strain of thought is Dr. Sicco Mansholt, former member of the European Commission. Also R. L. Heilbroner, 'Ecological Armageddon' in *Between Capitalism and Socialism*, New York, 1970, p. 283: 'Like the challenge posed by war, the ecological crisis affects all classes, and therefore may be sufficient to induce sociological changes that would be unthinkable in ordinary circumstances.'
10. On the need for extended public control of society and the 'different mold' in which capitalism 'will surely be cast' if it survives at all, see R. L. Heil-

broner, 'Growth and Survival', *Foreign Affairs*, 51, 1, October 1972, p. 150 ff.

11. Cf. Commoner, *The Closing Circle*, p. 271, and R. England and B. Bluestone, 'Ecology and Class Conflict', *Review of Radical Political Economics*, Fall/Winter 1971.
12. This in contrast to what Malcolm Stresser has stated: 'the startlingly cruel awareness of our environmental limitations has put the skids under almost every assumption of political organisation'. *The Politics of Government*, quoted in *The Ecologist*, February 1973.
13. J. Hardesty, N. C. Clement and C. E. Jencks, 'Political Economy and Environmental Destruction', *Review of Radical Political Economics*, Fall/Winter 1971, pp. 81-102.
14. Cf. by D. L. Meadows et al, *The Limits to Growth*, Report for the Club of Rome, Universe Books, New York, 1972, p. 175 ff; Commoner, *Closing Circle*, Chapter 10; H. E. Daly, 'The Stationary State Economy', *The Ecologist*, July 1972; England and Bluestone, 'Ecology and Class Conflict', and Colin Stoneman, 'The Unviability of Capitalism' in *Socialism and the Environment*, London, Spokesman Books, 1972.
15. H. C. Wallich, defending economic growth in *Newsweek*, January 1972; quoted by H. E. Daly, 'How to Stabilise the Economy', *The Ecologist*, March 1973.
16. Peter Bunyard, *The Ecologist*, March 1973, p. 112.
17. This would be nothing new insofar as the creation and maintenance of advantageous trade relations with the Third World has always been the essence of neo-colonialism. But the world market of raw materials which is rapidly turning into a sellers-market is already producing the first symptoms of an extraordinary and grave political concern in the rich industrialised part of the world. In 1972 Japan concluded an agreement with Iran for investments of around one billion dollars as development aid up to 1976; in 1973 the US concluded a new agreement with Iran for military aid and sales of arms for several billion dollars; early 1973 the US took the initiative for a conference of rich industrialised nations in an attempt to form a common front against oil-producing Third World countries; soon after the ceasefire in Indo-China in 1973 some big oil companies concluded an agreement with the Saigon government allowing them to drill for oil off the coast of South Vietnam; the role of the US in trying to maintain and strengthen 'cooperative' regimes in important raw material-producing countries is ever more openly defended with the argument of 'US interests'.
18. England and Bluestone, 'Ecology', p. 38, illuminatingly elaborate this tendency, which is already observable.
19. Cf. Colin Stoneman, 'Unviability of Capitalism', p. 60.
20. Cf. England and Bluestone, 'Ecology', p. 45 and Commoner. *Closing Circle*, pp. 207-208.
21. Daly, 'How to Stabilise the Economy', states pessimistically: 'Distribution is the rock upon which most ships of state including the stationary state, are very likely to run aground' (p. 95).
22. In the Netherlands in 1971, a proposal to provide funds for investigating the country's economic and financial power structure was voted down in Parlia-

ment. Commercial advertising for radio and television was maintained though a majority of the people, in a public opinion poll, had declared for its abolishment. In 1972 a Dutch Cabinet Minister, in a public speech, gave as his opinion that radio and TV bothered the people too much with political issues instead of 'sticking to their function of providing entertainment'.

14. Protection of the human environment and international law*

Another conflict of interests between rich and poor countries?

J. J. G. SYATAUW

* First published as 'Bescherming van het leefmilieu door volkenrecht. Nieuwe belangentegenstelling tussen rijke en arme landen?' *De Gids*, 134, 9/10, 1971.

International agreement and international law are vital if the nations of the world are to balance their actions with the realities of a resource-limited earth. The author examines the extent to which international law has succeeded in keeping pace with changing conditions and assesses its potential in this respect. The discussion of the relationship between resource use, competition, conflict and monopolisation shows similarity to the approach adopted by Van Benthem van den Bergh.

The problem of environmental pollution is not new; in some ways it is even old and stubborn, at least in international law. As long ago as the beginning of the 19th century treaties were concluded between states with the intention of regulating fishing and preventing the 'extermination' of the seas. In 1937, in his wellknown handbook on international law, Oppenheim discussed measures with which to prevent pollution of the oceans, which he referred to as 'a question not yet solved in 1937'. International law has thus long been concerned with problems of marine pollution and has attempted to define regulations and principles that would curtail actions by states and other subjects of law in this respect. In recent years, however, man has changed and damaged his environment to such an extent that the present situation differs considerably to that of 25 years ago. It might even be asked whether international law is still relevant to the issue.

Although environmental pollution is not a new problem, it has certainly become acute. Few issues, in fact, so kindle man's imagination and apprehension as that designated as environmental pollution, environmental protection, ecology, or related terms. The present worldwide dimensions of the problem cause it to be a subject of conflicting interest to different parts of the world: in particular between the rich, highly developed, industrialised nations and their poor and developing colleagues.

To what extent has international law, with its long experience in the struggle against environmental pollution kept pace with changing circumstances, and how can it meaningfully contribute to the struggle to maintain the ecological equilibrium?

THE 'GOOD OLD DAYS'

The great interest now shown in ecological balance and environmental protection is a very new phenomenon. Government measures at the national level and international conferences of statesmen and scientists are phenomena of the last 5 to 10 years. They followed a long period during which man felt little or no necessity for particular concern about the disturbance of the ecological balance which his own actions had caused. This applied especially to excessive population growth which increased the need for consumption articles and other goods, strong expansion of industry, and more intensive use of natural resources. Land, water and air appeared to be available in sufficient quantities, if not in abundance. Air and water were even considered as free or non-economic goods whose supply was inexhaustible and which might be used arbitrarily.

The air and water contamination which occurred even then was of little significance and was easily settled, whether by mutual consent or by the acceptance and application of rules based on custom. The classic example of intercession by international law and of its application to air pollution is the Trail Smelter Case, a dispute between the USA and Canada which was ultimately settled by arbitration in 1941. This concerned a complaint lodged by the US Government regarding the harmful action of sulphur-dioxide fumes emitted by a Canadian smelter, which caused damage to people and property on the American side of the border. In pronouncing judgment, the Court gave the now wellknown opinion that, under the principles of international law, no state has the right to use or to permit the use of its territory in such a way as to cause damage in or to the territory of another. This opinion has become the guideline for decisions in similar cases.

Sea and river pollution has long been a subject of international concern, not so much because of fear of direct violation of the human environment as of the threat posed by pollution to fish stocks and consequently to the fishing industry. To a lesser degree intervention has stemmed from the desire to protect birds and other animals living in or near the waters (including whales), while even then tourism demanded protective measures (clean beaches).

Measures taken in the interests of sea and river navigation also had less to do with fear of pollution than with navigational safety. Regulations regarding collisions on the high seas or in territorial waters, for example, were inspired more by questions of humanity (increased safety of passengers and crew) or of the assessment of liability (and the consequent obligation to pay indemnity) than by concern for contamination of the water by oil and other harmful substances.

The lack of any need to take stringent or radical measures suited –

or was even imposed by – prevailing opinion on the function of international law and the nature of international relations. The traditional view of international law left sovereign states with great freedom of action, the principal task of international law being considered to be to regulate and enable intercourse between nations. This being so, international law intervened in cases of abuse (such as pollution) only if they were excessive. Moreover, international intervention was hampered by the generally accepted principle of domestic jurisdiction, which was given very restricted interpretation, i.e. that a state need not countenance any international intervention in its domestic affairs by other states or by international organisations.

This means neither more nor less than that international law reflected the political views prevailing at the time: respect for the independence and the sovereignty of the states predominated over the interests of the international community which then showed neither solidarity nor unity. Moreover, these interests were not threatened by problems of environmental pollution to such an extent that drastic measures were thought necessary, whether or not by international law.

THE GREAT CHANGES

During the 1960s this situation underwent fairly radical change. Growing realisation that the longed-for scientific and technological progress might have strongly adverse effects for mankind, and that violation of the ecological balance might critically endanger man's existence, released a flood of emotion, interest and activity which caused the incidental, innocuous cases of water or air pollution to burgeon into a comprehensive problem of environmental pollution and environmental protection, concepts referring to human activities which directly or indirectly can create harmful change to man's natural habitat. Man's skill and activity has extended this natural habitat far beyond his immediate surroundings. 'Human environment' can now be understood to include everything that man can reach or influence and therefore comprises – in terms current in international law – the land and its subsoil, the air and outer space, and the water including the deep seas, the seabed and the subsoil of the seabed. The peculiar significance of each of these elements for the individual (for his direct physical needs and as the raw material with which to satisfy other needs) as well as in their own mutual cohesion (climatological, geographical or otherwise), clearly indicate the influence which they exercise on every human being, irrespective of country or nation.

It is understandable that prophecies of a threatening worldwide environmental crisis cause territorial boundaries to lose significance and people to begin to see the world as one entity. The ever more popular term 'Spaceship Earth' is very apposite in this respect. It is also frequently said that this comprehensive risk to our existence by environmental pollution has caused the continual contrast between the 'capitalist' and 'communist' worlds to lose much of its meaning and in fact to become almost senseless. In some ways these two blocs are growing towards each other, especially since they have been confronted with similar environmental problems. In both, realisation is growing that progressive environmental destruction will have catastrophic results for the living conditions of all people and in any event will negatively influence the standard of living. Irrespective of their different socio-economic systems, the economic activities of both have given rise to the detrimental byproduct of environmental pollution, thus showing the fallacy of the recently held belief that economic growth is the key to and magic formula of development, and that the economy must therefore be the basis of decision making. Both blocs now repeatedly proclaim that the remedy to the environment problem is to be found in calling a halt to the current economic and industrial growth rate.

Many arguments are cited in support of this opinion. For example, it has been calculated that unrestricted use of the world's natural resources, at the level presently applying in the west, will inevitably cause existing vital resources to become exhausted without any certainty that new sources can be tapped and exploited or old sources re-opened or replaced by substitutes. In addition to minerals and other raw materials, water, air, food, energy, recreation, etc. will become more and more scarce in the rich countries.

This coincidence of the interests of capitalist and communist countries places them (or most of them) as a group of rich countries in opposition to the poor and developing countries, whose development has in many ways lagged due to an insufficient growth rate. If the developing countries should be forced to stop or retard their growth process, the gap between the rich and the poor countries would not diminish but would remain the same or even become wider.

If such a situation by itself seems unacceptable for developing countries, they have many other reasons to consider it unreasonable and exploitative, an opinion that will make itself felt in the future when all countries will have to establish at the universal level (i.e. usually UN level) the rules of law with which these problems can be solved. This will be discussed further below.

The developing countries will produce many counter-arguments to show that they are being confronted with the necessity to restrain their economic growth at a most unpropitious moment.

In the first place, their standard of living is already low and their economic growth can hardly be called excessive. If environmental pollution is indeed caused by economic activities such as pollution and consumption, then it can easily be shown that their production and consumption are considerably lower than those of the affluent industrialised nations. On the other hand, they are possessors of much essential natural wealth (minerals as well as other raw materials) which is of great value to their development efforts. Furthermore, in contrast to many rich countries, they are so fortunate as to have such scarce commodities as clean air, pure water and unspoilt scenery, and do not yet experience pollution as an urgent problem.

Their most important counter-argument is that, as actual or potential polluters, they cannot be compared to the rich nations; in few metropolises in the developing countries can problems of garbage, stench, dust, noise, vibration and other so-called spillover effects of modernisation be said to be of serious dimension. This less unfavourable situation is not only due to a relatively lower degree of modernisation and industrialisation (car and industrial exhaust fumes do not yet form an insurmountable problem) but also to the fact that inhabitants of the developing countries seem more resilient and better able to cope with environment problems than do their more demanding fellow-sufferers in the west.

Finally, the lower technological and scientific level of developing countries means that their contribution to such environment-destructive activities as oil pollution, nuclear explosion and waste discharge is still quite negligible. In fact, there is no question of environmental pollution being caused by developing countries but rather of their being the victims of processes which the rich countries have usually set in motion. And this does not even take into account the terribly damaging effects of chemicals and other materials employed during hostilities as defoliants or water poisoners.

The risk of oil pollution, for example, is primarily caused by colliding and leaking oiltankers, most of which are owned by wealthy nations and which collect their valuable but dangerous cargo in the developing countries. The latter have come to realise that the hazards of oil transport must be checked. Their tendency to close their sea straits, territorial and other waters to oiltankers or to enforce strict regulations clearly illustrates their fear of the catastrophic results that oilspills may have for their peoples and their flora and fauna.

The testing of atomic and nuclear weapons is another activity that until recently was peculiar to the great industrialised powers. It is a particularly alarming thought that since the first big atom bomb experiments (Hiroshima and Nagasaki) the majority of above-ground tests have been held in areas (mainly seas and oceans) adjacent to developing countries and far from the rich nations. The protests held against the various experiments by the United States, United Kingdom, Russia and France unmistakenly demonstrate this alarm. Even China's less powerful tests, conducted in her own territory, gave rise to protest. The permanent danger of radiation is a risk that none of the developing countries wish to take, even though it is now claimed that the danger is reduced to a minimum owing to more accurate calculations by improved instruments.

The discharge of dangerous wastes into the sea is one of the new and major concerns of developing countries, particularly in view of the fact that they lack sophisticated instruments with which to do their own monitoring. Assurances that the waste, which is often radio active, is packed in absolutely leak-proof containers are not always convincing. The cases that have recently come to light of irresponsible and secret disposal of dangerous wastes in open sea understandably cause developing countries to wonder how often such disposals have taken place or are likely to be made in their surrounding seas. A law by which such activities may be regulated is clearly necessary.

The developing countries are of course also guilty of activities that are detrimental to the environment, as is well illustrated by the heavy deforestation and the gradual extermination of certain animal species (often for commercial purposes). Their major contribution to environmental change is their population growth which in some countries is of alarming proportions. However, population growth in itself need not seriously disturb the environment; the consumption pattern of the population concerned is equally important. It is obvious that a man's needs, consumption and pollution in a developing country by no means equal those of his materially better-off counterpart in a rich country. A recent UNESCO publication mentions that during his childhood an American consumes 20 times as much as an Indian and in the process causes 50 times as much pollution.

In view of the fact that at this stage of their development the developing countries are pursuing a higher rate of growth and that they nevertheless do not yet belong to the major polluters but rather to the victims of pollution caused by the rich nations, the exhortation to restrain or even to halt their growth process is neither opportune nor welcome.

This situation could change somewhat if a sharp curtailment of the economic growth of the rich nations could be coupled with a reasonable chance for continued growth of the poor countries. This would help determine the attitude that the latter will adopt when it comes to defining international legal norms with which to grapple with problems of pollution of the environment.

THE CONTRIBUTION OF INTERNATIONAL LAW

At the start of this paper we mentioned that international law has long been concerned with air and water pollution, an experience that will certainly be of benefit in attempts to solve present environment problems.

The present situation differs to the earlier one, however, in that everything indicates that the global environment has in reality become a unit which should always be considered in its totality. Although the economic or quantitative aspects of ecological protection often receive or demand the greatest attention (potable water, raw materials, the danger of unemployment), political, social, biological, ethical and other considerations are becoming more and more closely involved.

This totality is also given expression in the perceptible interdependence between the national and international human environments, which in no way implies that the nations concerned will not have different opinions about their respective interests. Regulations are therefore necessary with which the weighty and often conflicting interests may be reconciled in a manner that is both reasoned and impartial. Here too, international law can make a significant contribution in that one of its tasks has always been to regulate relations between states and other subjects of international law. Nowadays, the fact that international law is a useful weapon in any joint and coordinated attack on ecological problems is widely recognised. Lawyers in both national and international organisations are being assigned to study these problems in cooperation with other experts.

This estimable assignment is not without its own problems. The ability of international law to make satisfactory arrangements depends partly on many non-legal factors over which it has little or no control. It is thus unable to provide immediate answers to such fundamental questions as: will the population explosion hinder possibilities for development at national and international levels? does the present production pattern really have a destructive effect on the environment? should an immediate halt be called to economic growth in the interests of environmental protection? In other words, the strictly technical aspects of ecology are matters which international law has to leave to other scientific disciplines. But as soon as ethical aspects become involved, international law may be obliged to intervene in order to help find a just and generally acceptable solution. This is evidenced by its increasing albeit still hesitant intervention in the socio-economic development of the world community. It is expressed, for example, in the fact that international law deals with problems that touch upon the confrontation between rich and poor nations such as economic self-determination and claims to natural resources. To put it in another way, international law will be given general acceptance only when it fully appreciates and tries to reflect the political, social and other realities with which it is confronted in any particular case. Neglect of this essential condition has in the past caused lawyers and laymen alike to feel dissatisfaction with regard to international law.

In moulding rules of law, international law can make use of various methods, the two most important being the international agreement (or treaty) and custom. Both have their advantages and disadvantages. For example, to formulate law on the basis of custom is usually a slow process; moreover, it is extremely difficult to ascertain when and to what extent a custom is accepted and considered as binding. This is clearly a disadvantage in the urgent matter of environmental pollution.

In this respect, it is preferable for law to be laid down in the form of treaties, particularly multilateral treaties which are entered into at international diplomatic conferences attended by official representatives of many states; after all, the states are still the principal decision makers at the international level. The United Nations and its specialised agencies continually convene such conferences, which provide a relatively speedy method by which to formulate general and binding rules, to weigh interests, to determine standpoints, to evoke judgment by all participants and to clearly establish its results. International conferences have considerable advantages, particularly with regard to ecological issues, many of which are new, universal, complex, controversial and urgent. The value of legal solutions which are laid down in treaties is enhanced by the fact that the lawyers work in close collaboration with, and even under the supervision of, other technical experts.

During the past few years, international organisations such as United Nations, the specialised and other agencies, have shown unprecedented activity in holding international diplomatic conferences whose task is to examine the different aspects (including legal aspects) of environmental pollution. The most extensive research and the best results have probably been achieved in the area of water conservation, in particular of the sea and its riches. The following brief description may give some impression of the possibilities and difficulties involved in attempts to improve environmental control in general.

The General Assembly and the Economic and Social Council of the United Nations show continual interest in the marine environment. The Secretary-General has issued reports on marine pollution and on problems of the human environment. A special committee is engaged in the study of the peaceful uses of the seabed and the ocean floor. In 1969, the Intergovernmental Maritime Consultative Organisation (IMCO) drew up two treaties on damage caused by oil pollution of the sea, a subject that was also discussed at a special conference convened by NATO. In 1970 the Food and Agriculture Organisation held a conference on oceanic pollution, and the World Health Organisation discussed the harmful impact on the environment of chemicals such as DDT. UNESCO is currently looking into problems of joint scientific research on the marine environment. The Council of Europe pays particular attention to the protection of European waters against pollution. In 1970 again, the Latin American countries and the non-aligned nations (i.e. the majority of the Afro-Asian countries), in two conferences held in Lima and Lusaka respectively, issued statements regarding the sea and ocean beds in which they stressed the necessity to conserve the living marine wealth.

Important contributions are also made by individual scientists or institutions such as the International Law Association, the American Society of International Law, the Law of the Sea Institute of the

University of Rhode Island (USA) and the Alumni Association of The Hague Academy of International Law. The Club of Rome, a group of scientists, businessmen and industrialists who want to help to improve the human environment, is now also much in the forefront.

In effect, these organisations and scholars are embroidering further on the results of the UN conference on the law of the sea first held in Geneva in 1958 and reconvened in 1960, which re-examined the entire body of the law of the sea and subsequently laid down treaty regulations on the territorial sea and its contiguous zone, the high sea, fishing, and conservation of the living resources of the high seas and the continental shelf.

The next landmark will be reached at the UN Conference on the Human Environment to be held in Stockholm in 1972. This will be an intermediate step towards the next major UN conference on the law of the sea planned to be held late in 1973, at which this law will be re-examined and if necessary revised, amplified or- re-written.

In view of the difficulties enumerated above, what are the chances for the success of this conference? At present they do not seem completely favourable. The developing countries in particular have urged that it be held; others, including those of the Soviet bloc, have not shown much enthusiasm. Moreover, it is only since the 1958 conference that environmental problems have really made themselves felt and in the meantime the whole matter has become considerably more complicated. There is so little chance of reasonable consensus (for example on the necessary measures with which to conserve marine life) that it is doubtful whether many principal issues are sufficiently mature for discussion and decision.

It remains to be seen whether the conference will provide a reasonable chance for agreement and compromise or whether it will merely demonstrate the serious differences of opinion among major maritime powers and between rich and poor nations. At present, pollution problems seem to be most urgent in the rich countries. The tocsin has already been rung as a result of the ever-faster mortality of such inland seas as the Baltic, the Adriatic and the Mediterranean.

For developing countries, on the other hand, it is more important that they kill at birth any sign of pollution in their own territories. Conversely, they will make great efforts to protect their own natural resources and simultaneously to claim some of the wealth of the high seas and of the sea bed as their rightful share of 'the common heritage of mankind'. The hard commercial practices of some foreign fishing enterprises, for example, have already caused over-fishing and threaten the extinction of certain fish and other animals such as the whale and tuna, while indigenous fishermen are likely to lose their livelihood if their traditional fishing grounds are invaded by foreign fishermen with highly developed technical equipment.

The significance of the sea for military purposes gives direct evidence of conflicting interests and will unquestionably play an important role at the coming conference on the law of the sea. The developing countries have good reason to be uneasy about the secretive underwater activities of naval units of major maritime powers (submarines, deepsea vessels and underwater storage) whose probable use of nuclear weapons or oil may literally deposit the environmental pollution problem on their beaches, while the identity of the polluter who should pay for possible damages will be very difficult to ascertain.

Finally, two other important factors will determine the success of the conference: i.e. the way in which the matter is approached and the mental attitude of the participating countries.

As far as the approach is concerned, some experts want to see recognition of the totality of the environment expressed in a comprehensive approach to environmental problems by the conference, and advocate the prior design of a world environment strategy. For instance, the Lusaka conference, attended by more than 50 non-aligned countries, accepted a declaration on the seabed which supported the calling of the new conference at which issues would be discussed comprehensively rather than piecemeal. The declaration included other principles which characterise the attitude of the non-aligned countries toward environmental issues and the preservation of the sea's wealth. In their opinion, exploitation of the seabed should be undertaken in the interests of all mankind but with particular attention being given to the 'special needs and interests of the developing countries'.

However, others feel that the subject matter is so complex that a more pragmatic approach is necessary and that those problems should first be tackled which have a reasonable chance of success owing to sufficient consensus. In this way, a measure of success can be obtained which could form sufficient basis on which to grapple with the remaining and more controversial issues.

Another obstacle to the development of international law by the conference seems to be the great distrust with which diverse international circles regard measures for environmental protection. This is not surprising in view of the fact that the international law of the sea is in a transitional phase. Traditional law of the sea was based on the principle of the freedom of the seas, belief in the inexhaustibility of the sea's wealth, and the supposition that human activities could not appreciably alter the nature of that enormous mass of water. Traditional law of the sea not only guaranteed the right of all to sail the seas but also to exploit their living resources without disturbance.

It is understandable that the rich nations who contributed so much to the formulation of traditional international law still give it some preference. It is equally self-evident, however, that the developing nations are less in favour of it. The laissez-faire nature of the traditional law of the sea offers great advantages to technologically developed countries. Their superior technology enables them to exercise complete control over the exploitation of the seas, which again can place the developing countries in an economically vulnerable position. It is not surprising, therefore, that the latter seek new principles which may form the basis of the law of the sea.

In such a sphere it is almost inevitable that developing countries should regard environmental measures taken by the rich nations with some misgiving. Recently, a reported rise in the mercury content of a certain type of fish caused American demand to decrease significantly and in turn caused unemployment among the fishermen of a number of developing countries. As a result, at a London conference on sea pollution, the developing countries demanded more technical aid with which to set up their own measuring and monitoring instruments and to train the necessary experts – this with a view to reducing their dependence on the rich nations for data regarding the mercury content of fish. It is to be hoped that, despite the growing feelings of distrust, the coming conference will be able to achieve satisfactory results.

If these results are not forthcoming, however, the chance of conflict will become greater. In the absence of distinct regulations, nations will tend to take unilateral action to protect their own interests, giving rise to a deplorable fragmentation of the environment controversy which could far better be tackled at the international level. However, any state that adopts such unilateral measures may with some justification argue that prevention is still better than pollution.

15. Towards a stationary state society[1]

E. TELLEGEN

Among those contributions that indicate solutions to very real problems, this account stands out in setting clear objectives and in identifying some major ingredients of a strategy. Eight steps by which to achieve the steady state society are indicated and the actual order in which they should be implemented is discussed. The author also introduces the concept of absolute and relative limits to growth and passes sobering comments on our throw-away society that also throws away people. His plea for demobilisation may be compared with the views of several other authors on mobilisation.

1. DEFINING THE PROBLEM

As an outsider in ecological matters, a sociologist can be confused by the widely different interpretations of 'the' crisis in the relationship between man and his natural environment. Yet I think that most ecologists would agree that in modern industrial societies it is necessary to strive for a stabilisation of the population and of the production of material goods,[2] possibly in one or both at an even lower level than has already been reached at this moment. Such a 'stationary state' has been described as follows:

> By a 'stationary state' is meant a constant stock of *physical* wealth (capital), and a constant stock of people (population). Naturally these stocks do not remain constant by themselves. People die, and wealth is physically consumed, that is, worn out, depreciated. Therefore the stocks must be maintained by a rate of inflow (birth, production) equal to the rate of outflow (death, consumption). But this equality may obtain, and stocks remain constant, with a high rate of throughput (equal to both the rate of inflow and the rate of outflow), or with a low rate. Our definition of stationary state is not complete until we specify the rates of throughput by which the constant stocks are maintained. For a number of reasons we specify that the rate of throughput should be 'as low as possible'.[3]

Without denying the urgency of the population problem, I think it is useful to limit my sociological analysis mainly to the production problem. In modern industrial societies the production problem seems to be the more complicated of the two and the more difficult to solve. It will become clear that the problems of growth in production are related to problems of growth in other segments of modern society. Therefore, much more than stable production is necessary. We have to look for a stationary state society.

2. MOBILISATION FOR PRODUCTION

The development of productive forces in western societies is often seen primarily as the triumph of applying engineering or technical skills to the resources at hand, of avoiding waste and utilising social efforts as efficaciously as possible. But, as Robert Heilbroner writes, 'Long before a society can even concern itself about using its energies "economically", it must first marshall the energies to carry out the productive process itself. That is, the basic problem of production is to devise social institutions that will mobilize human energy for productive purposes'.[4]

Heilbroner describes how in western societies a traditional regulation of production and distribution was replaced by a regulation primarily based on the market mechanism. Essential for this social transformation was the dissolving of traditional bonds which might hinder the mobilisation of individuals for task-accomplishment within the productive system. 'A market society could not coexist with a form of legal organization which, for example, did not recognize the freedom of the individual to contract for employment as he wished'.[5] The development of the market economy brought the liberation of feudal bonds but also the loss of certain pre-capitalistic freedoms, like the freedom to use common grounds. The so-called enclosure movement in England made self-support for the tenants impossible. Heilbroner writes: 'The enclosure process provided a powerful force for the dissolution of feudal ties and the formation of the new relationships of a market society. By dispossessing the peasant, it "created" a new kind of labor force – landless, without traditional sources of income, however meagre, impelled to find work for wages wherever it might be available'.[6]

Whereas in societies with a traditional regulation of production and distribution these processes are strongly related to other aspects of social life, under a market regulation societies develop specialised institutions for productive activities in which individuals participate only as workers. The development of specialised productive systems implies 'the separation between the different roles held by an individual – especially among the occupational and political roles, and between them and the family and kinship roles'.[7]

This mobilisation of individuals for participation in the productive subsystem of society has not been reached without costs. Etzioni, discussing the concept of mobilisation in general, writes: 'Mobilisation of one entity often entails the de-mobilisation of some other'. In the case of the modernisation process within western societies, mobilisation for productive activities in specialised productive subsystems (factories) not only led to the destruction of pre-industrial skills and forms of labor organisation but also to the destruction of all sorts of social integration.[8] Therefore, the development of specialised institutions for personal care became necessary. In sociology these two different aspects of social life are often referred to with terms like 'goal achievement' and 'group maintenance'. In experimental research in small problem-solving groups, it was found that there almost always appears a differentiation between a person who presses for task accomplishment and a person who satisfies the social and emotional needs of members.[9] Later research in different types of organisations resulted in concepts like 'instrumental' and 'social' leadership, referring to different dimensions of leadership, although not necessarily divided over different persons.[10] In the analyses of complex societies it is also possible to distinguish between the achievement of some specific societal goal (like economic growth) and the maintenance and strengthening of the internal integration of society.

Within a society goal-attainment and internal integration can be based on small, all compassing social systems. Productive activities and the maintenance of social relationships can be institutionalised within the boundaries of the same institution, like the pre-industrial family. But it is also possible that different functions of societies become institutionalised in separate subsystems like factories, schools, medical centres, churches and nuclear families. This is what happened during the transfer from traditional regulation of production and distribution to market regulation, a process which is normally called 'modernisation'.[11]

This progress was not reached without costs. In fact, the industrialisation process has always met with strong resistance of which socialism became the ideological foundation, although some forms of socialism itself developed toward 'modernisation' or 'industrialisation' ideologies. One of the most famous criticisms of this process is to be found in Peter Kropotkin's *Mutual Aid*. In contrast to his Darwinian contemporaries, Kropotkin became impressed by the cooperative aspects in the life of animals and of pre-modern man. In his opinion, during the process of modernisation, cooperative tendencies had been repressed in favour of liberal individualism. In particular the modern state was considered by Kropotkin and other anarchists as the destroyer of cooperative tendencies among men. In his comparative study on modernisation, Barrington Moore concludes: 'there is no evidence that the mass of the population anywhere has wanted an industrial society, and plenty of evidence that they did not. At bottom all forms of industrialisation so far have been revolutions from above, the work of a ruthless minority'.[12]

Even if Barrington Moore's interpretation is correct, it seems hardly possible to deny the progress which has been made in western societies in the last centuries in the fulfilment of basic human needs. But if it is true that the mobilisation for productive activities and more generally the mobilisation for participation in large but specialised subsystems like schools and factories, does not go without costs, one has to wonder if there are no limits to this growth.

3. SOCIOLOGICAL LIMITS TO GROWTH

The notion of 'limits to growth' can, broadly speaking, refer to two different things. (a) An absolute limit. Growth cannot pass a certain boundary because then it will itself destroy the basis for further growth. (b) A relative limit. A relative limit is reached when further expansion of activities leads to a negative cost-benefit balance. In that case activities have more negative than positive effects and stability is more profitable than further growth. Ecological systems are self-regulating systems. They permit human activities, but 'growth' of human activities can reach a point where it interferes with self-regulation of nature. In that case, idleness which gives nature the chance to do its work may be more profitable than any sort of human activities. As Barry Commoner shows, even human activities which are intended to protect the environment often lead to new forms of ecological destruction. They must be considered as forms of positive instead of negative feedback.[13]

It makes sense to consider human social life in this respect as being part of 'nature'. Modernisation, both in its material aspect of introducing new methods of production and in its social aspect of developing a new type of society based on individual achievement within specialised subsystems, can bring and in fact has brought progress in the fulfilment of basic human needs like food, shelter and health. But in both material and social developments there are limits to growth. Not only absolute but also relative limits, in the sense that natural and social self-regulation can become over-exploited by the mobilisation of individuals for productive activities, so that mobilisation costs become higher than the benefits. That we come near these limits in the productive or 'goal attainment' institutions of our society seems evident from recent ecological publications. One of the most famous of these, the MIT report to the Club of Rome, is even entitled *The Limits to Growth.* But this title could also refer to developments in those institutions of modern societies which are primarily related to the interpersonal relations within society. It would be an appropriate title for a book on the spendings on health care and education. In the Netherlands, as in other western countries, expenditures in these fields have risen considerably during the last years. We come to limits in both fields: absolute limits because of lack of money, but also relative limits in the sense of sharply diminishing returns. The developments in both fields are described in two recent articles which are summarised below.

3.1 *The diminishing returns of medical care*

The problematic character of the growth of spendings on medical care is shown in an unpublished paper by the British physician John Powles, entitled 'Towards a theory of medicine of industrial man'.[14] Powles formulates his basic question as follows: 'Why is there such faith in the capacity of scientific medicine to conquer disease at a time when a rapidly increasing price is having to be paid for declining and marginal gains in health?' With the aid of statistical data the author shows that we witness a rapid 'medical inflation' in various industrial nations such as England and Wales, the United States and the Soviet Union. In all these countries there is an enormous increase both in the expenditures and in the workforce of medical institutions. What are the results of these efforts? Powles writes: 'It may be noted that it is precisely during the last two decades – when scientific medicine is alleged to have blossomed and when the quantity of resources allocated to medical care has been rapidly increased – that the decline in mortality that has been associated with industrialisation has tapered off to virtually zero. While it is true that female life expectancy is continuing to increase marginally, the picture for men is very sobering.' Powles' conclusions are supported by recent Dutch statistics which show a still rising life expectancy for women but a *declining* life expectancy for men. The stagnation of progress is caused by the growing number of patients suffering from what may be called 'diseases of industrial societies' because these diseases exist exclusively or are most common in industrial populations. They include arteriosclerosis (heart attacks and strokes); diabetes; and some forms of cancer and duodenal ulcer. Powles does not accept their common name of 'degenerative diseases'. 'They are more appropriately referred to as diseases of maladaptation – for whatever their individual causes, they may be considered as resulting from the fact that man's relation to his environment has become removed from that to which he is biologically adapted.' Powles quotes another author who called modern medicine 'cultural adaptation to biological maladjustment'. Yet contemporary health care is not strongly oriented towards amelioration of the physical and social environment of man. Instead of taking as its frame of reference an evolutionary-ecological perspective which recognises the optimalisation of the relation of man and environment as the most important base of health, health care is dominated by a 'belief' in an engineering style of response to illness and a reluctance to check its effectiveness. The massive expenditure on intensive cardiac care is taken as an example. 'The development of intensive cardiac care cannot be explained as a rational programme to reduce the toll from ischaemic heart disease. It has momentum which is almost detached from considering as rational as this. How different, functionally, are the activities involved from the rituals of the magicians of old? Both are active responses to forces threatening wellbeing.' From the viewpoint of 'effectively combating disease', the enormous amounts which are spent by 'the engineering approach' could be much better spent for preventive purposes. But besides the function of effectively combating disease medicine has always fulfilled and still fulfills a second function, which Powles calls 'helping to cope'. With the progress of industrialisation, traditional forms of helping to cope have been lost. 'Alone and mortal in an indifferent universe, industrial man seeks to screen off the void that surrounds him. He does not find it easy to face misfortune with a dignified resignation so that, when it does strike, "something must be done".' From a viewpoint of effectively combating disease a reorientation from the engineering approach toward an ecological approach is highly necessary. But it will not be simple to do away with or limit our 'much too expensive magic'. Powles' only hope for the future is based on the development from a growth society towards a stable society, which may be stimulated by the MIT report to the Club of Rome and other alarming reports about the ecological crisis. 'In a more stable society relatives could play a larger part in the care of the elderly and disabled. In a society that placed less emphasis on performance in a demanding productive apparatus, the insane and handicapped would not just be tolerated, but would find it easier to exist in the mainstream of society.' In this way, 'the "helping to cope" side of medicine might find expression following a relative switch in strategies to an ecological approach to the improvement of health.' The strategy suggested by Powles is a sort of de-modernisation process. Modernisation means mobilisation of individuals for functioning in specialised sub-systems. It leads to a weakening of stable relationships outside these institutions. The nuclear family is a small base as compared to comparable institutions of pre-industrial society. There is a tendency to base the expansion of health care on economic growth. People are mobilised for activities within the productive system to pay for the rising costs of medical care. Powles proposes, in fact, a process of 'demobilisation' in order to stimulate the development of new social relationships which might help to cope.

Before further discussing this strategy, it may be useful to look at comparable problems in the field of education.

3.2 *The myth of schooling*

One of the most widely shared beliefs in industrial societies is that schooling is a good thing. Yet there is also a growing criticism of the school system, a trend represented by men such as Paul Goodman, Paolo Freire, Ivan Illich and Everett Reimer. Reason enough to wonder if the enormously rising expenditures in this field really serve a worthwhile goal.

As in the case of medical institutions I will do little more than summarise a recent publication on the developments in this field, i.e. a paper entitled 'The Myth of Schooling', by Derek Phillips, an American sociologist who is now a professor of sociology at the University of Amsterdam.[15]

Phillips wonders why schooling should be 'a good thing', and discusses the following possible functions of the school system.

a. *The combating of illiteracy*

There can be no doubt that the school system has contributed to the attainment of this goal. Yet even 100 years ago, when about 57 percent of those aged 5-17 were attending school, the illiteracy rate in the USA was only 20 percent. Phillips does not mention the finding of the Brazilian teacher Paolo Freire that every adult person can learn to read and write in about 40 hours if the teaching is adjusted to his own daily situation. Although the school system contributes to combating illiteracy, its contemporary expansion cannot be explained by that function.

b. *Training*

The importance of the school system in respect to this goal is much more dubious. Phillips writes: 'It might seem at first glance that the association between schooling and training could be rather easily established. After all, we can look around and see an enormous increase in the number of lawyers, engineers, schoolteachers, nuclear scientists, skilled workers in a variety of work settings, and numerous other persons who are required to meet the needs of a highly industrialised society. It is frequently assumed that these increases in the proportion of jobs requiring highly technical skills are responsible for the vast increases in schooling found in America and other advanced societies. Yet the only empirical evidence on this matter which I could locate, indicates that only 15 percent of the increase in education in the United States during the twentieth century is attributable to an increase in the proportion of jobs with high technical requirements.' Probably there is 'over-education' for many jobs. 'An increased number of people appear to be performing jobs below the level for which their training was intended to prepare them.'

c. *To stimulate social mobility and social equality*

Research findings make Phillips sceptical about 'the widespread belief that formal education [schooling] serves as an avenue of upward mobility for the disadvantaged, for those whose parents are relatively poor and uneducated.' These findings show that 'changes in the numbers of people attending school and the number of years of school completed do *not* lead to an alteration in the social hierarchies within societies. Schooling, then, is apparently not an effective promotor of social mobility.' I think a more fundamental criticism of the school system is possible at this point. In *Class Inequality and Political Order*, Frank Parkin distinguishes two dimensions of inequality: one is the inequality in the *recruitment* for different social positions, the other is the inequality of *rewards* attached to different positions.[16] At best our contemporary school system contributes to the 'meritocratic' ideal of equality in recruitment. Even in this respect it is, as Phillips shows, unsuccessful. But the system does not pretend to contribute to the 'egalitarian' ideal of equality in rewards.

d. *Education for citizenship*

'One of the explicit goals of compulsory education was to provide a socialisation and enculturating process that would help make the student a good citizen and equip him to be responsible for himself and others.' Again Phillips does not believe that expansion of the contemporary school system can be considered as a contribution to this goal. He concludes even that 'life in the United States is in many ways more savage and less civilized than in earlier times when its citizens had far less experience with formal education'.

How can the enormous expansion of schooling be explained if this system seems to fail in more than one of its pretended social functions? One reason for this expansion is the situation of 'self-sustained growth' which has been reached by the school system. More education for the less privileged implies still more education for the privileged. So there is a rapid inflation in diplomas. Phillips writes: 'In short, the status value of a high school diploma has been almost totally diluted in the United States, and a similar fate awaits the college degree. We already can begin to see, for those who can afford it [those of high social origins], a trend towards the acquisition of advanced degrees as a means for protecting or guaranteeing a high position in society.' Another important function is that schools are places where children are cared for during large parts of the day. This 'baby sitting' function frees mothers to work or to engage in other activities. A third function mentioned by Phillips is that of keeping children out of the labour force.

The school system thus does not seem to be very successful in its functions. 'Learning' and 'education' may take place more successfully outside than inside the school system. Social equality can apparently better be achieved by income policy and changes in the division of labour. But the school system seems to be a necessary 'in-between' institution of industrial societies which need: (i) long preparation of disciplined functioning in the productive system, and (ii) integration of persons outside the productive system in organised subsystems; social relationships outside organised subsystems such as hospitals, schools, factories, are too incidental or too small in scale (nuclear family!) to 'bear' them. So we need schools, centres for aged and hospitals where people without work can spend their time. As in the case of medical institutions, a policy aimed at further growth to pay for rising costs seems irrational.

Everywhere we are confronted with the enormous social costs which a society has to pay for mobilising individuals to achieve in specialised institutions. The expenditures are enormous and there are growing doubts about their benefits. Specialised subsystems such as contemporary industrial organisations may be superior to any other form of productive cooperation, but schools are not always the best places in which to learn, hospitals not always the best places to cure illness,[17] mental hospitals not always the ideal location for 'repairing' crises in interpersonal relationships,[18] and institutions for the aged not always the best places in which to pass the last years of life. Our society could with some exaggeration be called a society of throw-away things and throw-away people.

This is not a plea to romanticise the past. There can be no doubt that the process of modernisation must be considered as positive when looked at from the viewpoint of fulfilment of basic needs; it has also broken down some forms of crude and primitive repression. But it seems that we have reached the limits of contemporary growth and that, in the name of real progress, we need to change developments in contemporary western societies. 'Goal attainment' in the form of productive expansion becomes a dubious aim when we realise that expansion of production has more negative than positive consequences. Productive expansion to pay for the rising costs of health care and schooling seems to be a mistaken policy if that expansion itself, by its social consequences, is a principal cause of the growth of medical and educational institutions. Once again I refer to Etzioni's discussion of the concept of mobilisation: 'Maximum unit-mobilisation, however, does not assure maximum realisation of the goals of the mobilising unit because some of these goals tend best to be served by activities of the sub-units; hence, these sub-units must retain some of the assets and manpower.'[19] The ecological and sociological limits to growth seem to necessitate demobilisation of the organisational sub-systems of industrial society to enable a strengthening of social relationships outside the organisational sub-systems. Both 'goal-attainment' in the form of productive activities and 'group maintenance' functions of society should be concentrated more than today outside the organised sub-systems of modern society.

4. A POLICY OF DEMOBILISATION

How can such development be stimulated? It must first be realised that expansion of industrial society cannot be considered as being encouraged only by a small, exploiting minority. Even if Barrington Moore is right and the process of industrialisation was forced by a small minority, nowadays widely different parts of the population regard themselves as dependent on further economic growth. Growth is considered necessary for more schools, new roads, larger local communities. We have reached a phase of self-sustained growth. Even the environment problem may easily become integrated in this self-sustained growth. It facilitates career-making for 'engaged' intellectuals, it stimulates traffic to local or international conferences and the selling of 'alarming' books. Woods are cut down, air is polluted and energy is used in the interest of discussing the environment topic. It is not only that business must grow to make a profit; there are many other motives for growth.[20]

And yet we have to stop growth. But in which way should this be achieved? Firstly, a strict regulation of the productive system seems necessary. States should be able to control which products are made and with which technology. The much-debated topic of 'nationalisation' of the productive system should be a matter of pragmatics rather than of principles. Even a nationalised industry may be growth-oriented. In *The Making of Economic Society*, Heilbroner discusses in addition to 'traditional' and 'market' regulation of production and distribution, the 'command' regulation. Unlike traditional but like market regulation, command regulation may be growth-oriented, as is shown by the Soviet example.

Secondly, apart from a democratically founded 'regulation from above', fundamental changes are necessary in the mobilisation of individuals. People in western societies should become much more independent of the productive system both for their income and for their sense of identity. This growing independence should motivate them to create new forms of less 'organised' productive activities and of social integration.

Measures necessary to stimulate such a development include: (1) lessening differences in income; (2) extension of collective facilities which stimulate personal creativity without damaging the environment; (3) abolition of obligatory forms of schooling; (4) free entrance at any age to schools and universities for purposes of general education;

(5) limitation of expensive and specialised education for professional qualifications, dependent on the social need for professional specialists; (6) introduction of a guaranteed income; (7) intrinsically unattractive labour tasks should be fulfilled in exchange for use of certain collective facilities (e.g. university students should work in unskilled jobs during a certain period); (8) abolition of full employment as a long-term political goal.

Of extreme importance is the movement for amelioration of the directly contiguous living area. Larger living communities – not necessarily in the form of communes – that do not do away with useful forms of division of labour, although they limit the splitting-up of living and working areas, may enable living at a lower productive and consumptive level, because (1) a larger number of persons may share the same goods and (2) more people may be present to help individuals with personal problems and less expenditure on professional help will be necessary.

A possible reason for opposition to these proposals might be that the ecological crisis makes it necessary for us to work more rather than less because we have to do away with some forms of labour-saving production. But even if this were so, the existing 'productive system' is not necessarily the framework in which these labour activities should take place. New forms of labour may develop outside as well as inside the economic system.

The above-mentioned measures do not form a political programme that could be realised after winning the next election. Of the eight measures mentioned, lessening differences in income, extension of collective facilities and the introduction of a guaranteed income seem to be the most urgent. The existing differences of income, related to our system of education and division of labour, block the development of a more rational division of labour and a better method of educating people. A guaranteed income, proposed long ago by Theobald and recently during part of his election campaign by McGovern, should at first mainly have a symbolic meaning. Starting with a low amount, it should not immediately replace higher existing payments for unemployment, retirement or ill health. But even as a small amount it would symbolise the principle of unconditional basic social security, which seems to be a requirement for the development of new social relationships. This development should also be stimulated by the extension of collective facilities. City centres, in particular, could fulfil many functions in this respect. A man-made environment of freely available collective facilities should in some way replace the free nature of the past.

The abolition of obligatory schooling should be the end rather than the beginning of a development. At first, schools should be more integrated in the rest of society and lose their sub-system isolation. During that period some extension of obligatory schooling could still be justified. But because of other developments in the sphere of income and labour and of the integration of schools in the social environment, obligatory schooling would be felt more as an unnecessary and regrettable onus. Abolition of this obligation would be the natural end of a development. In measures 4 and 5 a division is made between schools as facilities for general education and schools as institutions for training for special tasks. It should be a long-term policy to relate the high expenditures for the latter forms of schooling to the needs of society. But under prevailing circumstances such a policy is still impossible. The needs of society cannot be defined as the needs of our expanding military-industrial-educational-medical complex. After the introduction of such measures as 1, 2 and 7, we shall need to seek measures that enable a better division of unattractive tasks. I wonder if the market-mechanism will be very helpful in this respect. Forms of general work-service (comparable to military service) should at any rate be discussed.

Similar to the abolition of obligatory schooling, the doing away with a policy that aims at full employment is a natural end of a process rather than a commencing measure.

5. BAD AND GOOD UTOPIAN THINKING[21]

Ideas such as those presented above are often rejected as 'utopian'. In fact, labelling ideas as utopian usually serves as an ideological justification of the status quo and, in particular, as justification of belief in the institutions of industrial society and disbelief in the social abilities of individuals outside these institutions. Yet utopian thinking can be sterile and also support the status-quo. This is so if rejection of contemporary society is followed by a blueprint for a better society, without showing how the latter can be realised. Such utopian thinking can acquire totalitarian traits inasfar as it suggests that an elite of experts from different scientific fields should work to introduce 'the' new society. Thinking about 'the' old and 'the' new society can become ahistoric thinking. A society is not a 'thing' which can be replaced by a new 'thing'. Social life is an ongoing and ever-changing process. This does not mean that ideas about a better organisation of societal life are without sense. But they should be always related to contemporary social processes and in particular to tensions and conflicts within society. Utopian thinking is holistic thinking, thinking in which traditional boundaries are broken down. With Barry Commoner I think that we need such holistic thinking if we want to change the relationship of man and environment. But holistic utopian ideals should be related to actual problems of contemporary society. Those who think that social change is necessary because of 'the environment problem' should look for changes which also answer other urgent felt needs; needs such as changes in the treatment of psychiatric patients or in the situation of unskilled workers, to mention just two problems. Environmental policy should be related to the emancipation of repressed groups in industrial society.

Many urgent problems in modern society are not dealt with in this paper. What about population growth? 'Stop at two' is not the only solution. Much more attractive is a solution in the direction of demobilisation: do not stimulate people to marry and/or procreate if they are not by themselves motivated to do so. The existence of mobilisation in this direction in our society cannot be denied. Even 'stop at two' suggests that everyone should begin before stopping! But 'demobilisation' is not a simple solution that offers us an easy road to a happy future. An earlier crisis in industrial society has already led to the terror of fascism. This memory and the actual situation in the world should assure us that we face a dangerous future.

NOTES

1. I am grateful to Derek L. Phillips for helpful comments on an earlier draft of this article.
2. Even hot debaters such as Paul Ehrlich and Barry Commoner agree that the ecological crisis is partly caused by both population growth and developments in the production of material goods. Opinions differ as to the importance which is subscribed to both factors and in the interpretation of the damaging developments within the sphere of the production of material goods. Commoner argues that the influence of population growth has been largely overestimated by Ehrlich and others. As for the production of material goods, it is in Commoner's opinion not growth of production and consumption but technological change in the way of producing and distribut-

ing goods which mainly causes the destruction of the environment. Contrary to Ehrlich, Commoner holds that it is not 'affluence' but 'technology' that should be considered as the main contributor to environmental pollution within the sphere of production. The conflict between Ehrlich and Commoner at this point is partly no more than a matter of definition. Is it a change in 'affluence' or in 'technology' if we start to drink our beer at home out of tins rather than in a café out of barrels? Call it affluence or technology, we are confronted with a dangerous expansion of production within our society.

3. H. E. Daly, 'Towards a Stationary-State Economy' in J. Harte and R. H. Socolow (eds.), *The Patient Earth*, New York, Holt, Rinehart and Winston, 1971, p. 231.
4. R. Heilbroner, *The Making of Economic Society*, Englewood Cliffs, Prentice Hall, Inc., 1968, p. 6.
5. *Ibidem*, p. 65.
6. *Ibidem*, p. 60.
7. S. N. Eisenstadt, *Modernization: Protest and Change*, Englewood Cliffs, Prentice Hall, Inc., 1966, p. 3.
8. Such things as changes in geographical mobility, separation of work and living place, changes in religious organisation and also in work-associations are what I have in mind. For example, even the medieval guilds fulfilled social functions much more than contemporary trade unions.
9. D. Cartwright and A. Zander, *Group Dynamics, Research and Theory*, London, Tavistock Publications, 1960, p. 496.
10. C. J. Lammers, 'De sociologische studie van leiderschap in organisaties' [The Sociological Study of Leadership in Organisations], *Mens en onderneming*, XIX, May 1965, p. 142.
11. This process of 'modernisation' is not necessarily a universal phase in the development of every society. Communist China shows a very different development. In this society social integration seems to be less sacrificed in favour of individual mobilisation than was the case during the modernisation process in western countries.
12. Barrington Moore, *Social Origins of Dictatorship and Democracy*, Boston, Beacon Press, 1967, p. 506.
13. B. van der Lek, 'Politiek en milieu' [Politics and Environment]), *De Gids* 9/10, 1971, p. 5.
14. This and the following quotations are taken from J. Powles, 'Towards a Theory of Medicine of Industrial Man', discussion paper at the Third International Conference on Social Science and Medicine, Elsinore, Denmark, 1972.
15. These quotations are taken from the unpublished English draft of D. L. Phillips, 'De mythe van het onderwijs' [The Myth of Schooling], *De Gids*, 8, 1972.
16. F. Parkin, *Class Inequality and Political Order*, London, Paladin, 1971.
17. J. Roth, 'The Necessity and Control of Hospitalisation', *Social Science and Medicine*, 6, 1972.
18. E. Goffman, *Asylums. Essays on the social situations of mental patients and other inmates*, New York, Doubleday and Co. Inc., 1961.

19. A. Etzioni, *The Active Society*, New York, The Free Press, 1968, p. 392.
20. W. H. Starbuck (ed.), *Organisational Growth and Development*, Harmondsworth, Penguin Books, 1971.
21. This section is partly a reaction to critical comments on the original text of this paper made during the Man and Environment Course held in Leiden in 1972, and in particular to a written comment by Volkmar Kettnaker.

REFERENCES

Cartwright, D. and A. Zander, *Group Dynamics, Research and Theory*, London, Tavistock Publications, 1960.

Commoner, B., *The Closing Circle; nature, man and technology*, New York, A. A. Knopf, 1971.

Commoner, B., 'Response' in dialogue on *The Closing Circle*, in *Bulletin of the Atomic Scientists*, May 1972, pp. 16-56.

Daly, H. E., 'Towards a Stationary-State Society' in J. Harte and R. H. Socolow (eds.), *The Patient Earth*, New York, Holt, Rinehart and Winston, 1971, pp. 226-244.

The Ecologist – a Blueprint for Survival, by the editors of the *Ecologist*, Harmondsworth, Penguin Books, 1971.

Ehrlich, P., J. P. Holdren, 'One Dimensional Ecology' and 'One Dimensional Ecology Revisited. A Rejoinder'. Critique of *The Closing Circle* in *Bulletin of the Atomic Scientists*, May 1972, pp. 16-56.

Eisenstadt, S. N., *Modernization: Protest and Change*, Englewood Cliffs, Prentice Hall Inc., 1966.

Etzioni, A., *The Active Society*, New York, The Free Press, 1968.

Goffman, E., *Asylums. Essays on the social situations of mental patients and other inmates*, New York, Doubleday and Co. Inc., 1961.

Heilbroner, R. L., *The Making of Economic Society*, Englewood Cliffs, Prentice Hall Inc., 1968.

Kropotkin, P., *Mutual Aid* (first published in 1941, reprinted by Extending Horizons Books, Boston, undated).

Lammers, C. J., 'De sociologische studie van leiderschap in organisaties' [The Sociological Study of Leadership in Organisations], *Mens en Onderneming*, XIX, May 1965, pp. 131-152.

Lek, B. van der, 'Politiek en milieu' [Politics and Environment], *De Gids*, 9/10, 1971.

Meadows, D. L. et al, *The Limits to Growth*. A report for the Club of Rome project on the predicament of mankind, New York, Universe Books, 1972.

Moore, B., *Social Origins of Dictatorship and Democracy*, Boston, Beacon Press, 1967.

Parkin, E. *Class Inequality and Political Order*, London, Paladin, 1971.

Phillips, D. L., 'De mythe van het onderwijs' [The Myth of Schooling], *De Gids*, 8, 1972, pp. 544-558.

Powles, J., 'Towards a Theory of Medicine of Industrial Man', discussion paper at the Third International Conference on Social Science and Medicine; Elsinore, Denmark, 1972.

Roth, J., 'The Necessity and Control of Hospitalisation', *Social Science and Medicine*, 6, 1972, pp. 425-446.

Starbuck, W. H. (ed.), *Organisational Growth and Development*, Harmondsworth, Penguin Books, 1971.

Theobald, R., *Free Men and Free Markets*, New York, Doubleday and Co. Inc., 1963.

Theobald, R., *The Guaranteed Income. Next step in socioeconomic evolution?* New York, Doubleday & Co. Inc., 1967.

16. The ecological view of the steady state society*

ARIEL E. LUGO

* This paper was first outlined for presentation at the Philadelphia American Association for the Advancement of Science annual meeting in 1972. However, the ideas were tested and expanded during the first two summer courses on Man and Environment. I am grateful to all the course participants for their spirited discussions and resistance to accept the concepts that are presented. Other friends helped with the editing, typing and commenting on the manuscript. In no particular order they are: P. Murphy, K. Dugger, K. Lucansky, H. T. Odum, J. Dickinson, M. Brinson, H. van Raay, and Alma Lugo who did some of the art work. To all I am grateful.

This paper on the ecological view of the steady state society directly relates to the contributions by Weissmann, Tellegen and Du Boff. The author expresses what he considers to be the principal physical and biological constrictions that guide and control the behavior of matter, organisms, ecosystems, cities and societies. A comparison with Gerber's chapter seems apt for some conflicting views. The steps suggested to implement the steady state society are supplementary to those advocated by Tellegen.

INTRODUCTION

A common assumption in many of our economic models and everyday attitudes about man's dependency on natural ecosystems,[1] is that nature is a free commodity or an externality that can be assumed to remain in unlimited supply. In reality this is not true since we live in a universe where the laws of energy operate[2] and any action has an energy cost which is irreversible and is paid by some energy storage in the system. The services of nature have such energy costs, and nature's capacity to provide these services is limited by the solar energy influx into the earth. This flux is the solar constant with an approximate value of 2 g cal/cm^2 min. If the demands that man places on natural ecosystems exceed their capacity to convert solar energy into useful work, a situation could develop in which natural ecosystems become the limiting factor for the growth, development, and survival of social systems. Under these conditions, the real value of natural ecosystems will become obvious to all those who are directly dependent on their services. Figure 1 was constructed to illustrate the interdependency of man and nature. The essential components of the social and natural systems have been depicted using the energy language of Odum.[3] Symbols are described in Figure 2. The box on the left represents the natural ecosystems and its components, and the box on the right the social system and its components. Lines connect the components of each system which have interactions through the flow of energy and materials. Without studying the details of the diagram, it is immediately obvious that the social system on the right has many connections with the natural system on the left and vice versa. So large and extensive are in fact the interconnections that one cannot but consider the totality of the landscape when one talks about life support systems, and the future development of civilization.

One property of all living systems is their consumption of potential energy and the production of waste products. Where man has concentrated in high densities, these products are termed 'pollution' because they are considered to be detrimental to man and to the quality of his environment. When man is not concentrated in high densities, pollution is not a problem since the products of his activities are diluted in the atmosphere and/or surrounding waters and soil. When these products are in low concentration, they are recycled by the matter and energy processing functions of natural ecosystems. This relationship has a positive effect on the natural system that utilizes the waste products and on the social system that produced them and does not have to worry about their disposal. However, when the products are in high concentrations they become detrimental to both systems since the natural system is stressed by their high concentration and the social system loses environmental quality when wastes accumulate and stress its human population. We therefore view pollution as a symptom of imbalance in the landscape and a result of improper resource utilization. One must then examine ways to design viable systems of man and nature such that resources and natural systems are managed at optimal rates and for the benefit of a balanced and high quality landscape. In this paper I explore the ideas of a steady state society as one of the possible approaches for this design of balanced man-nature systems.

THE MEANING OF STEADY STATE

The concept of steady state as applied to thermodynamic systems implies continuous energy flow without any net accumulation of energy or matter in the system under consideration.[4] Steady states are also designated as stationary states and as systems in dynamic equilibrium. Many times they are confused with systems in equilibrium. Equilibrium implies the opposite of steady state. In equilibrium, a system possesses properties that are not changing with time (as do steady states) but these systems 'are in rest in the sense that their condition is *not* being maintained by the continuous expenditure of energy or effort of any form'.[5] Thus, in Figure 3 both systems are shown to have molecular distributions that do not change, but in one (A) there is no energy flow and the system is said to be in equilibrium while in the other (B) the flow of energy maintains the structural organization of the system and the system is said to be in steady state. In biological systems, equilibrium (absence of energy flow) is usually associated with death and the eventual degradation of biological structures into randomness. Steady states represent systems whose complex structural organizations depend on continuous energy flow for their maintenance. Transient systems exist between the two extremes (steady state and equilibrium) and exhibit either growth or decline.

In this paper, the thermodynamic concept of the steady state is used to describe the complex ecosystem composed of the social systems of man and the natural ecosystems that provide life support to man.

The term steady state society will be defined as the system of man and nature without net power density[6] increase (growth), designed for the long term survival of all its components and with a limited energy supply for its maintenance. Since steady state implies continuous energy flow without any net storage (growth), all the energies available to the steady state society will be allocated for replacement, repair, and maintenance of its parts and functions.

Let us consider a steady state forest. Such a system, while not increasing its total biomass or adding new species, is a very dynamic system with flows of energy and materials and constantly undergoing replacement and repair of worn-out parts. The rate of energy flow through a steady state forest approaches the maximum and optimal value for the site and thus allows the forest to maintain a competitive status in its landscape. For example, a steady state forest is the terminal system in a series of systems which successively replace each other when the area is disturbed by some environmental factor.

This process is known as succession and it represents one of the two most important processes of ecosystem development (the other one being evolution). The general trends that accompany the successional process are illustrated in Figures 4 and 5. They may be summarized briefly as follows: An early successional system is characterized by having low complexity and structural diversity but very high growth rates. As the system develops, its complexity and structural diversity increase, its growth rate decreases, and its work of maintenance increases. At any point in the development of the system, environmental factors such as fires, hurricanes, frost or man, may maintain the sequence at a given stage of complexity and structural diversity for as long as the environmental factor is operational. Man, acting like fire or wind but with premeditation, can manipulate succession to the level of complexity and productivity he desires. With or without man, however, natural selection operates on the ecosystem such that the combination of species most capable of coping with the prevalent environmental conditions, survive and form the communities of plants and animals observed in the steady state landscape.

The flow of energy and materials through the forest and through the proposed steady state society are the important functions which regulate the competitive status and health of the system. In natural systems where the available solar energy and nutrients are both limited and diluted, maximization and utilization of energy and matter flow leads to dominance and survival over competing but less efficient systems. Efficiency in this instance is measured in terms of net useful power gained for a given input of matter and energy (Figure 6).

ALTERNATIVES TO THE STEADY STATE

The two alternatives to a steady state are decline and growth. Decline leading to extinction is not discussed since I assume that survival and not extinction drive man's values. Growth, however, has many advocates and momentum in our current cultural traditions. By growth I mean the increasing use of energy and matter in a given area such that the overall power density increases without regard to the capacity of the area to absorb the increase. The idea of continuous growth has certain side-effects which are not conducive to a competitive and long-term surviving system of man and nature. Some of these are the simplification of the biosphere, increased dependence on high energy subsidization, high cost of life support, and the control of limiting factors.

To satisfy the growth of our society, we need to develop systems of high yield in both the agricultural and wood industries. To obtain high yield, we must reduce the number of species in diverse systems that usually have low net yields. The biosphere therefore must be simplified at the cost of biological diversity. Many ecologists agree that the stability of ecological systems is a function of their diversity. Thus (in the change to high yields) we may lose stability. By stability I mean the capacity of a system to return to steady state following a perturbation. In addition, we lose esthetics, protection of natural resources e.g. soils, the efficiency of mineral cycles, gene pools, 'clean' water, and we may lose the early-warning system of indicator species for toxic chemicals and radio activity in the biosphere. Underlining this discussion is the idea that the stability of the diverse ecological systems protects man and the quality of his environment but does not provide yield. If one develops natural ecosystems for yield only, these protective characteristics are lost as they are intrinsic to diversity only. The higher the intensity of management for yield, the lower the protective capacity of the system and vice versa.

If the diversity of the biosphere is drastically reduced and the 'free' services of natural systems are replaced with services provided by man through the use of auxillary energy sources, we become increasingly dependent upon the energy subsidy. A space capsule, for example, is dependent upon an outside energy subsidy. When a part fails in a subsidized life-support system, or when the energy source is exhausted, survival becomes uncertain. Thus, such subsidized systems represent a high risk and are undesirable for long-term survival.

Figure 7 shows that as a system grows in complexity, the number of possible interactions between its parts increases in a geometrical function. Since our social systems are organized units, the energetic cost of this organization and its maintenance also increase as the system increases in complexity. In primitive societies, man was a minor part of the larger natural system and natural systems, operating on solar energy, provided the life-support system for man. In our present-day urban systems, nature is greatly removed and man must provide most of the life support at a high cost of fossil fuel energy. Again, the space capsule represents an extreme example where man has provided all of the minimum life support systems. When the costs of life support in space are considered, it becomes apparent that continued growth at the expense of nature is prohibitive, given that our energy resources and capacities to provide the essentials for continued survival are limited and that costs may increase geometrically with the complexity of the system.

It has been calculated that in order to support an American for one year, 25 tons of materials must be extracted from the earth where they exist in concentrated deposits.[7] At this rate, an increase in growth and a desire to raise the standard of living of the world's people will eventually deplete the earth's deposits of concentrated resources. Since the flow of energy is coupled with the cycling of matter, when resources are concentrated and space is available, the maximum rate of energy and resource use is the best competitive strategy (maximum power output). This strategy is observed in the early stages of ecological succession (e.g. old fields) and in the early phases of human urban development. At subsequent stages in both developmental processes, however, resources become diluted and thus limiting (the cost of concentrating them becomes prohibitive). The delivery of maximum power output is now non-competitive while the efficiency of resource use (at a lower power output) becomes the strategy for survival. At this point growth must stop as it is limited by both energy and matter. This principle applies not only to the late stages of succession, but it is the prognosis for the future developmental stages of our social systems on the earth.

The consequences of systems based on continuous growth are best illustrated in the urban setting where the power density is highest and the ratio of natural areas to fully developed areas is low. The citizens detect the deterioration of their life quality in many subtle ways. Such things as employment, pollution, transportation systems, inadequacies of local governments, the obsolescence of machines and procedures for the delivery of services, the vulnerability for breakdowns in the function of the system, and the overall pace of life, are daily reminders that the system is too complex for man to manage. City budgets also reveal that the costs of maintenance are greater than the energies and resources available to do the job. Responsible leaders must carefully balance the alternatives of continuous and spiraling growth to those of an overall slowdown until maintenance catches up with the development of new structures. Usually the decision is to create new structures and to abandon the old ones to decay and degradation. The social problems of these decisions are familiar to all residents of large American cities.

PRECEDENTS FOR STEADY STATE

Natural ecosystems have evolved steady state regimes under different conditions over many eons. While species compositions have changed, these systems have been successful in the strategies of long-term survival and thus one must seek clues for the steady state society in these natural ecosystems. Natural ecosystems are units of life support which are self-perpetuating, self-designing, and self-maintaining as a result of their balanced processes of photosynthesis and respiration, with mineral cycling as the coupling mechanism and natural selection as the process that 'tunes' the systems structure and function with respect to its environment. For man to survive with nature in a steady state, he must couple his actions with the biogeochemical and energy-flow patterns of natural ecosystems.

As an example of this coupling process, I will use the leaf-cutter ants of the tropical wet forests of South and Central America (Figure 8). The leaf-cutter ant nest represents an analog of an urban city, with many similarities existing between these two apparently divergent types. For example, both systems are heterotrophic and draw food energy from diluted sources external to the system. To obtain and process their food both systems have evolved complex road networks and social organization. They also depend on monoculture agriculture (the leaf cutters culture and eat monospecific fungus gardens), and both systems produce refuse which must be discarded away from the system. Some of the mechanisms that allow the ants to survive in association with the forest are:

1. The ants have a positive feedback mechanism to their life-support system. This mechanism results from a service performed by the ants which is valuable to the system that 'feeds' them. This service, as shown in Figure 8, is their mineral cycling work which contributes to forest productivity. When man is in balance with nature he can establish these feedbacks by recycling his wastes and managing and protecting certain systems.

2. The ants use only a small amount of the system's total energy budget. They do not exploit or exhaust the leaf compartment of the system that provides their life support. They may become pests when introduced to simple systems such as plantations, but this can be explained as follows. In the natural forest, the ants are limited by the dilution of their food. Since they prefer certain tissues and at times, certain species of leaves, they can never find high concentrations of food in one place. In the plantation, where the diversity of species is lower but the number of each kind is higher, their food supply is concentrated and therefore easier to obtain. Under conditions of concentrated food supplies, growth is the desired strategy and indeed the ants become pests to the owner of the plantation.

3. A large portion of the energy budget of the ant is allocated for the

maintenance of the nest and the coordination of its operation. The nests do not overgrow the carrying capacity of the area and its maintenance seems to have preference over its growth. Nests are constantly maintained, with growth only as a secondary priority.

4. Each ant has a role in its society, thus all individuals contribute to the task of survival for the colony.

These are the characteristics of what we call ecosystem managers. Each animal species is an ecosystem manager in the sense that it has established a symbiotic relationship with the system to which it belongs. Other characteristics of ecosystem managers are that their numbers and demands on the system are deceivingly small, the feedback mechanisms work at a low power level but are timed precisely and at the location where they have the highest amplifying value for the system; they thus perform essential services for the system, and belong to and depend on the system for survival.

When one observes these ants clean their trails, carry their refuse away from the nest, and maintain complex but highly structured systems of communication, and of cutting leaves and planting, weeding, feeding, and harvesting the fungus for consumption, one wonders why man couldn't be as successful. Could man become a true ecosystem manager and design systems whose complexity, structure, and function are within the capacity of the surrounding environment?

STEPS TOWARD A STEADY STATE SOCIETY

In order to create a steady state system of man and nature, we first need a definition of development that is consistent with the ideas of the steady state. Critics of the steady state society believe that development is not allowed under this strategy. Contrary to this misconception, the steady state society will develop to the maximum level possible within the limits imposed by the carrying capacity of its environment. First let's define development and then the concept of carrying capacity as they relate to the steady state society.

To the pioneer, development was cutting the forest and building houses and cities. Today this idea remains in the minds of those that believe in continuous growth. For the purpose of this paper an area is underdeveloped if the power density is below its carrying capacity.

When the power density reaches carrying capacity it will be considered developed, and overdeveloped if its power density exceeds the carrying capacity. The delineation of the unit of area that is used to calculate the carrying capacity is a matter for national debate and priorities. Each nation represents a convenient political unit to distribute resources and energies. However, in our finite and complex earth, conflicts between nations have ecological bases when the allocation of resources within a given nation is subject to influence by another. I will discuss this point later but first I must define the concept of carrying capacity.

The concept of carrying capacity has its roots in population ecology and the logistic equation. In Figure 9 I illustrate the growth of a population without the constriction of the carrying capacity. Under these conditions growth is proportional to its food supply and the population's ability to reproduce. This occurs only under conditions of unlimited resources characteristic of early successional conditions when new areas are colonized. Analogies in the human experiences are the behavior of pioneer populations colonizing new environments or highly subsidized coastal areas in certain countries of the Third World. As I said, these conditions are temporary and soon some factor in the environment becomes scarce and limits growth. In Figure 9 this is illustrated by a tank with a limited quantity of a resource. The maximum number of individuals that the environment can support is termed the carrying capacity of the environment. Since environmental factors such as food, water, temperature or space are normally fluctuating, it follows that the carrying capacity also fluctuates and sometimes will be higher than at other times. For the steady state society this is important because if it is to develop to the carrying capacity of the environment it should develop to the condition of minimum carrying capacity and not to the highest level. If it develops to the highest level, it will suffer a crisis at the time that the carrying capacity oscilates to a lower level. It should be pointed out that in natural systems organisms exceed the carrying capacity only for brief periods. Man may exceed carrying capacity for a long period *only* if he has the energy resource to raise the natural carrying capacity. In the absence of such resource, he will also adjust to the natural level.

To calculate the carrying capacity of an area, all the elements required for life support need to be considered and quantified. For a given power level in the social system, resources are needed in some proportion to energy expenditure. Growth will then be limited by the resource in least supply. That resource is the determinant of the carrying capacity of the region. The region may exceed the carrying capacity if it decides to import the factor in least supply. This will have an energy cost, create a structural or cultural adjustment in the system, and the power density will increase. Another factor will then become limiting and the process may be repeated. Ultimately, energy and the capacity to recycle and organize the system will limit its growth. When an area exceeds its local carrying capacity, it does so at the expense of another area. When two areas draw from the same limiting factor competition develops and so does the potential conflict. In a resource-limited earth such as ours, this kind of conflict is certain to develop as the world's power density increases. Areas of potential conflict are the limited fossil fuels, limited water supplies, the use of the oceans, and the limited ores such as uranium, etc.

In natural ecosystems competition is avoided by maintaining each population within its environmental carrying capacity and by the development of symbiotic mechanisms between ecosystem components. Such symbiotic relationships could be a feature of a steady state society if the world leaders so desire. Perhaps an understanding of natural selection and survival would help in developing a spirit of symbiosis for the steady state society.

In the natural world, where processes are coupled to solar energy and the input of solar energy is limited, natural selection serves as the mechanism that 'tunes' the system such that energy is utilized with the greatest efficiency and for the generation of maximum useful work. Given two competing systems, that one which utilizes energy to its maximum potential will have a competitive edge over the one that is wasteful. When energy is abundant, some degree of waste is allowed and this may lead to creativity and experimentation of new designs for survival. But when energies are limited, efficiency of use is a more competitive strategy. Our leaders should realize that as energies become scarce, useless competition will lead to waste and poor competitive position for survival. If energies are allocated for uses that lead to maximum useful work, a more competitive position for survival emerges. Symbiotic relationships rather than competition lead to such useful use of energy.

In addition to the above considerations we need to educate people in the realization of the value of natural ecosystems, biological diversity, and the steady state. Many of our present-day attitudes and values neglect the role of nature as a life support system. Our economic systems assume that services of nature such as esthetics, diversity and 'clean' air and water have no value when, indeed, they involve a large energetic cost on the part of the ecosystems that provide these services. There is an important need for incorporating the life-support services of nature as a factor in the evaluation of their value to man. This incorporation may mean revising current accounting procedures to include energy flow as a more basic unit of measurement of value than the dollar. One of the limitations of dollar accounting is that in a landscape where human, natural, and fossil fuel energies all contribute to survival, the dollars only account for some of these energies and not for others. For those that they do take into account, they usually do so in disproportion to the actual amount of useful work that is generated by the energy. Some concrete examples where our classic economic accountings have failed in the past are in the assumption that certain natural energies are free externalities when in reality they represent limited energy resources. Economics do not reward natural processes in proportion to their contribution to the survival of the system of man and nature. The work of human procurement is usually rewarded but not the actual amplification value of that work. When the energy source becomes limiting the work of procurement increases, and the dollar value of the work increases while the energy delivery or amplification value, measured in net power, decreases. This is termed inflation, a current world problem.

Biological diversity allows natural ecosystems to survive and thus effectively provide a variety of life support functions. When one of those functions is the absorption of sewage from natural waters, its potential value to man is high. Moreover, the greatest value of diversity and natural ecosystems is survival, and the measure of this value is astronomical. Our chances of attaining such reward (competitive survival) are best assured through the steady state. The use of natural processes to do work for man is one strategy that will help in demonstrating the value of natural ecosystems. Natural processes have evolved under selective forces and contain miniaturization that allows for the efficient use of energy. Thus the use of these adaptations, when available, should have priority over technological alternatives which are usually costly and less efficient (i.e. sewage processing).

Finally, for the success of the steady state society, power must be limited and its density controlled. Since the availability of power will encourage new growth, and growth per se is not a property of a steady state system, power availability must be limited to a ceiling compatible with the continued operation of natural systems. As exemplified by the ants, man's energy budget must be a small fraction of the natural system's budget that provides for his life support functions. In addition, the concentration of large power expenditures without proper insulation stresses the natural ecosystems which are operating at lower energy levels. The addition of thermal effluents into waterways is an example of high energy additions to natural systems. These systems could be insulated if the heat was removed and used prior to returning the effluent to the waterway.

Once a power ceiling is achieved and its proper diffusion determined, energy must be allocated with first priority for the maintenance of existing processes and structures. New growth should be permitted only when surplus energy is available and within the predetermined ceiling. The restriction of the energy ceiling of the steady state society should be the capacity of the natural ecosystem to absorb the intrusion and still provide life support for man on a long-term basis.

These steps should result in the upgrading of life quality in contrast to the current degradation which occurs in proportion to uncontrolled development. Proper implementation of the steady state society leads to uncontrolled development. Proper implementation of the steady state society leads to a condition where all members of society become participating members, all human resources contribute towards the survival of the system, and the efficiency of energy use in the operation of the system increases.

THE STEADY STATE AND NATIONAL CONFLICT

As the carrying capacity of the earth as a whole is approached, the conflict between nations is bound to increase as they will find themselves in competition for limited resources. Perhaps at that time certain rules based on the survival of the whole and similar to natural selection in the natural world should be implemented without discrimination. Some examples of these rules would be: (1) Initially all systems survive as the diversity of the world as a whole is as important to survival as is diversity at a local level. (2) Each system is allowed to grow in proportion to its carrying capacity and its role for the totality of nations. Thus an area may exceed its local carrying capacity if it is performing an important role for the world. (3) Resource utilization within a system's boundary is determined by the local people provided that their outputs do not degrade the quality of another system. Thus each nation is assured clean air but must also return clean air. (4) The health of the natural system is the ultimate criteria for the establishment of developmental priorities. Any action which results in the lowering of the carrying capacity by harming the natural systems should not be allowed. (5) If conditions change such that the role of a system is no longer needed or is no longer important to survival, the system must change or be subject to a lower priority of resource allocation. While these measures seem too restrictive, it is my belief that stringent guidelines are needed for successful relations between nations. The methods of today lead to exploitation, reduction of human dignity and overload the capacity of the earth to support man.

The prospects for the steady state society are good because it represents the only solution to survival in a limited environment. As I have discussed, the growth alternative contains energy constrictions that are inherent to growth and inconsistent with a resource-limited earth. Already people are developing new cultural adaptations that direct our attention to the kinds of attitudes that will prevail in the steady state society. The desire to be in contact with nature, to ride a bicycle, to use human power, to recycle, to curb the automobile, and to limit population are indexes that point to the steady state. While they are still clumsy attempts of implementation, they do point a direction in which man rediscovers his harmonious balance with the natural world in which he evolved and on which he still depends for survival.

LIST OF FIGURES

The model in Figure 1 highlights all the natural flows which are doing work for man and thus represent those natural services which are directly responsible for sustaining life on the planet. They include:

1. Maintenance of the biogeochemical cycles (air, gases, minerals, water) which represent the raw materials of civilizations and of life.
2. Absorption of the wastes of man which include all the chemicals that we produce and which are absorbed by natural ecosystems. When the public service benefits of intact ecosystems are absent, these substances become dangerous and cause serious threats to our health and survival.
3. Photosynthetic products which support the biological diversity of the planet.
4. Climate moderation essential for the control of vital biological processes.

These services are free gifts of nature and are provided mostly by vast areas of natural systems adapted to one another and adapted to the performance of these work functions. These functions are stressed when the diversities of the ecosystems are reduced and when its processes are stressed by the physical or chemical actions of man. To date, we have taken these life support functions so much for granted that they may even sound trivial to the reader. If we consider the acceleration of human intrusion into these vital processes of nature (man as a geological factor, for instance), we might wonder when we shall reach the threshold point where we change conditions beyond the limits of our own adaptations to survive and those of the environment's capacity to sustain us.

Figure 2. Energy language symbols used in the construction of energy diagrams. Each symbol has a precise mathematical meaning. Details on these aspects may be obtained in the book by Odum, *Environment, Power and Society*.

Figure 3. Comparison between a system in equilibrium (A) and one in steady state (B). The system in equilibrium has no energy flow and its molecules are distributed randomly. This system will not change as long as it remains without an energy flow. System B has energy flow which is the casual force to organize its molecules into a pattern. In such systems the energy input is equal to the energy loss as heat (first law of thermodynamics) and the system will maintain the observed structure as long as the steady input of energy is available.

Figure 4. A generalized scheme of ecosystem development (succession). The earliest stages are on the left and the climax is on the right. Age of the system increases from left to right. The control of environmental quality also increases from left to right.

Figure 5. Relative changes in certain ecosystem characteristics during succession. Each characteristic increases over time except net production which decreases. Compare the changes in these characteristics with the events in Figure 4.

Figure 6. This is an energy diagram with statements illustrating the concepts of net power, efficiency, and effects of concentrated and diluted energy sources. Maintenance is shown to be proportional to the energy storage in the system.

Figure 7. The relationship between the number of components in a system and the possible number of interactions between components is shown. In the real world all the components of a system are not completely organized but it could be shown that even when only one relationship between components is considered, the complexity of the system also increases rapidly. Accordingly, the cost of maintaining such organization will also increase. The Figure was redrawn from Odum, ibidem. The dotted line illustrates a linear relationship.

Figure 8. Energy diagram showing some of the interactions between a leaf-cutter ant nest and the forest that supports the nest. The symbols are from Odum, ibidem. The diagram is redrawn from Lugo et al.[8] Leaf-cutter ants carry leaves and miscellaneous plant parts into their nest where the fungus cultures are kept and cultivated by fungus attendants. Maintenance ants do the work of trail maintenance and elimination of refuse. All ants eat the fungus. The nest of ants and fungus has three main roles in the forest: (1) grazing and pruning of plants, (2) rapid mineralization of leaves, and soil turnover, (3) provision of food and habitat for many forest species such as birds, mammals, and insects. The net result is an acceleration of energy flow in the forest as a result of the ants activities. All these activities are simplified in this diagram and details may be obtained in the original work. A similar model could be drawn for the relationship of social systems and natural systems.

Figure 9. Diagrams, equations, and graphs illustrating the concept of exponential growth and carrying capacity. In A, an unlimited energy source (J) feeds a population (Q) which grows at a constant rate (K). Since no provisions are made for a limiting factor, growth is exponential as shown in the graph and with the equation. The higher the population, the faster the growth. In B, three important changes are illustrated: The energy source is no longer unlimited, a constant gain amplifier is therefore not needed, and a limiting factor (P) is added to the equation. With limiting factors growth is no longer exponential and it thus reaches a steady state level. The point at which the curve levels is termed the carrying capacity which in the diagram is determined by P.

Figure 1

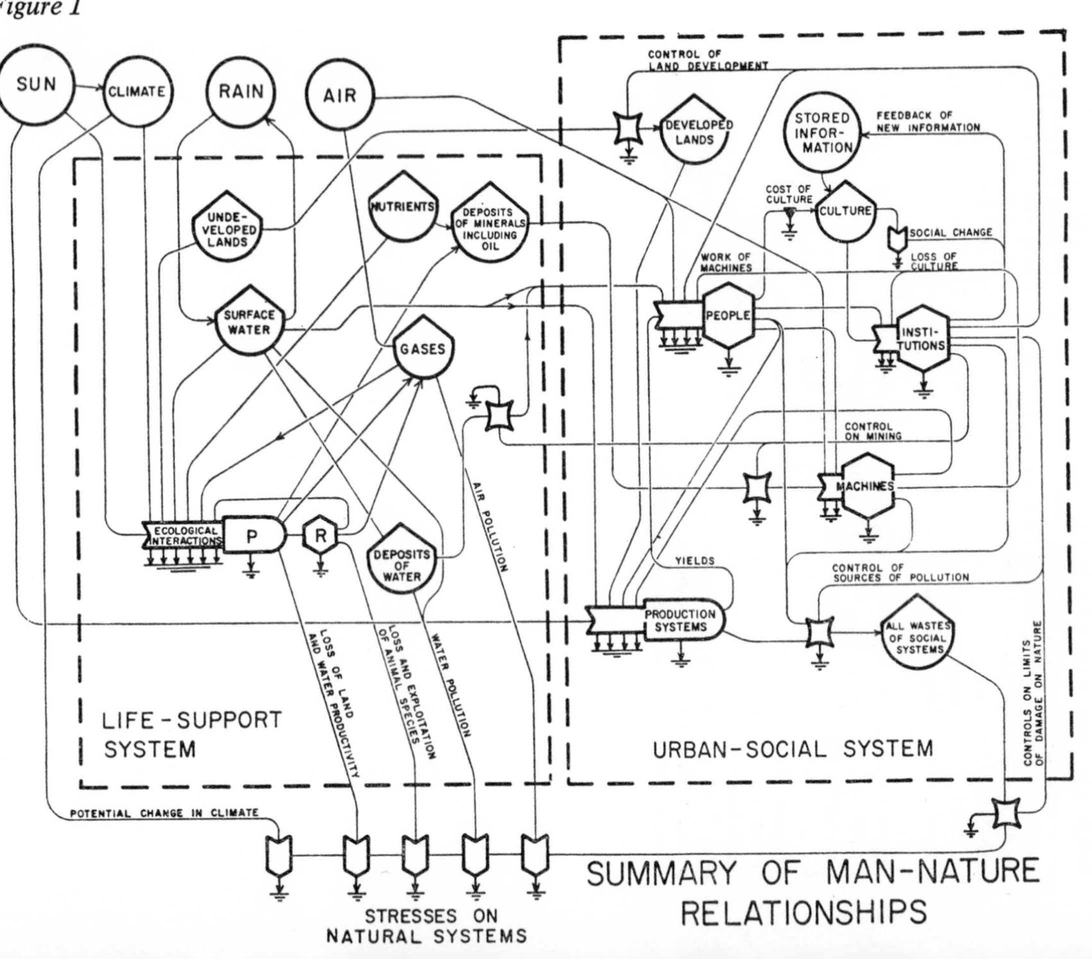
SUN
CLIMATE
RAIN
AIR
UNDE-VELOPED LANDS
SURFACE WATER
NUTRIENTS
DEPOSITS OF MINERALS INCLUDING OIL
GASES
ECOLOGICAL INTERACTIONS
P
R
DEPOSITS OF WATER
AIR POLLUTION
LOSS OF LAND AND WATER PRODUCTIVITY
LOSS AND EXPLOITATION OF ANIMAL SPECIES
WATER POLLUTION
LIFE-SUPPORT SYSTEM
POTENTIAL CHANGE IN CLIMATE
STRESSES ON NATURAL SYSTEMS
CONTROL OF LAND DEVELOPMENT
DEVELOPED LANDS
STORED INFOR-MATION
FEEDBACK OF NEW INFORMATION
COST OF CULTURE
CULTURE
SOCIAL CHANGE
LOSS OF CULTURE
WORK OF MACHINES
PEOPLE
INSTI-TUTIONS
CONTROL ON MINING
MACHINES
YIELDS
CONTROL OF SOURCES OF POLLUTION
PRODUCTION SYSTEMS
ALL WASTES OF SOCIAL SYSTEMS
CONTROLS ON LIMITS OF DAMAGE ON NATURE
URBAN-SOCIAL SYSTEM
SUMMARY OF MAN-NATURE RELATIONSHIPS

Figure 2

The energy language symbols

a. Passive storage

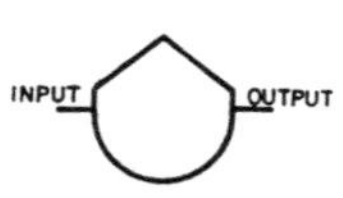

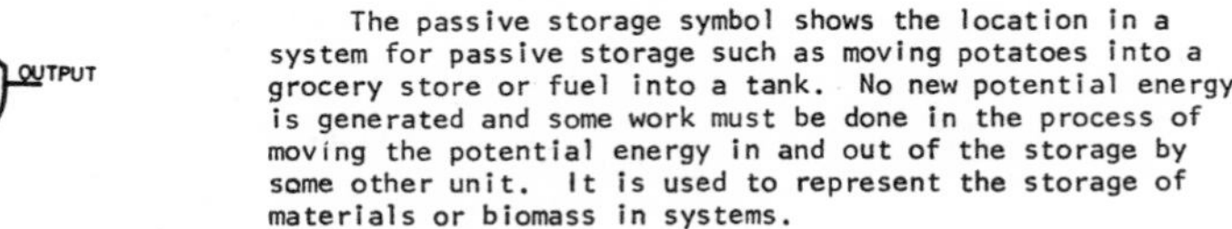
The passive storage symbol shows the location in a system for passive storage such as moving potatoes into a grocery store or fuel into a tank. No new potential energy is generated and some work must be done in the process of moving the potential energy in and out of the storage by some other unit. It is used to represent the storage of materials or biomass in systems.

b. Workgate

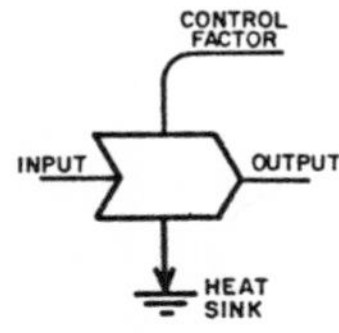

The workgate module indicates a flow of energy (control factor) which makes possible another flow of energy (input-output). This action may be as simple as a person turning a valve, or it may be the interaction of a limiting factor in photosynthesis. It is used to show the multiplier interaction of two system components.

c. Self-maintaining consumer population

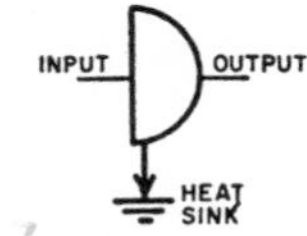

The self-maintaining consumer population symbol represents a combination of "active storage" and a "multiplier" by which potential energy stored in one or more sites in a subsystem is fed back to do work on the successful processing and work of that unit. It is used to represent populations of animals in ecosystems.

d. Pure energy receptor

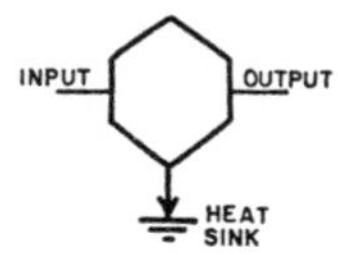

The pure energy receptor symbol represents the reception of pure wave energy such as sound, light, and water waves. In this module energy interacts with some cycling material producing an energy-activated state, which then returns to its deactivated state passing energy on to the next step in a chain of processes. This symbol is used to represent photosynthesis or chlorophyll light-reception in leaves and other photosynthetic tissues.

e. Plant population

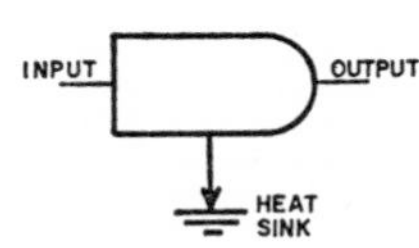

The plant population symbol is a combination of a "consumer unit" and a "pure energy receptor." Energy captured by a cycling receptor unit is passed to a self-maintaining unit that also keeps the cycling receptor machinery working, and returns necessary materials to it. The green plant is an example.

f. Energy source

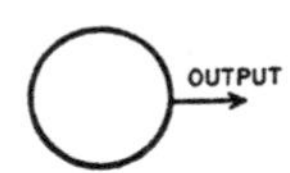

The energy source symbol represents a source of energy such as the sun, fossil fuel, or the water from a reservoir. A full description of this source would require supplementary description indicating if the source were constant force, constant flux, or programmed in a particular sequence.

g. Stress

The stress symbol defines the drain of calories of potential energy flow. When a system is stressed, some of the potential energy that was available to do the work is lost. The stress symbol is an inverted workgate with energy from the system being drained into a heat sink by an environmental factor (the stress) shown on the opposite side of the workgate. This symbol may be used, for instance, to show the effect of a pollutant on a stream.

ENERGY DRAIN
STRESS FACTOR
HEAT SINK

h. Two-way workgate

The two-way workgate or forced diffusion module represents the movement of materials in two directions as in the vertical movement of minerals and plankton in the sea. The movement is in proportion to a concentration gradient or a causal force shown operating the gate. The heat sink shows the action to follow the second law of thermodynamics.

DRIVING FORCE
INPUT-OUTPUT
INPUT-OUTPUT
HEAT SINK

i. Switch

The switch is used for flows, which have only on and off states controlling other flows by switching actions. There are many possible switching actions as classified in discussions of digital logic. Some are simple on and off; others are on when two or more energy flows are simultaneously on; some are on when connecting energy flows are off, and so forth. Many actions of complex organisms and man are ON and OFF switching actions such as voting, reproduction, and starting the car.

ON-OFF SIGNAL
INPUT
OUTPUT
HEAT SINK

j. Logic switch

The logic switch follows the same kinetics of the ON-OFF switch described above. In order for the logic switch to be operative, however, a certain value in the module controlling the ON-OFF signal must have been attained. When the threshold "T" is high, flow is off. For example, when simulating the effects of water level on a biological process, a threshold value, representative of a critical level, is used to turn the process ON or OFF. This symbol is useful in working with analog computers with logic boards.

T
INPUT
OUTPUT
HEAT SINK

k. Economic transactor

The economic transactor symbol is used for systems that have money cycles as well as energy flows. Money flows in the opposite direction to the flow of energy and the concept of price which operates among human bargains adjusts one flow to be in proportion to the other. Thus a man purchasing groceries at a store receives groceries in one direction while paying money in the opposite direction The heat losses of these transactions are small since the work involved is small. If there are complex structures regulating the transactions the costs of the coupling may be great.

$
$
PRICE
CALORIES
CALORIES
HEAT SINK

l. Box

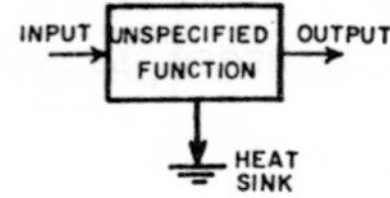

The box symbol is used when an unspecified action is being represented, or when the function is unknown or unimportant to the point being made. If the function is known, but no specific symbol is available, a box may be used with the function written inside.

m. Constant gain amplifier

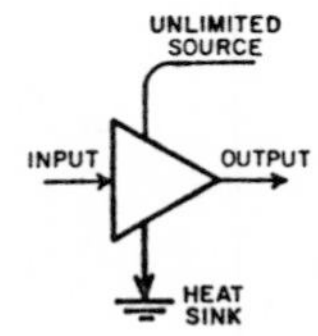

In this module the amount of energy supplied from the upper flow is that necessary to increase the force expressed in the system by a constant factor, which is called the gain. For example, a species reproducing with 10 offspring has a gain of 10 so long as the energy supplies are more than adequate to maintain this rate of increase. This symbol is used to represent exponential functions such as rapid population growth.

n. Heat loss in steady-state flow

This symbol is used to represent the energy losses associated with friction and backforces along pathways of energy flow. For simplicity, we consider the heat loss along a pathway to be understood and therefore omit it. Remember that all work results in a loss of heat.

Figure 3

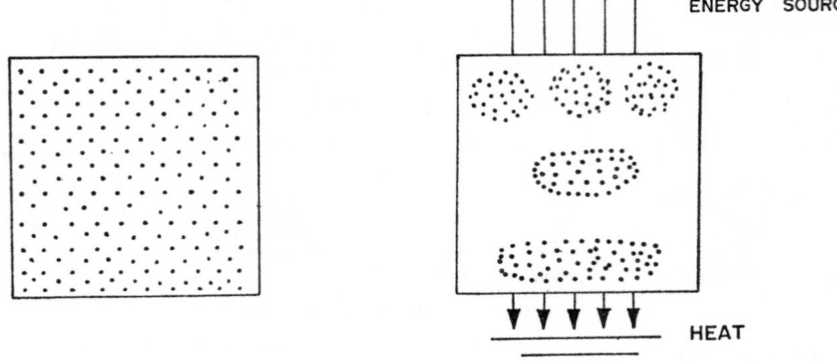

Figure 4

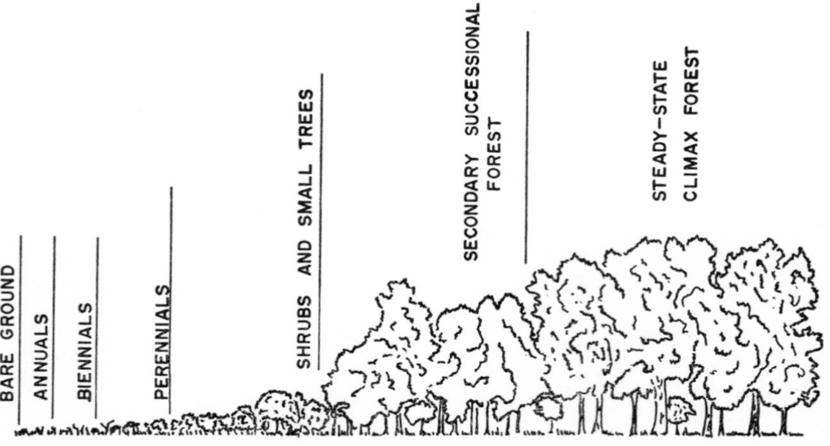

Figure 5

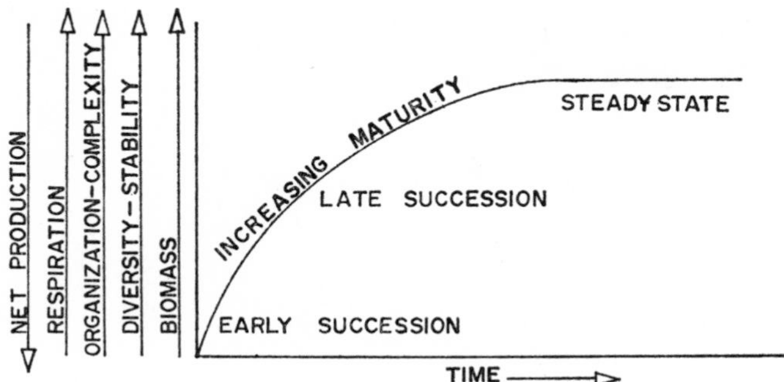

Figure 6

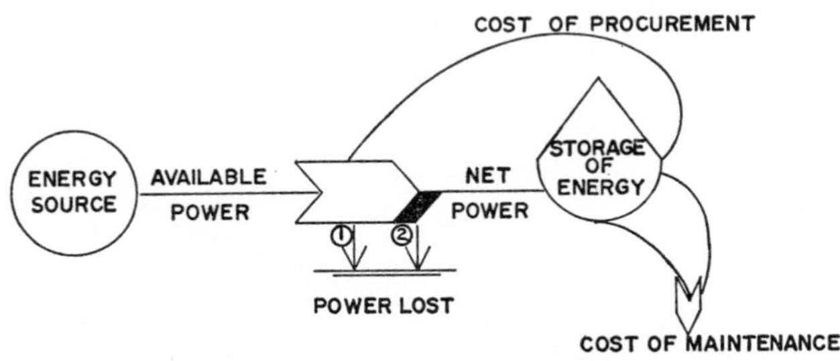

NET POWER = AVAILABLE POWER - POWER LOST

POWER LOST = ① INEFFICIENCY OF TRANSFORMATION FROM SOURCE TO USEFUL WORK PLUS ② LOSS DURING TRANSMISSION.

EFFICIENCY OF THE SYSTEM = $\frac{\text{NET POWER}}{\text{AVAILABLE POWER}}$

COST OF PROCUREMENT = AN INVERSE FUNCTION OF ENERGY CONCENTRATION AT SOURCE

Figure 7

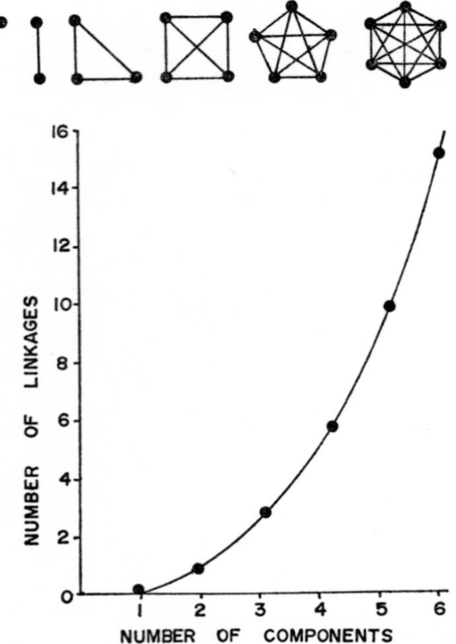

Figure 8

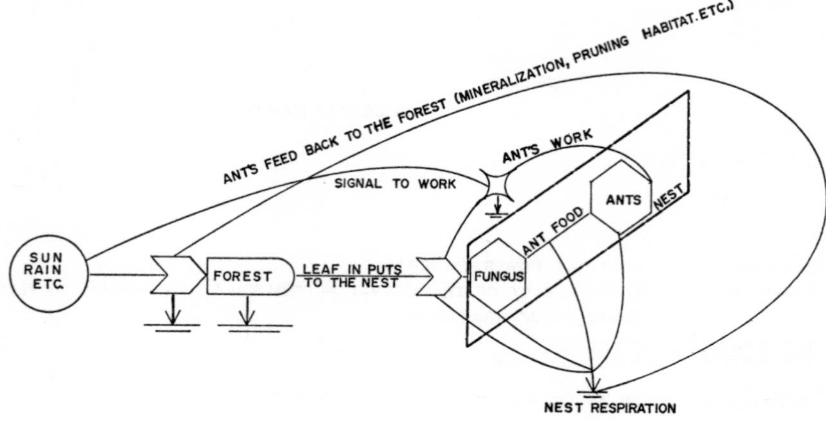

Figure 9

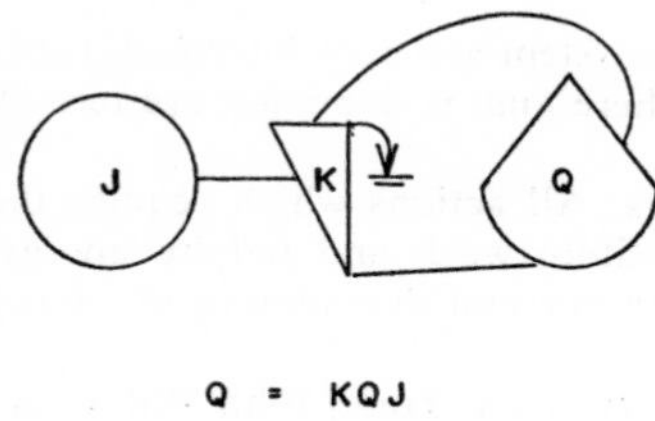

Q = POPULATION NUMBERS.

K = "INTRINSIC" RATE OF GROWTH.

J = UNLIMITED ENERGY SOURCE.

Q = KQJ

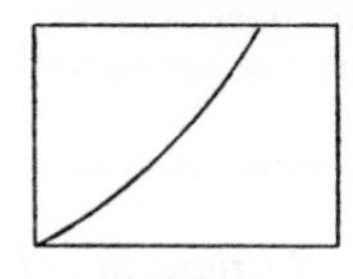

A

B

P

KQ

Q

J

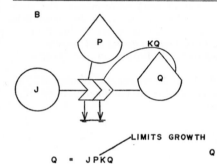

LIMITS GROWTH

Q = JPKQ

P = A LIMITED BUT ESSENTIAL RESOURCE

J = A LIMITED ENERGY SOURCE

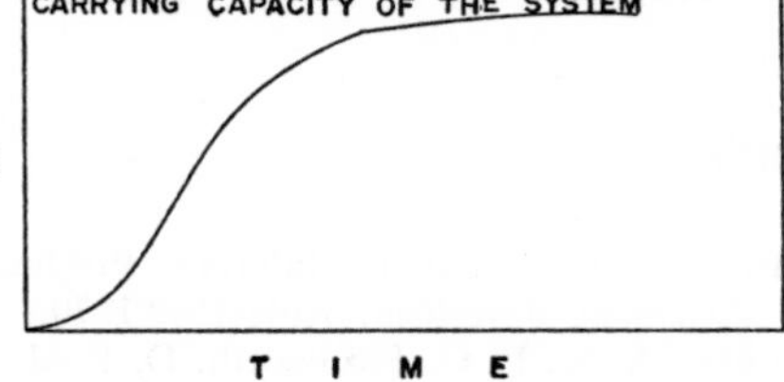

NOTES

1. In this paper the terms nature and natural ecosystem are used interchangeably to mean the systems without man. Systems where man is dominant are termed human or social systems.
2. Energy is defined as the capacity to do work. All actions which require the application of a force over a distance constitute work and require energy. The laws of energy are the conservation of energy and degradation of energy laws.
3. H. T. Odum, *Environment, Power and Society*, New York, John Wiley and Sons, 1971.
4. D. C. Spanner, *Introduction to Thermodynamics*, New York, Academic Press, 1964.
5. *Ibidem.*
6. Power is a measure of energy flow or rate of work performance. The term includes electrical power which is but one kind of energy. In this paper it is used to include all forms of energy. Power density refers to the flow of energy on a unit area basis (see Odum, *Environment, Power and Society*).
7. H. Brown, 'Human Materials Production as a Process in the Biosphere', *Scientific American*, September 1970.
8. A. E. Lugo, E. G. Farnworth, D. Pool, P. Jerez and G. Kaufman, 'The Impact of the Leaf Cutter Ant *Atta colombica* on the Energy Flow of a Tropical Wet Forest', *Ecology* (in press).

REFERENCES

Brown, H., 'Human Materials Production as a Process in the Biosphere', *Scientific American*, September 1970.

Lugo, A. E., E. G. Farnworth, D. Pool, P. Jerez and G. Kaufman, 'The Impact of the Leaf Cutter Ant *Atta colombica* on the Energy Flow of a Tropical Wet Forest', *Ecology* (in press).

Margalef, R., *Perspectives in Ecological Theory*, Chicago, University of Chicago Press, 1968.

Odum, E. P., 'The Strategy of Ecosystem Development', *Science* 164, 1969, 262-270.

Odum, H. T., *Environment, Power and Society*, New York, John Wiley and Sons, 1971.

Spanner, D. C., *Introduction to Thermodynamics*, New York, Academic Press, 1964.

17. Environmental realities: knowledge for action

HANS G.T. VAN RAAY
AND
ARIEL E. LUGO

In the two 'Man and Environment' courses that have so far been offered, concluding sessions were devoted to a stocktaking of the knowledge and insights gathered and to an appraisal of some practical implications for development planning and for educational efforts in the environmental field. Though differences of opinion and even outright disagreements still proved abundant, in this final chapter we have attempted to present some of the ideas that we consider fundamental to both course proceedings and the preceding chapters. The range of reflections, most of which were inspired by enlightening discussions with colleagues and course participants, no doubt reflects biases on the part of the two editors.[1] It should also be noted that this summary does not constitute a consistent and coherent body of analysis. Yet we hope that the ideas expressed will aid in the difficult job of integrating dispersed knowledge and will provoke others to refine and further extend the unifying elements contained in several of the observations listed.

1. Man is merely a component of the global ecosystem and the totality of interactions subsumed under the heading 'Man and Environment' is conditioned by the continued flow of energy.

2. Though each component, and that is particularly conspicuous of the human one, has unique properties which demand specialized investigation, it is clear that all systems must respect the laws to which matter and energy are subject.

3. Energy inputs coupled with prevailing efficiency of energy utilisation set a limit to the maximum amount of work which each system can accomplish and, in the case of ecosystems, the carrying capacity that can be reached.

4. Since the area of the earth, the amount of fossil fuel, and mineral resources are all finite, and since the magnitude of solar radiation is constant, it follows that the earth is limited in its physical resource base and that there is an absolute maximum carrying capacity for the earth as a whole.

5. Distinction should be made, however, between absolute and relative carrying capacity of the environment. The absolute global limit is that imposed by the physical realities of the ecosystem, while the

relative carrying capacity refers to a lower value as determined by efficiency of resource use.

6. Obviously, the concepts of absolute and relative carrying capacity can also be applied to subglobal entities which are treated as closed systems, in that a range of values can be conceived as related to specific environments and to different human responses.

7. But it should be remembered that the further development of any human system requires a continuously increasing flow of energy and products and that soon a stage will be reached where closed-ness breaks down and carrying capacities can no longer be understood in terms of a specific stretch of land of the global surface.

8. The progressive concentration of people and energy that is part and parcel of such developments tends to produce a host of adverse effects, such as excessive stress on the natural habitat, deterioration of life quality, increased disparities, etc.

9. This is not to say that concentration of people and energy is considered a bad thing in itself. Some measure of agglomeration is beneficial and indispensable for the efficient organisation and running of the human system and is also compatible with the requirements of the environment.

10. But the time has come to question the long-term survival value of excessive human agglomeration and concentration of energy and to emphasise more dispersed distribution of population and more diluted spacing of energy generation and consumption as feasible alternatives.

11. Time has also come to exercise greater care in the allocation of energy and other natural resources since these normally tend to be in low supply and limiting to development. In all such cases, energy expenditure and resource use should be made dependent on the net gains produced. Whenever energy and raw materials are limited, they should be allocated with the assurance that the maximum benefit is obtained from their use for the largest possible number of people of present and future generations. As Ghandi has stressed, 'Earth provides enough to satisfy every man's need but not for every man's greed.'

12. Although this principle seems evident, certain societies appear to utilise energy and raw materials in ways that seem wasteful to the outside observer. Experimentation with societal preference culminating in the consumerism of so many present-day societies, was perhaps warranted as long as there was a belief that virtually inexhaustible surpluses were available. But with increased awareness of acute scarcity of resources, survival priorities for mankind as a whole should become the major yardstick for allocation.

13. Unfortunately, the realisation is only slowly gaining ground that the survival of mankind as a whole is the ultimate value to which all other societal values should be subordinate.

14. Although in a system all components are somehow related and interdependent, the benefits derived from the interaction between social groups and nations are usually unequally distributed in that certain sections of society and certain nations gain more than others and tend to dominate the system at large. Monopolistic tendencies and growing disparities are particularly common in cases of widespread dependence on a limited resource.

15. Reduction of the polarisation of wealth and power is undoubtedly one of the great challenges that faces mankind and, implicitly, should be a main concern of those who are best able to affect the course of events. Particularly grave is the disparity between developed and developing countries and the role of the former in the creation of social injustice of global dimensions. The underdevelopment of a substantial portion of the global population constitutes a problem as serious as the deterioration of the natural environment and should receive equal attention.

16. The economic expansion of the 'West' and the attendant unjust exploitation of the labour and land resources of the developing countries has had serious environmental repercussions. The ill-considered introduction and application of a range of production technologies and institutional arrangements which maximized returns to outside investments has upset the resource base of many communities. This was aggravated by the relative fragility of several equatorial and tropical ecosystems.

17. This is not to say that technological progress and economic growth will, of necessity, progressively destroy the environment of many developing societies. On the contrary, if applied correctly and more explicitly in response to internal long-term needs and interests, both technological and economic advancement can be very conducive to the maintenance and restoration of the environmental balance.

18. Rapid population growth seems to be more a symptom than a cause of underdevelopment. It no doubt contributes to the environmental crisis, but so do many other things. There is ample evidence that the nature of production technology and the high consumption level of western societies are of larger consequence. The insistence by these societies that their less developed counterparts should apply birth control seems no more than an escape device and will lack credibility as long as its advocates remain unprepared to take effective measures at home.

19. The contention that developing countries would not be able to make substantive strides forward on the way to development without outside injections of capital and knowledge is incorrect, as is the idea that progress of the poor can only be at the expense of the rich.

20. It is obvious that a settling for less gain by privileged groups and nations could be very conducive to a more equitable distribution of wealth and power; however, judging by events on the international scene, there is little ground for optimism about the prospects of voluntary initiatives.

21. Given this unfortunate condition, improvement will be greatly dependent on those who are oppressed and exploited, and clearly related to their willingness and capacity to use their inherent power as part of an integrated system.

22. Notably, the skilful manipulation of scarce energy and metal resources so essential to the overall global economy, seems an effective means of advancement. However, initial successes should not detract attention from the danger that the final outcome may merely be one of higher price levels throughout, leaving the structure of international terms of trade unchanged. It should also be remembered that con-

siderable internal readjustments may be needed in the developing countries before the population at large can benefit from increased prices for primary commodities.

23. There is little doubt that the threat of concerted action by major producers of vital resources will prompt further search for new and possibly infinite energy sources and raw materials.

24. But even if infinite sources are found only part of the overall problem will be solved, i.e. of resource exhaustion and the resulting tensions.

25. Other problems such as environmental degradation, deterioration of the quality of life, alienation from nature and fellow man, emotional instability, etc., will remain or even be aggravated. In this context, it has been established that natural systems can only absorb a limited increase of externally-induced energy density before they oscillate into extinction. Though relative carrying capacities are by no means fixable by present standards and techniques, it would seem that man too can only be 'pushed' to certain limits of density, activity, and stress. If this assumption were at least partially valid, it would be of considerable consequence to planning and planners. It would imply that regardless of energy and raw material availability, the ultimate solution is still likely to lie in the mitigation of such trends as concentrating people in ever-larger agglomerations, increased activity and specialisation, continued emphasis on economic expansion and economies of scale, progressive uniformity of land-use, increased consumerism, progressive automation and bureaucratisation, etc.

26. An important principle to planning should also be that the natural systems provide essential services to man. It is submitted that these services and nature's capacity to perform them on a lasting basis should be secured by the proper planning of ecosystem stability through the maintenance of sufficient landscape diversity.

27. Many services of nature have so far been considered free services, but the time seems to have come, in Commoner's words, to 'internalise the externalities'. The suggestion that for certain purposes calories would be a better standard than monetary units, breathes the same spirit.

28. But it should be remembered that not all environment and development realities are quantifiable or to be measured in dollars or calories; a crucial concept such as the quality of life of communities and societies that occupy particular areas includes a number of qualitative aspects which escape our present capacity for precise quantification.

29. It is a disquieting paradox that continued insistence on improvement of the quality of life is often coupled to considerable tolerance regarding the deterioration of one of its major determinants, i.e. the quality of the habitat.

30. In this context, reference should also be made to limiting factors. Since ignorance of or insufficient allowance for these factors and the time in which they are in least supply is believed to have been frequent, it may be stressed that areal overdevelopment should be avoided just as much as underdevelopment of part of the world today. Areal overdevelopment cannot be but temporary and, in addition to overstressing and damaging the area's environment, will eventually tend to be detrimental to development elsewhere and to be at the root of much tension and conflict both within and between nations.

31. Adequate understanding of the human impact on the environment and of the proper balance between human and natural systems is still lacking; only recently have we begun to show serious concern for what is happening.

32. Although some significant progress has been made and the number of institutions that include environmental issues and development in their training and research programmes is increasing rapidly, we have not yet moved far beyond general principles.

33. If environmental realities are to become important as planning inputs, considerable intensification of training and research efforts is required. It seems obvious that UNEP, the timely offshoot of the UN family, can play a significant role in this respect.

34. In preparing curricula, it should be remembered that the complexity and diversity in the environmental field of study entail a real danger of overspecialisation, of narrowing the geographic scope of

investigation, and of knowledge being presented in slices, each of which is concerned with a particular domain of enquiry.

35. A high degree of specialist expertise is essential, but it is submitted that environmental training programmes would fail their objective if they did not succeed in also facilitating the establishment of overall comprehension.

36. Although no-one can be expected to be equally competent in all the complex fields that facilitate our insight into the man-environment totality, environment specialists should share a common core of knowledge including major contributions from all relevant disciplines. Simultaneously, the international and even global interwovenness of most environmental problems and developments should be adequately brought to the fore.

37. This agenda of items for incorporation in environmental training programmes will involve a degree of generalisation that frequently will lead to considerable sacrifices in depth and to serious oversimplification of existing situations; but to establish no general skeleton and frame of reference at all seems a far less attractive alternative. (For the curriculum of a six-week interdisciplinary and international course on 'Man and Environment' see Appendix A.)

38. Just as critical as the demand for more qualified personnel is the need to weaken or eliminate major inadequacies in problem-solving systems.

39. The absence of a supranational problem-solving authority is of particular consequence. Whereas most developments have implications for and repercussions on areas that extend beyond national boundaries and increasingly affect large portions of the global population and even mankind as a whole, effective levels of decision and policy-making continue to follow the political and administrative borders of old.

40. Admittedly, a world forum such as United Nations is instrumental in achieving recognition of an identity of interest and common acceptance of joint responsibilities of mankind as a whole, but we still seem far removed from the setting of common goals and priorities, let alone corporate action.

41. Supposedly more effective problem-solving entities such as national societies also seem to lack a clear vision of something new ahead, of ultimate aims, and of the direction in which development should proceed.

42. A range of possibilities for dealing with immediate problems is usually present as is a measure of consensus on guiding principles to be applied for the immediate future, but long-term perspectives are often lacking or, if present, tend to be of insufficient specificity to be of genuine significance to the planning process.

43. In the absence of agreement on and commitment to fairly narrowly defined ultimate aims, our ability to evaluate the performance of the system is greatly reduced for lack of a reference point.

44. Having no defined long-term objectives and being only to some extent aware of, but hardly in control over, the forces that make for the dynamics of the system and determine future development, many societies simply drift along; any future stage is thus rendered a chance result of continual flux and tension.

45. Planning and planners have no doubt enhanced the problem-solving capacity of societies and also, though to a much lesser extent, the ability to steer the process of societal transformation; but all too often the ideas developed and actions taken are mainly in the curative sphere and in response to existing development repercussions.

46. All too often, problems are treated in a fragmented manner by a multitude of committees and agencies which are inadequately co-ordinated.

47. An obvious demerit of such planning on what may be called a crisis basis is that, even if it is not too late for successful intervention, it is costly in money and energy. The longer preventive action is delayed, the more difficult and costly curative measures tend to become.

48. The replacement of passive planning in which 'the squeaky wheel gets the oil' by a more active form is made particularly complicated by a major structuring force of most societies, i.e. the power, often

hidden but yet extremely forceful, exercised by dominant interest groups.

49. It is submitted that as long as decisions by private interest groups have more impact and are of greater consequence than government initiatives in pursuit of the public good, comprehensive and sectoral planning and planners will find it extremely hard to move beyond the solving of immediate problems and to lead the way in initiating a development policy that is compatible with the long-term interests of the population and environment.

50. Although gaps in our body of knowledge clearly contribute to the planner's limited effectiveness in linking knowledge and action, it would seem that the difficulties involved in realising organised action are of more significance. Many of these difficulties originate in the manipulation of private interest groups.

51. This realisation may and has tempted certain societies to enhance the government's coercive capacity, with the implicit danger that the direction of development is now dictated by an all-powerful group of technocrats and bureaucrats and that the people are condemned to a passive state.

52. This passive status whereby people have little choice than to accept the status quo, clearly relates to the situation sketched elsewhere in this volume, i.e. of social alienation or lack of individual commitment to social purposes, with such possible repercussions as mounting social instability, social crisis, and even anomy.

53. Without denying the need for some measure of central control, it is clear that the ultimate source of transformation is the people and that any transformation involves far-reaching changes in awareness, attitudes and values on the part of individuals.

54. Any organisational structure for development that separates people from the actual decision-making process therefore entails the real danger of failing to achieve any substantive measure of consensus around important social tasks and any genuine effectiveness.

55. Accordingly, the operationalisation of such key concepts as social

mobilisation, participation, and dialogue, is imperative for constant innovative adaptation to societal and environmental needs now and in the future.

56. Global operationalisation hopefully being an ultimate reality, such subglobal entities as national societies seem obvious units for the initiation of this process.

57. It is clear that operationalisation at this level will require considerable adjustments in the planning structures that have evolved. Many traditional planning frameworks have tended to emphasise the national level of broad target-setting and general directives in particular, leaving a sort of vacuum between paper abstractions on the one hand, and real life conditions and down-to-earth action on the other, inducing a high degree of fragmentation and ill-coordination of development efforts.

58. This subnational vacuum is presently being entered by regional development planning, whose interest lies in the integrated analysis and guidance of societal and spatial processes of change as mainly influenced by differentials in population and human activity, in socio-political power, societal values and expectations, and in environmental potentialities and constraints. It is suggested that this form of planning offers considerable scope as catalyst and amplifier of developments which are compatible with the capabilities, hopes, and aspirations of the people and with the long-term survival of their habitats.

NOTE

1. While assuming exclusive responsibility for errors in thinking and interpretation, we share with colleagues and course participants of the two 'Man and Environment' courses the possible merits of this inventory. We particularly wish to thank James Morrison of the University of Florida for his assistance in the compilation of several ideas on organisational aspects.